THE GREAT AMERICAN RV COOKBOOK

WILLIAM & LORETTA MARSHALL

Johnson Books: Boulder

First Edition
1 2 3 4 5 6 7 8 9

ISBN 0-933472-92-7
LCCCN 85-060640

Printed in the United States of America by
Johnson Publishing Company
1880 South 57th Court
Boulder, Colorado 80301

CONTENTS

To Marc and Matthew, our young sons and traveling companions, who adventurously sampled *almost* everything as we ate our way across America.

FOREWORD

Bon Voyage! Bon Appétit!

We've always thought those two well wishes go together. So when we joined the ranks of millions of Americans who take their kitchens with them on vacation and business travel, it was only natural that we would think that on-the-road cooking was a marvelous opportunity to explore the bounty and rich culinary heritage of America. And it is—far beyond our first imaginings—a wondrous array of eating adventures spread from coast to coast: the creative cookery of the Pacific Cornucopia, memorable meals from Mountain and Desert, the hearty fare of the Heartland, the cosmopolitan cuisine of the Cradle of Liberty, and the delights of Dixie. Not coincidentally, these are the divisions of the heart of this book—a Sampler of Great American Recipes at their simple best.

In profiling some of the "brightest ideas of the current, extraordinary American food scene," an article in *House Beautiful* described the much-acclaimed new American cooking as a movement "characterized by respect for and reliance on first-rate ingredients, an interest in native products and a fair amount of cooking over charcoal." All of which is a quite apt description of RV cooking at its finest, whether what's on the menu is a traditional favorite or an innovative creation.

By far the hardest part of preparing this book has been choosing from the wealth of good eating that is enjoyed on the road in our country. But we tried, with the help of countless friends and friendly RVers, to give you a choice of tempting tastes from every state for every occasion. In each regional chapter there are *Eye Openers* for casual and special mornings; *Soups, Salads, and Sandwiches* for midday to midnight; *Main Events* for anywhere, any time; *Asides* to round out your menus or for regional munchies; *Sweets* from simple to simply spectacular; and *Cheers*, traditional refreshers and

restorers. And, along with the basics of outdoor cooking, we've also included a roundup of regional *Over the Coals* recipes.

On the other hand, we haven't overlooked the challenges of on-the-road cooking: the built-in limitations of the RV kitchen, the reality of trying to create dishes rivaling those of the passed-by restaurants from convenience store shelves, the feast-and-famine situation that RVers often encounter, and the delicious dilemmas of dealing with the unfamiliar fruits of land and sea. *Before You Get on the Road* includes advice on outfitting the RV kitchen and stocking the pantry to make your travel cooking as easy and efficient as possible. *Roadside Ramblings* is a treasury of travel tips on coping with everything from changing altitude to varying water supplies. And, in *Living on the Land*, you'll find an extensive three-part guide to America's bounty.

All of the recipes in this book have been designed for the minimum of effort, ingredients, equipment, and cleanup. For your convenience, we have used market amounts when possible, and all recipes, unless otherwise noted, are planned for four people—an amount easy to double or halve.

Whether you've logged 10 or 100,000 miles in your traveling kitchen, whether your RV is a recreational vehicle or a required vehicle, whether you are an overnighter or a full-timer, there are wondrous eating adventures on your route. *The Great American RV Cookbook* is your personal triptik to the good eating of America, old and new. Wherever your travels may take you, we wish you

Bon Voyage! Bon Appétit!

Loretta & Bill Marshall

BEFORE YOU GET ON THE ROAD

As the RV cook you are expected to satisfy mammoth appetites stoked by the great outdoors in a miniature kitchen and to transform whatever you discover en route into mouthwatering delights with a miniscule pantry. And you're supposed to perform these feats with a few pots and a handful of tools.

You are not alone if you sometimes feel that you need a magic wand more than a wooden spoon. But if you start with an understanding of what it takes to make your RV kitchen function effectively and select your basic equipment and supplies with care, you won't need magic to fill this tall order, just some foresight, a little imagination, and a spirit of adventure—the same ingredients you'll find in the best of your trips.

Getting to Know Your Kitchen

Now you can take almost everything with you on a trip, *including* the kitchen sink. Compared to tent camping, your RV kitchen is an incredible step up from the campstove, cooler, and supply box: a luxurious mess tent with running water (probably both hot and cold), a real refrigerator (or efficient icebox), a range that's ready in an instant, and, quite possibly, even an oven—all with a window on the world and out of the rain, flies, and heat.

However, if you compare your RV kitchen to your home kitchen, it may be something of a surprise. Make no mistake about it, RV kitchens are small, whether you have a pop-up tent-trailer or a posh 33-foot motorhome. The RV-kitchen appliances tend to dominate the RV so they seem almost like the ones at home. But look at yours again with a tape measure in hand.

Rangetop and Ovens: Your RV rangetop may have 2 to 4 burners, but they are small, and the average rangetop is about half as big as the average home range. Normally, this doesn't make much difference unless you actually try to use all the burners at once and have anything but small pans. Pans with long handles (usually considered a desirable feature) can be unwieldy on this petite top. And don't even think of setting something that isn't heatproof on an unused surface of the range as you may do at home: since the radius of heat hasn't been miniaturized, you're likely to end up with a plastic bowl or lid welded to your rangetop. And remember, when you're cooking with gas you are using up oxygen: *open a window or vent.*

If you have an oven, now you are really talking *small*—5-inch height clearance maximum and, if you are lucky, 14 inches wide. Forget the turkey. Forget the standing rib roast. Forget the bundt-pan meatloaf or cake. In fact, don't count on a 2-layer cake or 2 pie pans unless you measure your oven first—they won't fit in most RV ovens. Write down the exact internal dimensions of your oven and broiler, taking note of any design oddities (a slope up at the back of the rack, brackets that cut into the pan clearance space), and carry them with you when you shop for baking pans and oven foods. Don't forget you have to allow for air circulation around the pans.

Many RVers consider their ovens an oversized toaster (which it can function as) or an expensive pots-and-pans cupboard (which it should double as). Though most RVers avoid using their ovens when the weather is very hot (since the oven can quickly turn the RV into a sauna), an RV oven can expand your cooking possibilities almost any other time. It can warm your morning with fragrant, freshly baked biscuits, cornbread, or coffeecake. Can take over when your cookout has been rained out. Or bake a cherry pie from cherries you picked yourself. All of which make it a remarkably versatile cupboard/toaster. And, even with its limitations, once you get used to it, you will probably use your oven about as often as you do on ordinary days at home base if you happen to be camping in the fall or winter or in cool country.

If you have the time and an oven thermometer, check the accuracy of your oven temperature: your oven may not be finely calibrated. Add that to a slightly inaccurate setting, and you may be baking at 300° when you think you're baking at 400°.

If you're one of the lucky RVers who have a microwave oven, you'll find it endlessly useful as much for a cool convenient stand-in for the rangetop as for conventional oven uses. Once you have microwaved asparagus or corn on the cob, you may never want to cook fresh vegetables any other way. The RV microwave ovens are the same as the smaller home microwave ovens, but since there is considerable difference between microwave oven models, consult your manual for specifics.

Refrigerator: The thought of having a ready supply of cold drinks, fresh steaks, crisp lettuce, and ice cream has sold more than one owner on the RV life. We don't have to tell you how nice it is having this marvel on board, but it too may not be as large as you think it is. For example, what is commonly called a 10-cubic-foot refrigerator, actually has a capacity of somewhere between 6.5 and 7.5 cubic feet. This discrepancy comes from a general misinterpretation of the model numbers: for example, *Dometic's* 1303 is often referred to as a 13-footer, but the owner's manual identifies the capacity as 7.6 cubic feet. And that's one of the largest RV refrigerators available. They range on down to about 3 cubic feet.

Your home refrigerator is probably between 16 and 22 cubic feet, which means that, at best, your RV refrigerator is only one-half the size of the one at home. Most of us are dealing with considerably less space; our 3-footer is one-seventh the size of our home refrigerator.

And then there's the freezer space. It may be ample for a 2-week family trip to the wilderness, or it may be so small you have to make a choice between a package of frozen vegetables and a quart of ice cream (in our RV, the ice cream always wins).

This all means you have to use the space you have as effectively and efficiently as possible to meet your needs, and you must be ruthless about refusing space to seldom used items or leftovers that are probably going to be thrown out eventually anyway.

The efficiency and temperature of your refrigerator/freezer can fluctuate with several variables—extreme weather, the energy source, whether you've had to turn it off briefly when you couldn't get leveled up. Consequently, food storage of highly perishable items may be less than optimum; try to use them sooner than you do at home. Incidentally, if your refrigerator has undifferentiated space except for the freezer, the area near the freezer is the coldest and can be used for the most perishable foods.

Cupboards, Counters, and Sinks: The rest of the RV kitchen is a diminuitive version of an ordinary kitchen sans garbage disposal and dishwasher.

We find it touchingly optimistic that RV designers put 16-bottle spice racks in kitchens with pint-size pantries. What's worse, there are pantry cupboards that won't even take some standard-size food packages. Measure yours and assign space accordingly.

RVs are subject to the universal law: The need for storage space will always exceed the storage space available. In RVs it happens much sooner than in other places. On the other hand, there is no rule that food must be stored in designated pantry space. But remember, canned goods are heavy and should be stored low (and don't *ever* put anything glass in an overhead cupboard).

You may find your RV counter space the most dramatic difference from home base—our RV has *zero* counter space! Most RVers with double sinks have a cover for one to add some counter space (it is especially useful if the sink cover is a cutting board). In addition, small cutting boards can serve as portable work space set almost anywhere.

Helping to make everything work is that kitchen sink. If you do what your mother probably told you a thousand times and clean as you go, you'll find that this assemblage of undersize equipment and appliances will work efficiently as a comfortable compact kitchen where you can create satisfying exciting meals with ease—with the help of *The Great American RV Cookbook*, of course.

Outfitting the RV Kitchen

Whether you have purchased or rented your RV, you have made a considerable investment. Now is not the time to skimp. Don't raid the junk drawers and the back of your home kitchen cupboards for discards and rejects; if they aren't earning their keep in your kitchen at home, they have even less chance of doing it on the road. On the other hand, your on-the-road equipment needn't be expensive. A complete new set of basic RV kitchen equipment will probably cost you less than a tank or two of gas.

Every piece of equipment you add to the RV kitchen should be easy to store, easy to use, easy to clean, and essential; each item must earn its keep by being consistently used or doing something important that nothing else does. Of course, what is essential to you and your family is not necessarily essential to someone else—a corkscrew, popcorn popper, pressure cooker, citrus juicer, thermos, stovetop toaster.

Good cooks can make a case for a dozen different knives and a number of special-purpose pieces of equipment. Entire catalogs and stores are devoted exclusively to the needs of cooks. But as one of the most prestigious of the suppliers, Chuck Williams of *Williams-Sonoma*, puts it, "You really don't need a souffle dish to do a souffle. It would work in a dog dish." While we'd all like to cook with a bit more stylish equipment than that, the point is that you don't need a lot of fancy equipment and tools for every purpose. Mr. Williams, a noted gourmet cook himself, is said to cook with only two or three saucepans and a single knife. In other words, there are a lot of things that you probably have in your home kitchen that are nice but not necessary.

The Basic Set of Cookware. The shared road wisdom of fellow RVers and our own experiments conclude almost unanimously that the best choice for RV cookware is inexpensive, nonstick aluminum.

We have a battery of fine copper cookware that we use at home base, but we wouldn't dream of trading our RV's nonstick aluminum pans for it for on-the-road cooking.

You can readily buy the nonstick aluminum pans in supermarkets, variety stores, and discount stores anywhere. They are lightweight and, best of all, easy to clean—an absolutely essential consideration when attempting to conserve water on the road. In addition, one pan is often used for two or three things during a single meal; a nonstick pan just needs rinsing and it's ready to go again. Since you will probably use your oven, if you have one, for storage, look for pans that do not have large projecting knobs and oversize handles. Both *Mirro* and *Foley* make pans that would be good for your basic set.

You also need something for boiling water (though you can use a saucepan). Choose a compactly designed kettle that will store in your oven if you can. *Farberware* makes a very handsome, small, stainless steel, wood-trimmed teakettle if you'd like something special.

If you have an oven, even if you don't plan on baking, you should have at least one 9-inch nonstick baking pan (a round cake pan—or 2—will nestle in your skillet) and a baking sheet with a lip around the edge. Cookie sheets ordinarily do not work in RV ovens, even if they fit, because they cut off the air circulation. However, a large round pan—like a pizza pan—will work because the heat can circulate. A pizza pan will double as a cookie sheet and a baking dish for many foods, and, of course, it can be used for pizzas. It will also catch drips, keeping your oven clean. Finding a large pizza pan that will fit your oven can be a challenge. Keep in mind that there are subtle differences in pans of seemingly the same size—sloping sides, handles. Don't go by the label dimensions. Measure the *actual* size of the pan—a fraction of an inch can make one pan fit where another maker's "same" size pan doesn't.

1-quart nonstick saucepan with lid
2-quart nonstick saucepan with lid
10-inch nonstick skillet with lid
1- to 2-quart teakettle
9-inch nonstick round cake pan (1 or 2) and/or
   9-inch pie pan
Large pizza pan

Basic Tools: All of the tools we recommend as basic equipment are available nationwide at supermarkets and variety stores, but you may have to look awhile to find the ideal tool for your needs. We went through 3 funnels and umpteen stores before we found the one that fit right in our small storage drawer. However, looking for just the right kitchen gadget is inexpensive fun shopping that you can do in a big-city boutique or a small-town general store. Look for tools with fairly short handles for easy storage and remember that you are using nonstick cookware.

Tape measure (a small pocket metal one)
Cutting board
All-purpose knife (about a 6-inch blade)
Paring knife
All-purpose scissors (*Fiskars* will cut almost anything but bones)
Can opener, can piercer, lid lifter, and corkscrew in some combination of tools
Vegetable peeler
Cook's spoon (nylon or wood)
Pancake turner (nylon)
Cheese grater (a particularly practical choice is a plastic one that fits over a bowl; it will also do double duty as a strainer)

Basic Storage Equipment: A recreational vehicle is a *vehicle*. When you move, your containers, packages, and equipment shift, slide, tip, fall over, and, if not securely contained, spill. And when you stop, the cupboards (especially overheads) and the refrigerator should be opened cautiously—be ready to play catch.

Glass bottles especially are potential mess makers for they are not only heavy but are breakable and can spew contents and glass shards all over your RV. Most refrigerators have some contained shelf space on the door but that is limited, so you need an assortment of unbreakable tight-lidded containers for all the usual purposes and also to keep some standard items that you ordinarily store in their original containers, for example, mayonnaise. Spend some time with your empty refrigerator and assorted sizes and shapes of containers determining which combinations fit your refrigerator shelves best. It will save a lot of shifting around when the refrigerator is full.

Unfortunately, you'll have a hard time buying the hands-down most efficient containers for liquids, although you may be able to get them free at your local hospital. The 1-liter and 2-liter plastic saline-solution and distilled-water bottles manufactured by *McGaw* that are used in hospitals have ideal dimensions for most RV refrigerator doors and have tightly fitting caps. You'll have to make an effort to get them and work at taking the labels off once you have them, but they work so well for storage and mixing (you can shake them vigorously with no leaking) that they are worth the bother.

Spatula (a Viennese spatula will double as a scraper and as a knife for frosting cakes or cutting in nonstick pans)
Plastic colander (use for straining and draining cooked foods, salads, the dishes)
Egg whisk (choose a fairly small one)
Tongs
Set of nesting measuring spoons
Set of nesting measuring cups
2-cup liquid measuring cup
1-quart plastic shaker with tight lid (for mixing shakes, batter, puddings, drinks—*Jell-O* sells one as an instant pudding shaker)
Basting and pastry brush (nylon bristles are easy to clean)
Nutcracker (doubles as jar opener or lobster/crab cracker)
Small plastic funnel
Set of plastic nesting bowls with lids (use for mixing, storing, serving, dishwashing—*Rubbermaid* makes individual lidded bowls that can be combined to make a nesting set: 2, 4, 6, 8, 12 cup; a second 12-cup bowl is particularly useful)

Assorted 1-cup to 4-cup plastic containers with lids
4 1-liter plastic bottles (for juices and other beverages
2 2-liter plastic bottles (for drinking water, decanted jug wine, or other beverages)

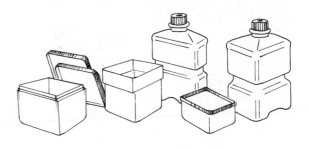

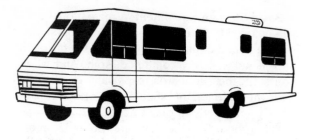

"Class A" Set: To make the basic set of equipment into a deluxe set, add a few more pieces of cookware that will expand your cooking options and a few tools to make your work easier.

5-quart saucepan or Dutch oven with lid (preferably a lid that fits the skillet)

9 by 13-inch nonstick baking pan

2 6-cup nonstick muffin pans (2 will store in half the space a 12-cup pan takes but will usually fit side-by-side for baking—measure your oven)

Apple corer (if you eat many baked apples)

Divided spice shakers (a great space saver; several assortments of spices are sold by United Industries)

Ladle

Mouli grater (preferably the plastic model made in France; with the various cylinder blades you can use the grater for everything from slaws to snow cones)

Small pepper grinder

Strainer/spatula

Timer

Special Options: If you plan on doing *any* cooking outside, check the chapter on cooking over the coals for basic equipment.

If you have a microwave oven you may find some special microwave cookware useful. As always, try to get as much mileage as you can out of all equipment. Check to see if your nesting bowl set and/or dinnerware is microwave-safe so you can use it for double duty. Or look into the lightweight unbreakable microwave baking pans on the market that can also be used at lower temperatures in the conventional oven.

If you have a very small freezer, take along an ice cube tray with a removable divider for freezer "pies."

If you usually plug in or use a generator, a small portable electric mixer can be a work saver. (We don't expect you to have one with you for any of the recipes in this book.)

Last, and best, choose a few pieces of equipment just for fun. Pick anything from a wok (*Sears*

makes an easy-to-store streamlined model) to a wafflemaker (you can use a stove-top Belgian waffle iron without electricity). But make it something you're really going to use. You won't mind finding room for a wafflemaker if waffles are an everyday family breakfast favorite or you top them with

creamed chicken one night and strawberries and cream another. Even if you're willing to drink instant coffee most of the time, you can treat your favorite coffee fan to a cup of freshly brewed coffee with only a little more effort if you have a 1-cup permanent coffee filter (*Rittergold* makes one that easily rinses clean and takes only a few inches of storage space). These custom options will put your personal stamp on your kitchen and remind you that all your time in the kitchen should be enjoyable.

Indispensable Disposables: Perhaps the most dramatic difference between the way we use our kitchen at home and on the road is our attitude toward disposables. At home we recycle aluminum cans and bottles, store leftovers in reusable containers, use cloth napkins and dishtowels, get out the inexpensive roll of paper towels only if someone has dumped over a glass of milk or a mirror needs polishing, and wouldn't even notice if we were out of aluminum foil. On the road, being out of foil is second only to being out of gas, we use clothlike paper towels whenever possible for cleanups and dishes, and on extended trips cans and leftovers are likely to end up in the nearest trash receptacle.

We're still conservation-minded; but on the road we are conserving water, energy, space, time, and ourselves.

Disposables are extraordinarily useful traveling companions that will make your on-the-road cooking and cleanup *much* easier: with some recipes in the book, you'll end up with only the forks in your hands to wash at the end of the meal.

Matches, regular and fireplace lengths

Aluminum foil

Sealable plastic bags, sandwich-size, 1-quart, 1-gallon (*Ziploc* bags are convenient and reliable even with liquids)

Plastic wrap (choose a brand that's microwave-safe if you have a microwave oven)

Heavy-duty paper towels ("super towels" like *Job Squad* can actually be used for washing and drying dishes and as scrub cloths; add a nylon scouring sheet cut into small squares for tougher jobs and you don't need any other cleaning equipment)

Small garbage bags

Setting the Table

Your choice of tableware has a lot to do with your style of RVing in general—casual, rustic; elegant, sophisticated. But don't be misled by the RV ads into stocking your cabinets with fine crystal and china. Choose plastic or break-resistant tableware like *Corelle*, or use disposables. Many RVers who spend considerable time in their RVs get by comfortably using disposable tableware almost exclusively. If you are planning to use paper plates, get a set of paper-plate holders, woven bamboo or plastic. (About the only time anyone seems to object to paper plates is when steak is on the menu; try having some heavy-duty disposable plates for those occasions.)

In any case, you will need several cereal/soup bowls for salads, desserts, snacks, serving, etc. There are disposable/reuseable thin plastic bowls sold as partyware that will fit the bill for a renter or for short trips. Or get something more substantial. Make sure they and any pieces of dinnerware you buy nest well for compact storage. Depending on the design, tableware can take inches or feet to store.

For beverages, paper cups are essential and, on some occasions, the more expensive clear-plastic disposable party glasses are nice. If you want "crystal," try the handsome acrylic tumblers and stemware designed for poolside use (*Epic Products* makes acrylic wineglasses elegant enough for imported vintage champagne). If you plan to depend on disposable cups, stow a set of camper's plastic nesting cups somewhere, just in case.

For hot drinks we like *Solo Cozy* cups, disposable plastic cups that fit into permanent plastic holders with handles. The refills cost about the same as paper cups, but the *Solo* cups are more stable and endlessly useful as small bowls for foods as well as for both hot and cold beverags.

Although it's nice to have a small bag of plastic spoons, knives, and forks on hand, they are not satisfactory flatware substitutes for any extended use; for one thing, if you're going to reuse them, they are hard to keep clean. We also advise against the gadgety picnicware that combines utensils—ever try to eat soup with a spork? Fortunately, a simple set of stainless flatware is inexpensive. Look for moderate-sized utensils.

When you are setting a camp table, smooth plastic placemats that can be wiped or scrubbed clean or a patterned cloth tablecloth that can be tossed in with any laundry load make dining more pleasant.

Add paper napkins, a plastic pitcher, and an unbreakable tray/platter or two and you're all set.

Stocking the Pantry

Obviously there are considerably greater differences in how we stock our pantries than in basic cooking equipment. Otherwise we wouldn't be writing a book featuring the regional specialties of our country. But to provide a common base,

we have compiled three pantry lists that include the ingredients most frequently called for in the recipes in the book.

You don't necessarily have to take the entire contents of a package with you: unless you're planning to do a lot of baking, you're not going to need 5 pounds of sugar or flour.

Basics: The basic pantry list consists of the items we have assumed you have on hand. All but the perishable dairy products can be stored in the RV in any season without refrigeration.

Butter (or margarine)
Buttermilk baking mix (our choice: *Bisquick*)
Cinnamon
Cornstarch (a small supply will do unless you make gravy with it every day)
Cooking oil (an all-purpose cooking/salad oil)
Eggs
Flour (all-purpose flour or instant flour)
Instant chicken and beef bullion (cubes or granules)
Milk (you might keep a small box of instant dry milk on hand in addition to fresh milk)
Mixed herbs (make up a multipurpose mix of your favorite fine herbs—dill, basil, chives, chervil, and/or parsley—for salads, vegetables, and other dishes)
Pepper
Salt
Sugar
Vanilla extract

Tip: Keep a small cache of "emergency" supplies in a sandwich bag tucked away in your pantry: a book of matches and a couple of restaurant packets of sugar, salt, pepper, lemon juice, etc.

The Dependables: These common ingredients, often called for in this book, are things you probably usually have on hand anyway.

Brown sugar
Confectioners' sugar
Instant minced onion
Grated Parmesan cheese
Ketchup
Lemon juice
Mayonnaise (or salad dressing)
Prepared mustard
Sherry (a small bottle)
Soy sauce and/or bottled teriyaki sauce
   (our choice: *Kikkoman*)
Tabasco or other hot pepper sauce
Syrup
Vinegar
Worchestershire sauce

The Versatiles: These versatile products are useful in so many recipes, you may find it convenient to keep them on hand if you can find room.

Bacon (you can store unopened canned bacon like canned ham)
Condensed soups—cream of chicken, cream of mushroom
Corn muffin mix (our choice: *Jiffy*)
Gelatin dessert mix—lemon, berry
Herb-seasoned stuffing (herbed bread-crumb dressing) and/or herb-seasoned croutons
Instant rice
Italian salad dressing (our choice: *Newman's Own Olive Oil and Vinegar Dressing*)
Miniature bottles of brandy and liqueurs
Orange marmalade
Pancake mix
Pastas—plain, packaged dinners
Picante salsa (our choice: *Pace*)
Spaghetti sauce (our choice: *Ragú* or *Newman's Own*)

Of course, this is just the beginning for *your* pantry list: now you have to fit in coffee, tea, cocoa, crackers, cereal, peanut butter . . .

Preparing for Your Trip

Just as you take swimming suits when headed toward the beach in warm weather and sweaters or coats if you're off to the high country, pack your kitchen with the specifics of your trip in mind.

Think about the weather you are likely to encounter, your destinations, who is going, the length of the trip, what you'll be doing: if you're heading south in the summer, you are unlikely to be doing much baking. But if you're going north for the fall color, you may enjoy making corn muffins and oven meals—don't forget the special baking pans. Going to the seashore? Pack the 5-quart pan for clams, crab, lobster. Taking the children? Lay in a supply of wholesome nibbles and pack the campfire pie cooker.

Advance shopping and food preparation can vary dramatically from the approach of our neighbors who pack *everything* they are going to eat for the next two weeks to people like us who enjoy the serendipity of living on the land—we've taken off for several-week trips with practically bare cupboards. (If you take our tack, just make sure you have the first day's meals along and *always* have an easy "emergency" meal or two with you that anyone who can open a can or read a package can do—there are days like that in everyone's travels.)

For short trips, cooking in advance makes a lot of sense. At the least, you can take advantage of the conveniences of your home kitchen to do some of the work before getting on the road. For example, prewash your salad greens and shred a supply of cheese in your food processor and bag it by the cupful or in 2-ounce batches.

But beyond that, it depends a lot on how large your freezer is and how much you prefer doing work in advance of your trip. The favorite packing strategy of our relatives who go on long hunting trips to remote areas is to spend the week or so prior to the trip stocking their freezers with batches of lasagna, casseroles, chili, etc. (Of course, you can do the same thing with commercially prepared frozen dinners.)

We think, for most circumstances, easy on-the-road cooking is far less trouble all around and a lot more fun. One of the nicest things about RVing is having all the comforts of your own home with you. But if you eat like you've never left home, you'll be depriving yourselves of one of the most delightful dimensions of travel—the adventure of new eating experiences.

A SAMPLER OF GREAT AMERICAN RECIPES

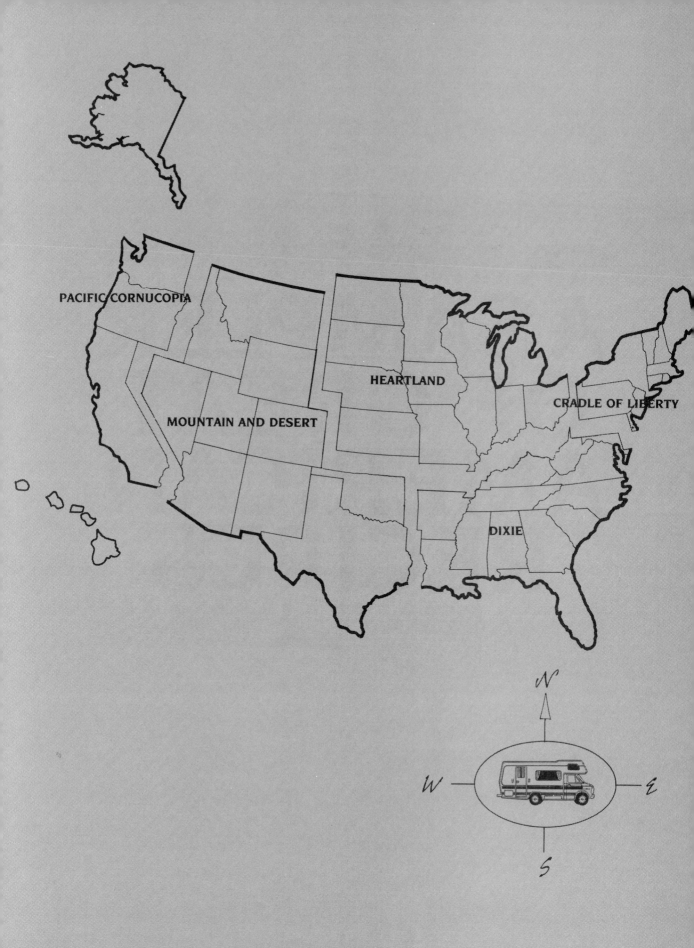

Creative Cookery

PACIFIC CORNUCOPIA

We begin our cook's tour of America with the creative cookery of the Pacific because it is so much in the spirit of RV cooking. Far West food is the fun and festive food of beach picnics, fiestas, luaus, potlaches, and patio parties. The cooking is casual but as cosmopolitan as it comes. And, from the beginning, the wondrous bounty of land and sea has inspired its cooks from the tropical islands of the Pacific to the arctic reaches of the North.

But whether they are creating a salad for a starlet or making lumberjack breakfasts as big as the redwoods, the cooks of the Pacific seem to be blessed with more than bounty: they have a spirit of adventure. The imaginative mingling of cultural traditions has led to Mission-style cooking—and to the New Cuisine. The creative use of ingredients has led to the Hangtown Fry—and the California Black Olive Quiche. And, perhaps more to the point, as a *Newsweek* article describing the glorious food of one creative Pacific Coast chef pointed out, even failures can be fun when cooking is an adventure.

The cardinal rules of the New American Cooking as practiced in the Far West are the same that led to old classics like Caesar Salad and Crab Louis: *Use the best fresh ingredients and don't be afraid to invent*—our first and best recipe for the on-the-road cook.

EYE OPENERS

All recipes serve four unless otherwise stated.

Jade and Gold Breakfast Salad

Fresh fruit is a sunny way to start the day all over America, but breakfasters in the Far West do far more than slice a banana on their bowls of cereal. Chilled slices of pastel-hued melons, fresh green and purple figs in sour cream, broiled pink and gold grapefruits, and a rainbow of berries drizzled with cream are only the beginning. With a glorious palette of fruits, the creative cooks of the Pacific Cornucopia practice the fine art of salad making even at breakfast.

1 ripe pineapple
1 ripe avocado
¼ cup lime juice
¼ cup honey

To prepare the pineapple: Slice off the bottom and the frond. Quarter the pineapple. Cut the core off each quarter and discard. Cut between the shell and pineapple flesh, leaving the flesh resting on the shell. Slice horizontally into large bite-size sections (quarter rings).

To prepare avocado: Halve avocado lengthwise, then twist gently to separate halves. Whack a sharp knife directly into seed and twist to lift out. To peel each half, place cut side down in palm of hand and strip the peel away with the other hand. Cut crosswise into crescents.

Mix lime juice and honey in a disposable cup. Place each pineapple quarter on its shell or on a plate. Tuck avocado crescents between pineapple slices and drizzle with honey-lime dressing.

Midsummer Fruit Bowl

1 ripe pineapple, cut into chunks
1 pint fresh berries or
sweet pitted cherries
½ pound green and/or red grapes
1 pound other fresh fruits (sliced
peaches, plums, nectarines)
1 cup California rosé wine

Combine fruit with the wine in a large bowl and chill for at least an hour. Serve this bountiful fruit bowl with bakery croissants for a luscious light brunch.

California Black Olive Quiche

Quiches continue to find favor on chic American menus, but they are just as likely to show up on the tables of folks who couldn't care less whether what they eat is "in" as long as it tastes terrific. And there are those who like quiches because they are easy one-dish meals. Whatever your reason, this classy classic will make you feel like you're breakfasting in a Beverly Hills mansion. (Of course, in Beverly Hills breakfast can come at any hour of the day.)

1 9-inch deep-dish pie shell (unbaked)*
4 ounces Swiss cheese, finely diced or shredded
6 bacon slices, cooked crisp and crumbled
1 6-ounce can California ripe pitted olives, drained
4 eggs
2 cups (1 pint) half-and-half (light cream)
Salt and pepper
Nutmeg

Preheat oven to 375°. On bottom of pie shell arrange cheese, crumbled bacon, and olives. In a 1½-quart bowl, beat eggs, half-and-half, and generous sprinklings of salt, pepper, and nutmeg until well-mixed. Pour over cheese, bacon, and olives. Be careful not to overfill the shell, as you may have a bit too much filling. (Tip: It is sometimes easier to pour the custard filling when the pie pan is already in position on a baking sheet on the oven rack.) Bake on a baking sheet in oven until top is golden and a knife inserted a few inches in from the edge comes out clean (about 30 to 45 minutes). Serve with Sunshines or a white or rosé California wine or champagne.

Variations: Without the olives, this recipe is a basic *Quiche Lorraine* with cheese—good all by itself or as a basis for other quiche combinations. Quiche fillings are limited only by imagination—chopped spinach seasoned with mustard and tarragon, sliced mushrooms and shallots, cooked crab or lobster moistened with sherry. (Allow about a cup of filling in place of the olives and/or bacon.) One simple substitution we often make in the basic quiche is to replace the crumbled bacon with 4 ounces of cooked ham, thinly sliced and diced.

*If you are making the quiche in a *standard* 9-inch pie pan, reduce the amount of custard to 3 eggs and 1½ cups half-and-half.

Hangtown Fry

California lore has it that a '49er came into a Hangtown establishment with a poke of nuggets and asked for the finest, and most expensive, meal possible. Since eggs and oysters were the most prohibitive items on the menu, the Hangtown Fry was created. The still popular dish was originally made with the small Pacific Coast Olympia oysters, now so rare that you have to strike it rich to afford them today, too.

16 large oysters, shucked
Flour
Butter
8 eggs
¼ cup whipping cream
1 cup grated Parmesan cheese

Roll oysters in flour and fry in a skillet in butter over medium heat until just delicately browned. In a bowl mix eggs, cream, and Parmesan cheese. Pour over oysters and cook until eggs are set. (You can do this like an omelet or as slightly scrambled eggs.)

Three Capes Crab Strata

We considered calling this "Have-You-Lost-Your-Mind?" Souffle. But the only thing tricky about this souffle-puff is, if you make it ahead, finding overnight refrigerator space for a baking pan. Try the puff as a delicious showpiece for a leisurely brunch in any cool Pacific campsite. (It will serve 6.)

12 slices white bread
½ cup (1 stick) butter, softened
8 ounces of fresh cooked
    Dungeness crabmeat *or*
    1 6½-ounce can crabmeat,
    drained
8 ounces (about 2 cups) Tillamook
    Cheddar cheese *or* other sharp
    Cheddar, grated
4 eggs
3 cups milk

Remove bread crusts and butter bread slices on both sides. Lay 6 slices in a rectangular baking pan. Sprinkle with cheese and crabmeat. Top with remaining 6 slices of buttered bread. In a bowl, beat eggs and milk together until well-mixed. Pour over the "sandwiches." Refrigerate overnight or let stand at least an hour at room temperature.

Preheat oven to 325°. (If the strata has been refrigerated, let it warm up at room temperature while you are preheating the oven.) Bake 1 hour. A knife inserted a few inches from the edge will come out clean when the strata is ready. Cut in squares and serve hot.

Note: If you wish to reduce this to 4 servings, use a square deep pan and 8 slices of bread, but use the full amount of crab and cheese, reduce the eggs to 3 and the milk to 2½ cups.

Zucchini Frittata

Vegetables also have their place in the morning sun. Old World versions of the Italian frittata finish this omelet-like dish under the broiler, but it's tasty, and much cooler, as a stovetop breakfast or lunch.

4 small zucchini, trimmed and
    sliced
2 tablespoons cooking oil
1 shallot, sliced thin (optional)
Salt and pepper
¼ teaspoon dried basil *or*
    pizza seasoning *or*
    mixed herbs
6 eggs
½ cup grated Parmesan cheese

Heat oil in a skillet over medium-high heat. Add zucchini and shallot slices and cook covered, stirring from time to time, until zucchini is tender and slightly transparent (about 5 to 10 minutes). Midway through the cooking, generously season the zucchini with salt and pepper and add the herbs. When the zucchini is cooked to your preference, break in the eggs and stir in the Parmesan cheese. Scramble the eggs well with the zucchini slices and cook until the eggs are set. Serve immediately.

Variations: If you are making the frittata as a side dish, reduce the eggs to 2 or 3. You can substitute other summer squashes for all or part of the zucchini or add other sliced vegetables—mushrooms, sweet onions, or fresh mild green peppers.

"Birthday" Pancakes

When one of our youngsters had a birthday on the road, we started the day with these fun fanciful pancakes. They enjoyed them so much that they manage to declare a "birthday" on every trip we take—like several for a favorite stuffed Mickey Mouse that travels with us.

Pancake batter mix for 12 to 15 pancakes, made according to package directions
Black jellybeans
Cherry fruit roll-ups

Use ⅓ cup batter for face, ⅛ cup batter for each ear; fry pancake as usual. Use 1 black jellybean for nose and 2 halves for eyes. Cut a smiling mouth out of cherry fruit roll-up and shape 1-inch strips of roll-up into a perky bow tie.

Variations: For unbirthdays, make features with squeezed-on syrup or raisins. Once you start sculpting with pancakes, it's hard to stop—we make teddy bears, elephants, crabs. Now a round pancake seems odd.

SOUPS, SALADS, AND SANDWICHES

Oregon Coast Cioppino

Cioppino, the seafood stew California made famous, is enjoyed on up the Pacific coast to Canada in many delightful variations with whatever fish and shellfish is available. The name, coined probably by the Italian-American fisherfolk who invented this Mediterranean-inspired stew, means roughly "chopped a little," and little bits of chopped this and that have made most recipes for this American classic complicated. But start with a good spaghetti sauce and you'll have this great stew on the table in 15 minutes.

2 15½-ounce jars chunky spaghetti sauce with extra tomatoes, garlic and onions*
1 cup white or red wine
1½ pounds Oregon trawlfish (perch, snapper) fillets, cut in bite-size pieces (about 1 inch)
1 cup (4 ounces) tiny cooked shrimp
12 steamer clams (optional)

In your largest skillet or saucepan (it will be a tight squeeze in a 10-inch skillet or 2-quart pan), heat sauce and wine over medium-high heat until simmering (use a lid to keep stovetop clean). Stir in fish and simmer gently for about 10 minutes or until fish is almost opaque. Add scrubbed steamer clams in shell, cook until clams open. Stir in cooked shrimp and heat just for a moment and serve. (If you are omitting the clams, stir in the shrimp when the fish is done.) You can sprinkle some parsley or chervil on the stew for color if you have it, but the cioppino makes a hearty meal in a dish with no further embellishment. For the full wharf-side restaurant treatment, add sourdough bread and a dry red wine.

*Ragu Gardenstyle Spaghetti Sauce is our choice for this recipe, but a regular spaghetti sauce will work well also.

Pacific Oyster Stew

The subtleties of perfect and properly made oyster stew vary from region to region and, as always, from cook to cook. In New York they often add a little Worcestershire sauce, and celery seed or a dash of *Tabasco* show up in other recipes. The one thing that oysters stew is not, is stewed—and various culinary techniques have been devised to prevent the oysters from being overcooked, sometimes involving juggling scalded cream in multiple pans. This family recipe, popular along the Pacific Coast, is the soul of simplicity and to our taste about perfect—although you might like to add a tablespoon of sherry.

30 medium oysters, shucked (use more or less depending on size of oysters)
¼ cup (½ stick) butter
1 teaspoon paprika
1 cup oyster liquor, white wine, or water
2 cups (1 pint) light cream (or use milk with a bit more butter)

Melt butter in saucepan, stir in paprika and liquid, and bring to a boil. Reduce the heat, add the oysters, and simmer until their edges begin to curl and they plump up (about 3 to 5 minutes). Stir in cream and cook only long enough to heat without boiling. Salt to taste. Serve with a pat of butter floating on top of each bowl.

Crab Louis

This world famous Pacific Coast creation was served at the Olympic Club in Seattle in 1904 to Enrico Caruso, *or* orginated at Solari's in San Francisco about 1914, *or* was an innovation at the Bohemian Restaurant in Portland, Oregon, that same year. When you make it you'll understand why everyone wants to claim this classic crab salad that is still featured in fine restaurants.

1½ pounds cooked Dungeness lump crabmeat, picked over
4 cups shredded lettuce
2 hard-boiled eggs, quartered
4 tomatoes, quartered
1 avocado, peeled and sliced (optional)
***Louis Dressing*:**
1 cup mayonnaise
½ cup sour cream*
¼ cup chili sauce
2 tablespoons grated onion

On a large platter (or individual serving plates) arrange a bed of lettuce. Heap the crabmeat on top. Garnish with eggs, tomatoes, and avocado. Combine the dressing ingredients. (If you have them on hand, add 2 tablespoons of fresh chopped parsley and a sprinkling of cayenne.) Pour Louis Dressing over the crab salad and serve.

*Traditional Louis recipes call for a cup of whipped cream.

Caesar Salad

According to Hollywood folklore, a group of movie people spent a Fourth of July weekend during Prohibition in Tijuana (the Mexican border town had no liquor restrictions). The Caesar Salad is supposed to have been created for them by one Caesar Cardini, a restaurant owner whose larder was temporarily bare except for a few esoteric ingredients. The fame of Caesar's Salad spread across California and the continent.* All of which should be an inspiration to you the next time your pantry is paltry.

1 head romaine lettuce, washed and torn into bite-size pieces
1 egg
1 2-ounce can anchovy fillets with capers
2 tablespoons lemon juice (½ large fresh lemon)
¼ to ½ cup oil
½ cup grated Parmesan cheese or Romano cheese
Salt and pepper to taste
1 cup garlic-cheese croutons

The secret to Caesar Salad is an egg coddled for 1 minute, which is not hard to do. In small saucepan bring 2 inches of water to boiling. Turn off heat and lower whole egg in its shell into the water. Let stand 1 minute. Lift out of the water.

In a large bowl combine the romaine (it should be cool and crisp), anchovies (including the oil), lemon juice, ¼ cup oil, and grated Parmesan cheese; break in the coddled egg. Toss until well combined. Season to taste with salt and pepper and add more oil if needed. Sprinkle on garlic-cheese croutons and gently toss again. Serve with Margaritas to toast adventurous traveling eaters then and now.

*In 1951 the International Society of Epicures in Paris gave Caesar Cardini an award for "the greatest recipe contribution of the United States in 50 years."

Newport Shrimp Salad

A refreshing first course for a seaside meal.

½ pound small cooked Pacific salad shrimp, shelled and cleaned
1 head lettuce, washed and torn into pieces
Other salad greens, sliced avocado, and tomato wedges as desired
1 1-ounce slice of Swiss cheese, cut into matchstick strips
1 cup bottled Italian dressing
1 cup herbed croutons (optional)

Rinse shrimp and drain excess water. In a small refrigerator container mix Italian dressing and shrimp and marinate in refrigerator for 20 minutes to an hour if convenient (or longer). Pour shrimp and marinade over greens, other vegetables, and cheese and toss. Top with croutons.

Salad Loretta

Four of the Pacific Cornucopia's finest products make this delicate, delicious salad our favorite.

½ pound fresh perfect
mushrooms, cleaned and thinly
sliced
1 cup high-quality bottled Italian
dressing*
1 fresh lemon, squeezed
(or substitute 2 tablespoons
lemon juice)
1 teaspoon dried mixed salad
herbs
Salt and pepper, preferably
freshly ground
1 small head Bibb lettuce
(or Big Boston lettuce), washed
2 ripe avocados

Put mushrooms in a refrigerator container. Mix Italian dressing, fresh lemon juice, salad herbs, and generous sprinklings of salt and pepper. Pour marinade over mushrooms, toss gently, and chill at least one hour. (You can keep mushrooms for up to 2 days in the marinade, but they become "cooked.")

Just before serving, arrange lettuce leaves as cups. Slice or halve and peel avocados. Arrange avocado halves or a fan of avocado slices on lettuce cups. Spoon chilled marinated mushrooms over each serving.

Variation: Marinated Mushrooms for an antipasto tray can be made by chilling small whole cleaned mushrooms in the above Italian dressing and lemon mixture.

*Loretta's choice is *Newman's Own Olive Oil and Vinegar* Dressing.

Coronado Spinach Salad

1 to 2 pounds fresh spinach
washed and dried thoroughly
4 slices bacon, diced
4 hard-boiled eggs, sliced
2 small scallions (green onions)
including tops, sliced into
small pieces (about ¼ cup)
2 teaspoons brown or white sugar
2 tablespoons vinegar
Salt and pepper (preferably
coarsely ground)
1 cup croutons (optional)

Tear spinach into bite-size pieces and put in a bowl. Cook diced bacon in a skillet over medium-high heat until crisp. Reduce heat and stir in sugar, green onions, and vinegar. Bring to a boil, remove from heat, and let cool a little. Pour over salad and toss. Season to taste with salt and pepper. Top with sliced eggs and croutons and toss again gently.

Variations: If you are serving the salad as a side dish, you may want to omit the hard-boiled eggs. Chefs often add a personal fillip to this salad from a handful of fresh mushrooms slices or pine nuts to the Hotel del Coronado's brandy-flamed finale.

California Poppy Seed Salad

There are so many excellent bottled dressings on the market today that a dressing has to have star quality to warrant special attention. This one has.

1 16-ounce can mandarin orange
  sections, drained
1 16-ounce can grapefruit
  sections, drained
2 avocados, peeled and sliced
Poppy Seed Dressing:
½ cup oil
1 teaspoon prepared mustard
2 tablespoons lemon juice
2 tablespoons honey
1 tablespoon poppy seed
Salt and pepper to taste

Put mandarin orange sections, grapefruit sections, and sliced avocados in a bowl. Mix remaining ingredients (use a disposable cup) and pour over the fruits. Gently toss the salad and serve.

Variation: Other fruits—sliced kiwis, strawberries, pineapple—can be added.

A Pair of Pears with O'Henry's Dressing

The famed pears of Oregon's Rogue River Valley and pear-shaped avocados from California are the handsome pair that make this winning combination.

2 ripe pears, chilled and sliced in
  lengthwise wedges
2 ripe avocados, peeled and
  sliced in lengthwise wedges
Lettuce leaves
O'Henry's Dressing:
1 8-ounce carton sour cream
¼ cup (2 ounces) blue cheese,
  crumbled

On individual serving plates, arrange pear slices and avocado slices alternately in a decorative pattern on a bed of lettuce leaves. You can make overlapping fans or the petals of a flower. Mix sour cream and blue cheese. Pour a little of the dressing on each salad and pass the remainder.

Variations: Bottled blue cheese dressing may be substituted for for the O'Henry's Dressing. Canned drained pears can be substituted for the fresh pears.

San Francisco's Avocado and Bacon Sandwich

Avocado and bacon sandwiches, one of the most popular sandwiches in California, are even more distinctive when made with thin slices of San Francisco's world-famous sourdough bread instead of the usual whole wheat or white toast (and you don't have to plug in or heat the RV oven).

8 slices sourdough bread (cut on the diagonal if a thin loaf)
Mayonnaise
1 ripe avocado, peeled and sliced
½ pound bacon, halved and cooked crisp
1 large tomato, sliced
Salt and pepper

Spread bread with mayonnaise on one side. Divide avocado slices, bacon, and tomato slices among the sandwiches and arrange in layers, sprinkling salt and pepper to taste on the avocado and tomato. Top with remaining bread, cut in halves or quarters to serve.

Variation: Add thinly sliced sweet Spanish onion and/or lettuce leaves.

Solvang Sandwich

There are parts of the Pacific region that can make you feel like your RV will have to pass customs. Some like San Francisco's famed Chinatown are in big cities; others are off the beaten track like Solvang, a Danish town north of Santa Barbara. Not surprisingly, the Solvang Sandwich, which features the avocados grown near there, is served Danish-style—open-face.

4 large slices rye, pumpernickel, or white bread
Butter
2 ripe avocados, peeled and thinly sliced
½ pound small cooked shrimp, shelled
1 tablespoon lemon juice
¼ teaspoon dill weed (optional)
2 ounces crumbled blue cheese
1 2-ounce can rolled anchovy fillets, drained

Spread bread with butter. Arrange rows of avocado slices and shrimp on bread. Sprinkle with lemon juice and dill weed. Crumble blue cheese on each sandwich and garnish with anchovies.

Vineyard Steak

A kissing cousin of Steak Diane, easy Vineyard Steak will do justice to a choice cut of fine Western beef.

4 tender serving-size steaks (filet, rib, club, or sirloin)
2 tablespoons butter
2 tablespoons finely chopped shallots or scallions (green onions)
⅔ cup California red wine
Salt and pepper

Heat butter in skillet until foaming has almost stopped. Pan-broil steaks in butter until desired doneness (about 3 or 4 minutes on each side of a 1-inch-thick steak for medium rare). Transfer steaks to plates and salt and pepper to taste. Pour excess fat out of pan into a heatproof disposable container. Add finely chopped shallots and wine, and bring to boil over very hot flame, scraping all the pan juices up from the bottom of the pan with a wooden or plastic spatula. Boil for about a minute and pour over steaks. Serve with the rest of the bottle of wine and salad.

Note: If you have to do the steaks in two batches, because your skillet is small (or the steaks are big), do the first steaks all the way through using half of the shallots and wine. Start over with fresh butter for the second batch.

Variations: You can substitute ⅓ cup of sherry or brandy for the wine. A gourmet variation of this recipe, *Steak Henry* IV, tops the steaks with hot artichoke bottoms filled with Bearnaise sauce.

Chicken Waikiki

Add a tropical fruit salad and an island punch to this luau in a pouch and you'll feel like doing the hula wherever you are parked.

4 large pieces of chicken breast (about 2½ pounds of split breasts with ribs)
Flour
Salt and pepper
6 tablespoons butter
1 bunch fresh spinach, washed and picked over
2 tablespoons chopped scallions (use two or three onions with just a little of the tops)
½ cup dry white wine
4 teaspoons soy sauce
½ teaspoon ground ginger
8 to 12 mushrooms, cleaned and sliced

Skin chicken pieces and rinse in cool water. Pat dry with paper towels. Lightly flour the chicken pieces and salt and pepper generously. Melt about half the butter in a skillet over medium-high heat and brown the chicken on both sides, adding more butter as needed and turning the pieces with tongs several times. Mix the wine, soy sauce, ginger, and chopped scallions in a small container (a paper cup or measuring cup will work well). Tear off 4 pieces of aluminum foil about 12 inches square. On each foil square place a layer of about 8 large spinach leaves. Lay a browned chicken piece on the spinach. Top each chicken piece with ¼ of the mushroom slices and ¼ of the soy-wine mixture (about 2 or 3 tablespoons). Cover with about 6 more spinach leaves and fold foil to make a sealed pouch. Bake about 1 hour in a preheated 350° oven or over medium-hot coals until chicken is cooked through. Serve chicken in pouch accompanied by white or wild rice.

Sweet and Sour Meatballs

Among the many international cuisines that are appreciated in the Pacific Cornucopia, few have had the widespread popularity of Americanized Chinese recipes.

Meatballs:
1 pound lean ground beef
1 cup herbed bread-crumb dressing or croutons, crushed to fine crumbs*
1 egg

Other ingredients:
2 tablespoons butter
1 9½-ounce jar sweet and sour sauce
1 small green pepper, sliced thin
1 13¼-ounce can pineapple chunks
1 carrot, sliced thin (optional)

Mix together beef, stuffing, and egg, and make walnut-size meatballs. Melt butter in a skillet and brown meatballs. Continue cooking meatballs over medium heat for a few minutes. Stir in sweet and sour sauce, pepper, carrot, and the pineapple juice from the can of pineapple. Cover and simmer for 10 minutes, stirring from time to time. Stir in pineapple chunks and heat through. Serve over rice.

*Put the dressing or croutons in a sealable plastic bag and mash with anything heavy or tap with the back of a heavy spoon.

Sweet and Sour Sauce

If you don't happen to have a bottle of sweet and sour sauce on hand, you may have the makings for this Northwest Coast version or for the Simple Sweet and Sour Sauce from Hawaii.

3 tablespoons sugar
1 tablespoon soy sauce
1 tablespoon dry white wine
2 tablespoons vinegar
¼ cup pineapple juice
2 tablespoons ketchup
1 tablespoon cornstarch

In small saucepan, over medium heat, combine sugar, soy sauce, wine, vinegar, pineapple juice, and ketchup; bring to a boil. Mix cornstarch in ½ cup water until smooth and add to sauce. Stir mixture until thickened.

Simple Sweet and Sour Sauce

2 tablespoons vinegar
4 tablespoons sugar
2 teaspoons Worcestershire
   sauce
1 cup ketchup

Mix and stir into skillet with meatballs.

Polynesian Prawns in Pineapple Shells

You won't regret passing up the posh hotels when you have this at a tranquil oceanside campground.

1 ripe medium pineapple
1 pound large raw prawns or
   large raw shrimp, peeled and
   cleaned*
¼ cup (½ stick) butter
1 10-ounce package frozen snow
   peas or ½ pound fresh snow
   pea pods, washed and trimmed
1 medium green pepper, thinly
   sliced
Sweet and Sour Glaze:
1 cup (1 10-ounce net weight jar)
   orange marmalade
2 tablespoons soy sauce
2 tablespoons vinegar
1 teaspoon ground ginger

Cut pineapple in half lengthwise, right through the frond. Cut pineapple out of shell, leaving uncut pineapple shells ½ inch thick. Cut the core out of the pineapple and discard; cut remaining pineapple into bite-size chunks.

Melt butter in a skillet over medium heat (don't let butter brown). Fry prawns just until they begin to become pink (about 5 minutes). Add pineapple chunks, snow pea pods, and green pepper; cook, stirring occasionally, for several minutes. Combine glaze ingredients and pour over prawns mixture. Cook, stirring now and then, until the green pepper and pea pods are tender. Spoon into pineapple shells and serve with Luau Punch or Hawaiian pineapple wine.

*You'll enjoy the prawns more if you do the shelling and deveining outside of your RV. That step tends to leave a lingering odor.

Dungeness Crab Linguini

We were on our honeymoon when we first made this dish in a motel room on Bodega Bay on the north coast of California. It surpassed many of the expensive restaurant meals of our wedding trip and whetted our appetite for cooking on the road. We still fix this memorable linguini with the first crab of a trip.

**Crabmeat from 1 or 2 cooked
  Dungeness crabs
2 6-ounce packages *Noodle Roni
  Parmesano*
1 cup milk
½ to 1 cup (1 to 2 sticks) butter
½ cup white wine**

Melt ½ cup (1 stick) of the butter in a skillet and warm the crabmeat in the hot butter. Stir in milk, wine, and more butter (if you use 2 crabs, you will probably need another ½ cup butter); heat through but do not boil. Stir in sauce packets.

Meanwhile, cook noodles in boiling water for 5 minutes. Drain. Combine drained noodles and crab mixture in whichever pan is larger. Serve with a salad, sourdough bread, and California white wine.

Silver Salmon Columbia

Since we fish for recipes the way other people fish for fish, this is our version of a fish story.

We had bought a couple of handsome fresh silver salmon commercially raised in the Northwest, planning to have a cookout in our campsite near the gorgeous waterfalls of the Columbia River. But, as often happens in this region, it rained. Assuming not *all* the fish caught around there were record-breakers, we went local-recipe-fishing for an easy way of dealing with small salmon. At the Vista House on the Columbia River Gorge we came up with a real winner when a local lady shared this dandy technique: Poach salmon in milk. That's it. Period.

According to our source this can be done in the oven as well as on the stovetop. The trick is that the milk boils up, making a bubble that keeps the salmon's delicate flavor and moistness intact.

Well, we went right back to our RV and tried it, and, sure enough, it worked like a charm! Which goes to show that a recipe doesn't have to be complicated to be special—but if we didn't believe that, we wouldn't have written this book.

**2 to 4 pan-size silver salmon
  or other salmon or trout,
  cleaned
Milk**

Rinse fish and pat dry with paper towels. Put as many of the fish as will fit in the skillet. Pour milk over the fish until they're almost covered. Bring milk to a boil and reduce the heat so that it continues boiling, but doesn't boil over. Cook until fish flakes easily (about 15 minutes for average pan-size fish). Repeat with remaining fish. Serve the poached salmon hot or cold with pan sauce (it tastes like cheese) and your favorite fish sauce—tartar sauce, lemon and butter, sour cream and dill weed.

Poached Pacific Perch

Subtly and simply enhance fresh fish fillets with this New Cuisine recipe.

1 to 1½ pounds fresh Pacific
    perch or other mild fish fillets
2 tablespoons butter
1 cup California white wine
1 teaspoon dried mixed salad
    herbs *or* 1 teaspoon dill weed,
    chopped chives, or dried
    tarragon
Salt and pepper

Rinse fillets and pat dry with paper towels. Melt butter in a skillet over high heat. Add fish fillets and cook for a minute or two on each side. Pour wine over fillets; sprinkle with herbs, salt, and pepper. Bring wine to boil. Reduce heat, cover, and barely simmer until fish flakes easily in thickest part (about 10 minutes). Serve with pan sauce and a bright bouquet of gently cooked fresh young vegetables.

Snappy Oven-Fried Snapper

2 pounds Pacific snapper or
    other mild fish fillets
½ cup high-quality bottled Italian
    dressing (or substitute ½ cup
    oil and 1 teaspoon salt)
1 cup grated Parmesan cheese
1 cup herb-seasoned stuffing or
    croutons, crushed to fine
    crumbs*

Rinse fish and pat dry with paper towels. Cut fish into serving-size pieces. Put the fish and the Italian dressing in a large sealable plastic bag. Allow the fish to marinate for 20 minutes if you have the time, turning once midway. Preheat oven to 500°. Remove fish from marinade and roll fish in cheese, then in crumbs. Bake on an oiled foil-lined baking sheet. Bake until fish flakes easily when tested with a fork (about 15 minutes.)

*Put the stuffing or croutons in a sealable plastic bag and mash with anything heavy or tap with the back of heavy spoon.

Alaskan Salmon in a Bag

Among the myriad ways Alaskans fix salmon is one so simple that it ought to be in your bag of tricks.

Whole salmon (no longer than the
    longest dimension of your
    oven), cleaned
Butter, softened
Salt and pepper

Preheat oven to 450°. Rinse the salmon and pat dry inside and out with paper towels. Measure salmon at thickest point. Spread a coat of butter over both sides of the salmon. Salt and pepper generously. Put the salmon in an ordinary clean brown paper bag. Close the bag by folding the open end over an inch or two and securing with paper clips or wooden clothespins. Put the bagged salmon on a baking sheet (to catch any drips) and bake until salmon flakes easily when tested with a fork near the backbone (allow 10 minutes for each inch of thickness). Cut the bag to serve fish.

Seawife's Halibut

This is such a simple way of making batter-fried fish, you may never stop at a fish-and-chips place again.

**2 pounds halibut, cut in 2-inch
pieces
1 cup pancake mix
¾ cup beer
1 cup cooking oil**

Heat oil in a skillet over medium-high heat until hot but not smoking. In a bowl, stir beer into pancake mix (if you happen to be doing this on very dry land rather than seaside, you may need more beer to make batter of normal pancake consistency). Dip halibut pieces in batter and fry several at a time until golden (about 3 minutes on each side).

Variations: In place of the beer, some "seawives" use 1 cup milk and 1 egg. This recipe is equally good for other filleted fish—Pacific cod, perch, snapper.

ASIDES

Quilcene Quickies

The prized Quilcene oyster retains its delicate flavor when cooked with this quick trick (so do other oyster varieties).

**Oysters, freshly shucked or
drained
Flour, seasoned with salt and
pepper
Mayonnaise
Fine cracker crumbs (saltine,
club, or similar soup cracker)
Butter**

Use three paper plates or small bowls for the seasoned flour, mayonnaise, and crumbs. It's best to work with small amounts of flour, mayonnaise, and crumbs, making or adding more of each as you need it, since any surplus should be discarded.

Melt about 2 tablespoons of butter over medium heat in a skillet. Roll each oyster in seasoned flour until coated; then coat oyster lightly with mayonnaise (use your fingers or a knife to smooth it on more or less evenly); and then roll oyster in crumbs. Cook coated oysters until light gold (about 5 minutes on each side, a little longer if they are very large). Add more butter as needed for additional batches. Serve the oysters as they come from the pan or with cocktail sauce.

Snow Crab Ball

Popular up and down the Pacific Coast, crab appetizers are a delectable way to stretch a small amount of crab. This one is as special as it is simple—as easy as making a snowball.

1 6-ounce package frozen snow crabmeat, thawed and drained
1 8-ounce package cream cheese, softened
2 teaspoons dried chopped chives
Garlic powder to taste
½ cup chopped blanched almonds

Mix cream cheese, chives, and garlic powder. Fold in crabmeat. Shape into a ball (if you shape the crab mixture in a piece of plastic wrap you can keep your hands neater). Roll crab ball in almonds. Serve with crackers or bread sticks.

Variations: A crab appetizer that is popular in Southern California can be made with most of these same ingredients (omit the almonds). For *Hot Crab Dip*, mix cubed cream cheese, crab (you can use drained canned crab), and seasonings in a small saucepan. Over low heat, stir and heat until cheese is melted and dip is smooth. Optional additions to Hot Crab Dip are 2 tablespoons of sherry, 1 teaspoon prepared mustard, and seasoned salt to taste. If you want to thin the dip, add mayonnaise.

Jelly Blossoms

This salad-in-a-can makes a pretty accompaniment to grilled steaks, fish, or chops, and is especially fun for children.

1 20-ounce can pineapple slices
1 3-ounce package fruit-flavored gelatin (lime, lemon, or orange are good)

Open can of pineapple and drain juice. Dissolve fruit-flavored gelatin in 1 cup boiling water. Pour gelatin mixture into can, almost to top. With a fork or knife, jiggle the fruit slices a little to get the gelatin between the slices. Refrigerate until gelatin is set. (If you think about it a half hour or so later, jiggle the partially set gelatin between the slices again.) To unmold salad, open other end of can and wrap with a hot wet cloth for a moment or two. Use the lid to push out the salad. Slice between the pineapple slices.

Tips: If you are going to be driving while the gelatin is setting, don't fill the can too full and put a plastic sandwich bag or plastic wrap over open end and secure with a rubber band. Mix the leftover dissolved gelatin that doesn't fit in the can with the drained pineapple juice for a fruit "punch" or pour the mixture into ice cube trays or popsicle molds for a treat.

California Guacamole

Southern Californians eat as much Mexican-style food as the people of the Mountain and Desert region, although, understandably, California's dishes have more emphasis on fresh vegetables and fruit. One that has achieved farflung fame is California's guacamole. Guacamole can be eaten as a salad mounded on lettuce with tomato wedges, as a filling for tostadas and tacos with shredded lettuce and chopped tomato, as a sauce on hamburgers and Mexican dishes, and as a dip.

Guacamoles can be delicate or dynamite for different tastes and occasions. Though we've made guacamole countless times, we've seldom made it the same twice. Here's a classic guacamole recipe to get you started.

2 fully ripe avocados, peeled and halved
1 4-ounce can chopped green chilies (or less to taste; start with a tablespoon)
1 tomato, chopped
1 tablespoon lemon or lime juice
1 small clove garlic, minced *or* garlic powder (optional)
Salt

In a small bowl, mash avocados with a fork* and mix in other ingredients. Salt to taste. Serve immediately with tortilla chips or vegetable dippers.

Variations: Crisp, crumbled bacon; a small minced onion; a dash of *Tabasco* sauce; and/or a sprinking of chopped chives, dill weed, cilantro, or parsley can be added. Make a milder guacamole by stirring in ¼ to ½ cup of sour cream or mayonnaise.

*Don't feel bad if you don't have a food processor, neither did the originators of guacamole—it's supposed to have a coarse texture.

Guacamole Pronto

An avocado is good plain with no more embellishment than a squeeze of lemon or lime (or a dash of tequila) and a sprinkle of salt. So it doesn't really need much to make it a special dip. You can do this guacamole in a minute.

1 fully ripe avocado, peeled and halved
2 to 4 tablespoons picante sauce

In a small bowl mash avocado with a fork. Stir in picante sauce to taste. Serve with tortilla chips.

Artichoke Parmesano

1 14-ounce can artichokes, drained and shredded
1 cup mayonnaise
1 cup grated Parmesan cheese

Preheat oven to 350°. Arrange shredded artichokes in a baking pan (a pie pan or cake pan). Top with mayonnaise and Parmesan. Bake for 20 minutes. Serve with an assortment of crackers and California wines. (This is more a spread than a dip.)

Note: It's not quite the same, but you can make this in a saucepan on the stovetop. Heat everything together until bubbly.

Variation: To serve Artichoke Parmesano as a side dish rather than as an appetizer, reduce the mayonnaise and Parmesan cheese to ½ cup each and quarter the artichoke hearts instead of shredding. Bake as directed above.

Monterey Bay Artichokes

Most American artichokes come from the fields around Castroville, California, near Monterey. If you are driving through the region, succumb to the temptation to pull off at one of the farms and buy some—a really fresh artichoke is as special a treat as fresh corn.

Choose artichokes that are firm, heavy, and look fresh. Brown-tinted leaves have been "winter kissed" but their flavor is unaffected.

Artichokes come in all sizes. Don't immediately reach for the largest unless you are sure you have a pan they'll fit into. We met one Texas couple who pack a large pot especially for this stretch of coast and their favorite RV meal—steamed crabs and artichokes served with melted butter and lemon. If you haven't been that far-sighted, you can still enjoy whole artichokes: 1 or 2 medium artichokes will steam in an average 2-quart saucepan if you trim the stem flush with the bottom and trim an inch or so off the tops of the leaves.

2 medium whole artichokes, thoroughly washed and trimmed
Salt
Optional additions: 1 or 2 tablespoons of lemon juice, 1 clove of garlic, peppercorns, bay leaf, 1 or 2 tablespoons of olive oil mixed with wine vinegar, and/or a pinch of oregano

It is not necessary to trim the artichokes if they will fit in your saucepan whole, although usually all but an inch of the stem is trimmed off. (If you are trimming the tips of the leaves, scissors will help.) Pull off tough or discolored bottom leaves. Place the artichoke in enough boiling salted water to cover (about ½ teaspoon of salt for each quart of water). Add any combination of the optional additions—our favorite is peppercorns and oregano when we have them. Cover and simmer until a leaf pulls out easily (about 20 to 30 minutes). Drain and serve hot with melted butter, lemon butter, or hollandaise; or serve cold with mayonnaise or other salad dressing dip. *Capered Mayonnaise* is especially good: stir 1 teaspoon capers into ½ cup of mayonnaise.

If this is your first artichoke, here is a step-by-step eating guide: 1. Pull off a leaf, dip the bottom in sauce, and draw the leaf through your teeth so you get the tender flesh at the bottom. Have a bowl or plate nearby for the "used" leaves—by the time you're done, you'll wonder where they all come from. 2. Eat your way down to the very tender leaves. As they start to change color, you are nearing the choke, stop. 3. Scoop out all the choke—sharp purple-tinged leaves and hairy center—and discard. What is left is the artichoke bottom or crown, considered the best part. 4. Cut the bottom into pieces, dip in sauce, and finish it off.

Variation: Steamed artichokes are made the same way as boiled artichokes exept that only an inch of boiling water is used. Steaming may take up to 10 or 20 minutes longer than boiling.

DESSERTS

Fresh Berry Desserts

The fabulous berries of the Northwest are famed for their flavor and abundance. A handful gathered on a walk can be sugared and sprinkled on cereal or ice cream, and a pint needs nothing more than cream and sugar to make a delightful dessert. But if you have a windfall of berries, it's fun to do something a little special (which will also make them last longer). Use any wild or cultivated sweet berry—strawberries, blueberries, blackberries, Marionberries, raspberries—in these incredibly easy, elegant desserts.

Fresh Berry Mousse

½ to 1 cup washed, hulled, crushed fresh berries
2 cups fruit-flavored yogurt (matching or complementary fruit)
1 8-ounce or 9-ounce container whipped topping, thawed

Combine fruit and yogurt in a refrigerator container. Fold in whipped topping. Freeze about 4 hours, then leave in refrigerator for ½ hour before serving. Keep leftovers frozen.

Variations: If your freezer space is limited, spoon mousse into individual serving containers like paper or plastic cups before freezing. For a *Fresh Berry Cream Pie,* spoon mousse into a graham cracker or unbake nut crust before freezing.

Fresh Berry Summer Pudding

Close your eyes when you taste this old-fashioned fruit pudding and you'll think you're in a charming bread-and-breakfast inn—come to think of it, you are.

4 to 6 slices white bread
1 scant quart (2 pints) soft berries (raspberries, blackberries, strawberries, currants)
1 apple, peeled and thinly sliced (optional)
Sugar

Use a 1-quart bowl with a snap-on lid for the pudding mold. Line the bowl with bread: trim crusts, cut a circle for the bottom, and cut wedges to fit around the sides. Wash berries (if you are using strawberries, hull them; if they are very large, halve them). Simmer berries, apple slices, and sugar to taste (about 5 tablespoons) with 2 tablespoons of water in a covered saucepan for about 5 minutes. The fruits will be juicy but not stewed. Spoon into bread-lined bowl as full as possible. Snap on the lid and wipe up edges. Chill pudding for several hours or overnight. To serve, unmold, cut in wedges, and pour on country cream or milk.

Note: If you omit the apple, increase the amount of berries. You can use a combination of berries—one popular combination is raspberries, strawberries, and blueberries. Frozen unsweetened berries, defrosted, can be substituted.

Fresh Berry Jewel Dessert

1½ to 2 cups fresh berries, washed
1 3-ounce package fruit-flavored gelatin (matching or complementary fruit)
1 cup fruit-flavored yogurt (matching or complementary flavor)
2 tablespoons sugar (optional)

If berries are tart, sugar them. In a refrigerator container dissolve package of gelatin in 1 cup boiling water. Add 1 cup cold water, and stir in the yogurt until evenly mixed. Chill mixture until thick (about 1 hour). Stir in fresh whole berries. Chill until set. Serve with whipped cream topping and a whole berry atop each serving.

Strawberries Romanov

This international classic is at its best when made with the fine fruits of the Pacific Cornucopia.

1 quart fresh ripe strawberries
¼ cup confectioners' sugar or granulated sugar
1 cup fresh orange juice
⅓ cup Grand Marnier or other orange liqueur
1 4-ounce carton whipped cream topping *or* 1 6½-ounce can whipped cream topping (use 2 cups)

Wash and hull strawberries and put them in a refrigerator container. Sprinkle with sugar, orange juice, and Grand Marnier. Chill in the refrigerator for at least 1 hour. To serve, drain off some of the liquid, spoon whipped cream over strawberries, and toss until berries are coated.

Variations: Strawberries Romanov are often presented in a clear bowl with the cream spread on top rather than mixed in. If you aren't going to eat all of the strawberries at one time, it's better to top the individual servings with whipped cream topping at serving time.

Mount Hood Cherries Jubilee

Oregon's lush orchards produce the beauties that are featured in this classic French dessert—one of the easiest show-off desserts in the world.

1 17-ounce can Oregon pitted dark sweet cherries
3 tablespoons sugar
3 tablespoons cornstarch
¼ cup Grand Marnier or other brandy
1 quart vanilla ice cream

Stir sugar and cornstarch together in a skillet and slowly stir in the syrup from the can of cherries. Cook sauce over medium heat, stirring continuously, until mixture thickens and bubbles. Stir in cherries and reduce heat to very low. Dish ice cream into four bowls. To flame Grand Marnier, heat the liquor in a small saucepan and carefully ignite* the liquor. Carefully pour flaming brandy into cherries and stir. Serve over the ice cream immediately. Voila!

*Turn off the range-hood fan to avoid sucking flames into the hood. Use a long match if you have one and stand back when you light the liquor.

Washington Apple Pie

Almost without exception, when we ask anyone to name typical classic recipes of their state, high on the list—no matter which state—is apple pie. Trying to determine who makes the *best* apple pie is even more of a dilemma. Montana claims to have the best pies of any kind, but its claim is disputed by at least 49 other states. Colorado tried to settle the matter by holding a national pie-baking contest recently, but winners from all over the place confused the matter further.

Well, in the interests of diplomacy (and so you would have an apple pie recipe with you in case you don't carry yours in your head) we have decided to give the Great American Apple Pie Award to the state that raises the most apples.

6 to 7 cups thinly sliced, peeled tart cooking apples (about 5 medium)

1 cup brown or white sugar or a mixture of both

1 teaspoon cinnamon or apple pie spice

1 teaspoon grated lemon peel (optional)

2 tablespoons butter

1 15-ounce package refrigerated pie crusts (2 9-inch pie crusts)

Preheat oven to 425°. In a small container mix the sugar, cinnamon, and lemon peel. In a bowl gently combine the apple slices and sugar mixture until the apple slices are well coated. Line a 9-inch pie pan with pie crust. Heap the apples into the pie shell. Dot with butter. Cover with second pie crust, fluting edges to seal well. Cut slits in the top and bake until crust is golden and juices are bubbling (about 30 to 40 minutes). If the crust seems to be browning too fast, reduce heat and cover with foil.

Tip: We like to brush the top crust with milk and dust with a bit of sugar before baking.

Palm Springs Stuffed Dates

Make the most luxurious and simple sweets around with plump dates from the Coachella Valley in California.

California dates, pitted

Whole shelled Brazil nuts *or* almond paste or marzipan (available in packages or cans)

Sugar

Stuff each date with a whole Brazil nut or a small nut-size ball of almond paste. Roll in granulated sugar. Paradise!

Note: Packaged dates are fresh dates—they pick them when they are very ripe and naturally "candied." As fresh fruit, they should be stored in the refrigerator if possible.

Della Robbia Wreath in Nectar

We won first prize in the Great Jell-O/Family Circle Recipe Swap with this beautiful and simple dessert that can be enjoyed on special occasions year-round. It is especially festive and appropriate if you happen to be spending the holidays in sunny California or Hawaii.

Fruits in Snow:
An assortment of the most beautiful fresh fruits you can find: green and red grapes, strawberries, apples, pears, oranges, tangerines
Lemon juice
1 egg white, slightly beaten
Sugar

Nectar:
1 24-ounce bottle California claret
1 3-ounce package lemon Jell-O
½ fresh lemon, thinly sliced
1 teaspoon ground nutmeg

To make *Fruits in Snow*: wash and dry whole fruit; cut unpeeled apples and pears into wedges and dip cut sides in lemon juice to prevent discoloration; peel and separate citrus fruit segments; lay fruit pieces on wax paper and dampen each section with small amount of slightly beaten egg white and sprinkle liberally with granulated sugar. Allow frosted fruits to set for a few moments before arranging fruit in an artistic Della Robbia wreath shape on a large round platter. Wreath should be refrigerated if prepared much in advance of serving.

To make nectar: In a small saucepan, heat one cup of claret wine to slow simmer and add the package of lemon Jell-O, stirring until dissolved. Add remainder of bottle of claret, lemon slices, and nutmeg. Bring the nectar to a slow simmer. Serve the nectar in individual cups with the wreath in the center of the table. Each person dips the fruit in the nectar with a fork. Afterward, any remaining nectar is sipped as a warm after dinner drink.

Variations: For a less formal cold weather dessert, leave the saucepan of nectar on the stove and let everyone "poach" the fruit to taste in the simmering nectar. Fruits in Snow is a beautiful way to serve fruit by itself or as a garland around a baked ham, chicken, or pork roast.

Island Fruit Candies

These wholesome sweets from Hawaii make great trail snacks.

1 cup raisins
1 cup pitted dates
1 cup pitted prunes
1 cup walnuts
½ cup crystallized ginger
Confectioners' sugar

Chop the fruit, nuts, and ginger as fine as possible (if you have a blender, use it). Mix everything together and shape into walnut-size balls with dampened hands. Roll the balls in confectioners' sugar.

CHEERS

Fresh Berry Shakes

In the far northern countries and the Far North of our country, all kinds of fresh berries are used to make refreshing shakes—nectarberries, salmonberries, blueberries, strawberries, raspberries.

2 cups fresh berries
4 cups (1 quart) cold milk
Sugar or honey

Wash and hull berries. Chop berries into very small pieces. In a shaker with a tight lid, vigorously shake milk, chopped berries, and sugar or honey to taste (about 3 tablespoons for sweet berries) for about a minute. (It may be easier to make 2 shakes at a time.) You can also make the shakes with an egg beater in a bowl or in a blender, if you have one.

Sunshines

Whether you call it a Mimosa, Happiness, Bellini, Orange Blossom, or Sunshine, by any name this delight is a classy way to have your breakfast orange juice or to entertain brunch guests in the grand style. Both ingredients should be icy cold.

1 quart orange juice
1 25-ounce bottle California
    champagne

Mix the ingredients half-and-half in each glass, varying either direction for individual preferences. Float a flower on top for a resort hotel touch.

Notes: Even vineyard owners don't use their best champagne for this drink. And, unless you happen to have a surfeit of oranges, juice made from frozen concentrate seems to be at least as good as freshly squeezed.

Luau Punch

1 quart orange juice
1 20-ounce can chunk pineapple
    in heavy syrup
½ cup lemon or lime juice
½ cup sugar (to taste)
3 cups rum
½ cup curaçao or Grand Marnier
    or peach brandy
1 25-ounce bottle champagne
    or 1 32-ounce bottle club soda

Chill everything. Mix all ingredients except soda or champagne in a large pitcher or pan. Top off individual drinks with soda or champagne after pouring punch over ice in each glass. Makes 10 big drinks, enough for a luau for four. If you are making Luau Punch for a crowd, pour everything into large container, adding a couple of trays of ice cubes and, just before serving, the soda or champagne.

Variations: If you omit the rum and curaçao, this is a very nice luau punch for non-drinkers and for children. You may want to add more sugar. You can, of course, make either version with fresh pineapple.

Summer Sangría

Summer and sangría are almost synonymous in some parts of the West. Sangrías range from gentle coolers of wine and soda with a squeeze of fruit juice to heady mixtures of brandy, wine, and macerated fruits. Occupying the happy territory in between, a pitcher of this easy sangría is a refreshing complement to a variety of summery foods at almost any time on a hot lazy day.

1 25-ounce bottle inexpensive
  California burgundy or claret
1 6-ounce can frozen lemonade
  concentrate
1 32-ounce bottle lemon-lime
  soda or club soda (add sugar
  to taste with club soda)
1 orange, sliced
1 lemon, sliced
1 lime, sliced

In a large pitcher or bowl, dissolve lemonade concentrate in wine. Add a tray of ice cubes and the sliced fruits. Pour in lemon-lime and serve.

Variations: We prefer a stronger, tarter sangría with a double the amount of wine. You can also add many other kinds of sliced fruit—peaches, strawberries, papayas, mangoes, pineapple—except apples.

Tequila Sunrise

Californians say this pretty drink first rose in the City of Angels, but its popularity has shone far beyond. For each Tequila Sunrise you will need a clear, preferably tall, 8-ounce glass.

1 teaspoon grenadine
1 jigger (1½ ounces) tequila
Orange Juice

Pour grenadine in bottom of glass and fill with ice cubes. Add tequila. Fill with orange juice but do not stir.

Martinis To Go

According to San Francisco tradition, America's most famous cocktail originated around 1860 at the Occidental Hotel, when famed bartender Jerry Thomas created the drink for a traveler on his way to Martinez, California.

Over the years, martinis have grown drier and drier. They were originally 1 part gin to 1 part dry vermouth; they are now sometimes made as dry as 10 parts gin to 1 part vermouth. You may want to make up a bottle to suit your taste before you leave home (these will be about 7 to 1; increase vermouth to ¾ cup for martinis about 4½ to 1).

1 32-ounce (1 quart or 1 liter)
  bottle gin
½ cup dry vermouth
1 fresh lemon

Pour out ½ cup of gin from the bottle and reserve for another use. Replace with dry vermouth. Peel the lemon in a long continuous spiral. Add the lemon peel to the bottle and recap. You can either chill the whole bottle in your refrigerator or stir each drink with ice cubes and strain into a glass.

Note: Be aware that there are martini-purists who agree with Bernard de Voto that you can no more keep a martini in the refrigerator than you can keep a kiss there.

Memorable Meals

MOUNTAIN AND DESERT

Straddling the mountainous backbone of the country, the Mountain and Desert region is a land of contrasts: vast open areas where you can drive all day and see nary a soul and breathtakingly primeval wildernesses, metropolises of startling cultural and technological achievement and some of the fastest growing urban areas in the country. It is a land where the deer and the antelope still roam and where space technology is a major industry. A land still fed on simple chuckwagon favorites and, like the nineteenth-century Argonauts, on the best that money can buy.

Some people say the Mountain and Desert region is where the East ends. Some say it's where the West begins. It certainly shares the culinary and cultural heritages of both with a strong flavor accent from south of the border. There are cities in the region that have more than 2000 restaurants to satisfy the multiplicity of local tastes. The most regionally distinctive cooking is a legacy from Spanish Colonial and Mexican settlers. Spicy Hispanic dishes are common throughout the Southwest but with notable variations—Tex-Mex cooking is as different from Nuevo Mexican as Italian is from French.

But the hands-down favorite food from Big Bend to the Big Sky Country is, without doubt, beef. This is the picturesque West of film and the real West of genuine cowboys—this is Cattle Country.

In Utah we interviewed two octogenarians of pioneer stock about the popular foods of the region. "Meat and potatoes," one lady answered, "we've always eaten meat and potatoes."

"How did you have them?" we asked.

"We raised them."

"No, we meant how did you fix them?"

"We cooked them."

And for much of the West that is still *the* favorite recipe.

EYE OPENERS

New Mexico Huevos Rancheros

Breakfast in the Mountain and Desert region can be anything from *Cream of the West* in Montana to biscuits and gravy in parts of Texas, with steak and eggs a rugged Western favorite from border to border. The regional enthusiasm for potatoes shows up on breakfast tables as hash browns and pan fries. And there are all the usual American breakfast standbys. Not as common are the popular spicy breakfasts of the Southwest that may curl your eyelashes as they open your eyes. Whether you spell it chile, chili, or chilli, the spicy green or red pepper teams with eggs in zesty ways to start the day.

8 corn tortillas
2 + tablespoons oil
2 cups green chile salsa*
8 eggs

Heat 1 tablespoon of oil in skillet over medium heat. Fry tortillas one at a time about 1 minute on each side, adding more oil as needed. Drain the tortillas on paper towels and keep warm in a lidded pan or foil. Heat 1 cup green chile salsa to simmering in the same skillet. Carefully break in 4 eggs, cover skillet, and poach in the sauce until the whites are set but the yolks are still soft. Top a tortilla with an egg and sauce and serve immediately. Repeat with remaining sauce and eggs for second helping. Huevos Rancheros are often accompanied by extra chile sauce, refried beans, and warm flour tortillas.

Variations: Some cooks like to fry the eggs in butter and top with warmed chile salsa (about a cup for 2 eggs). And you can use blue-corn tortillas or flour tortillas.

*We recommend a fine local product like *Territorial House Gourmet Green Chile Salsa* made in Corrales if you can get it.

Sangre De Cristo Omelet

6 eggs
1 tablespoon butter
1 8-ounce bottle picante salsa
  or green chile salsa
6 to 8 ounces of Monterey Jack
  cheese, grated

Melt butter in skillet over medium-high heat. Break eggs into hot butter and scramble until eggs begin to set. Stir in ½ cup of the salsa and the shredded cheese, cover skillet and cook until cheese is melted and eggs are set. Serve with warm buttered flour tortillas and extra salsa.

Tip: There is a lot of flexibility in this tasty recipe—more or less of anything isn't going to mess it up. We use a half egg shell to measure the salsa (1 for each egg) and save washing a measuring cup.

High Country Quiche

On a cool morning or evening in the mountains, warming the RV can be an appealing idea. One exceptionally appetizing way to do it is with this crustless quiche. We were first introduced to it at an elegant Boulder, Colorado, cocktail party and have enjoyed it as an easy on-the-road breakfast, brunch, lunch, or supper ever since.

1 pound Monterey Jack cheese, shredded
1 4-ounce can chopped green chilies, drained
4 eggs, mixed up with a fork in a cup or bowl

Preheat oven to 300°. Butter a pie or cake pan. Arrange cheese and green chilies in baking pan and pour eggs over top. Bake for one hour or until quiche is lightly golden and a knife comes out clean. Serve for brunch, lunch, or supper main dish or hearty side dish or appetizer.

Variation: Add or substitute for the chilies, a 4-ounce can of sliced mushrooms, drained. If omitting chilies, you may want to add salt and pepper to taste or a pinch of herbs.

Tentacion Timbales

Our simple recipe for baked ham and eggs with chilies was selected as one of the Top 100 Pork Recipes in the James Beard/Woman's Day Creative Cookery Contest which attracted 22,000 entries (one of Loretta's complex recipes won first prize in that contest). You do need a muffin tin or two for these.

8 slices cooked ham (packaged Danish-style boiled ham works well)
¼ cup whipping cream
1 4-ounce can chopped green chilies, drained
8 eggs
Salt and Pepper
Fresh or dried chopped chives (optional)

Preheat oven to 350°. Lightly butter 8 of the muffin cups (muffin pans with non-stick surface work especially well). Into each cup, carefully place 1 ham slice, folded into a square, to make a small flat-bottomed ham cup. Pour about 1 teaspoon of cream in each cup and add 1 teaspoon of chopped chilies. Break 1 egg carefully into each cup. Sprinkle with chives, salt, and pepper. Bake until eggs are firm, but not hard (about 15 minutes). Loosen each timbale by running knife around side of muffin cup. Serve with warmed sweet rolls.

Variation: If you want something very fancy and you have a blender, make *Eggs Marco with Jade Sauce*. Add a ripe avocado cut in chunks to *Blender Hollandaise Sauce* (see index) and blend until smooth. Serve Jade Sauce over hot timbales.

Country Breakfast-In-A-Skillet

There is a lot of flexibility in this easy breakfast recipe. More or less of any of the ingredients can be used if your package happens to be a different size, or the aroma attracts an extra guest or two, just add a few more eggs.

¾ **pound ground breakfast pork sausage**
1 **10-ounce package frozen shredded hash brown potatoes**
6 **eggs**
4 **ounces (about 1½ cups) longhorn or other Cheddar cheese, shredded**
Salt and pepper

Brown pork sausage in a skillet over medium-high heat. Break sausage into small pieces as it browns. Add shredded frozen hash browns and continue cooking until golden (about 15-20 minutes), stirring occasionally to prevent sticking. When hash browns are golden, stir in eggs and cheese. Continue stirring occasionally and cooking until eggs are set. Salt and pepper to taste.

Saddle Biscuits

Miniature breakfast "burgers" are fun for eating on the go or wrapping in foil for a warm snack on the trail.

1 **package (10 biscuits) refrigerated biscuits**
¾ **pound ground breakfast pork sausage**
Butter

Bake biscuits according to package instructions (or see *Skillet Biscuits*). Shape sausage into 8 to 10 3-inch patties. Cook patties in a skillet according to package instructions. Sandwich sausage patties between hot buttered biscuit halves and serve immediately or wrap in double thickness of foil.

Sundae Muffins

The easiest breakfast muffins ever and just the thing to cheer you up if you discover half-melted ice cream in your freezer.

1 **cup vanilla ice cream, softened**
1 **cup *self-rising* flour**

Preheat oven to 350°. When oven is ready mix ice cream with flour into a lumpy dough. Spoon into buttered 6-muffin tin. Bake for 20 minutes. Serve the warm muffins with your favorite preserves.

Variation: For *Fresh Berry Sundae Muffins*, stir ½ cup fresh berries, blueberries, for example, into the dough before spooning into the tin. Muffins may take a few more minutes to bake.

SOUPS, SALADS AND SANDWICHES

Rio Grande Chili Con Carne

Few American dishes are more hotly debated (pun intended) than the Southwest's famous "bowl of brimstone." Oklahoma-born Will Rogers once said he judged a town by its chili, Texans hold annual chili cook-offs and argue whether to bean or not to bean, while New Mexicans have chile societies to discuss the relative merits of green and red chili. No one can even decide how to spell it. The red Texas stuff is usually spelled *chili*, the firey green sauce ladled on dishes in New Mexico is usually spelled *chile*, and the peppers themselves—whole, ground, or otherwise—are generally called *chilies*. Since in this recipe we're talking about a bowl of the cattle country's favorite warmer-upper, *chili* it is.

There must be at least as many chili recipes as cooks in the Southwest since everyone we know seems to have several for different circumstances. This is *our* favorite quick chili. You can find recipes more time-consuming and complicated than this one but not many that are much better.

1 pound lean ground beef
1 15½-ounce jar chunky garden-style spaghetti sauce with extra tomatoes, garlic and onions
1 tablespoon chili con carne seasoning (or more to taste—up to 3 tablespoons)
1 15-ounce can chili beans *or* pinto beans *or* red kidney beans

Brown meat in skillet over medium-high heat. Drain off excess fat into a heatproof disposable container. Stir in spaghetti sauce, chili seasoning, and beans and heat until boiling (cover skillet to keep down spattering). Simmer a few minutes and serve hot with cold beer.

Montana Calico Bean Soup

½ pound of fully-cooked ham, trimmed and cubed
1 15-ounce can Great Northern white beans
1 15-ounce can dark red kidney beans
1 16-ounce can green lima beans
1 15½-ounce jar chunky garden-style spaghetti sauce with extra tomatoes, garlic and onions (or other spaghetti sauce)

In large saucepan (at least 3-quart), mix ham, undrained beans, and sauce and bring to a boil. Reduce heat to low, cover, and simmer for 15 minutes or longer. Serve with bread or crackers for a warm satisfying meal-in-a-bowl after a day in the Big Sky Country.

Roadside Stand Gazpacho

2 large tomatoes, chopped
1 large cucumber, peeled and
 diced
1 medium green pepper, seeded
 and chopped
1 small onion, peeled and
 chopped *or* 1 tablespoon
 instant minced onion
½ cup bottled Italian dressing
2 12-ounce cans tomato juice
Tabasco sauce
Salt and pepper

Combine chopped vegetables, Italian dressing, and tomato juice in a large refrigerator container. Season to taste with *Tabasco* sauce and salt and pepper. Cover and refrigerate until well chilled (3 hours or longer). Add your finishing touch to the bowls of gazpacho with any of the following popular garnishes: a dollop of sour cream and chopped almonds, herb or garlic croutons, a slice of lemon, chopped olives, or chopped chives.

Variation: If you have a blender, blend half of the vegetables with half of the juice and then mix the remaining ingredients as above.

Gazpacho Pronto

For each serving, mix 1 6-ounce can mixed vegetable juice or tomato juice with ¼ cup mild picante sauce and sprinkle with pepper. Serve over ice cubes.

Garden Gazpacho Salad

Your market finds will keep their fresh flavor for days in this tangy salad that makes an ideal complement for simple hamburgers, steaks, fish, and sandwiches.

1 12-ounce can mixed vegetable
 juice
½ cup picante sauce (or
 substitute more vegetable
 juice)
1 3-ounce package lemon gelatin
2 cups of chopped fresh
 vegetables*
Salt and pepper
1 teaspoon dried salad herbs
 (optional)

Heat 1 cup of vegetable juice to boiling. Remove from heat and stir in lemon gelatin until dissolved. Stir in remaining vegetable juice, picante sauce, and herbs. Put mixed chopped vegetables in 1-quart refrigerator container. Pour juice-gelatin mixture over vegetables. Stir gently and salt and pepper to taste. Refrigerate until set.

*Any mixture of non-leafy salad vegetables are good: tomato, cucumber, jicama, green pepper, celery, onion, avacado.

Roundup Bean Salad

Judging from local cookbooks and potlucks, bean salads are popular across the country in colorful combinations of green beans, yellow beans, garbanzos, red kidney beans, pinto beans, Italian flat beans, Great Northern beans, etc. They can be as simple as the quick salad we often make from one can of beans (garbanzos or a green bean variety tossed with vinegar and oil) or have assorted ingredients and five different kinds of beans as one charmingly misnamed Ohio recipe called Three-Bean Salad does. You can buy the most usual mixture of beans as a spicy bottled salad, but Roundup Bean Salad is special enough to make yourself and is a refreshing contrast to the highly seasoned main dishes popular in this region.

1 16-ounce can cut Blue Lake
  green beans, drained
1 15½-ounce can garbanzos (ceci
  beans), drained
1 15-ounce can pinto beans in
  plain sauce, drained
½ cup bottled Italian dressing
2 or 3 scallions (green onions)
  with tops, trimmed and
  chopped
Salt and pepper

Mix everything in a refrigerator container (at least 1½-quart), cover, and chill for an hour before serving. (This is a good make-ahead salad that keeps well.)

Rainbow Salad

This Irish salad made its way to the High Plains along with a great number of the Irish and their traditions. (Colorado's St. Patrick's Day Parade is the second largest in the country.)

1 green apple
1 large carrot, peeled
1 green pepper, seeded
1 small cucumber, peeled
1 cup of sliced celery
½ cup mayonnaise
Salt and pepper
1 hard-boiled egg, chopped
1 teaspoon dried parsley

Cut all vegetables into small slices. Mix well with the mayonnaise. Salt and pepper to taste. Sprinkle with parsley and chopped egg.

Rangeland Steak Sandwiches

Thick sirloins and T-bones sizzling on the grill, whole steers roasting slowly over a firepit, plump burgers searing in a skillet, chunks of lean meat simmering in a kettle—since the days when the Native American shared life on the plains with the buffalo, the people of the Mountain and Desert have been stilling the pangs of hunger with choice meat. And as far as many Westerners are concerned, a good choice for anytime is steak.

4 small tender ½-inch thick
   boneless steaks, trimmed
Butter
Salt and pepper
4 hamburger buns

Melt a tablespoon of butter in a skillet over high heat. Add steaks and sear on both sides. Turn heat down a little and cook steaks to desired doneness. Sprinkle generously with salt and pepper and remove steaks from skillet. Butter cut side of buns and pan-toast the cut sides in the skillet for a few moments. Serve steaks immediately in the warm buns with the usual burger extras—sliced tomatoes, lettuce leaves, sliced onion, etc.

Italian Meatball Heroes

Community spaghetti dinners, family-run pizzerias, Italian markets, and homemade noodles and ravioli available in supermarkets hint at the Italian influence in the mountainous areas of the West where many Italians made their home after the turn of the century.

Meatballs:
1 pound ground beef
1 egg
1 cup soft bread crumbs (made
   from the scooped out center of
   the Italian bread or from
   ordinary sandwich bread)
½ cup grated Parmesan cheese
2 tablespoons water
1 teaspoon dried basil
1 teaspoon dried parsley
½ teaspoon salt
Generous sprinkling of pepper

Other ingredients:
2 tablespoons oil
1 15½-ounce jar homestyle
   spaghetti sauce
1 fresh loaf unsliced Italian
   bread* sliced horizontally
   into upper and lower halves
   and slightly hollowed out

Put all meatball ingredients in a bowl and mix well. Shape into 1½-inch balls (not too firm). In a skillet, fry the meatballs in the oil over medium-high heat until well browned. Drain off excess fat into a heatproof disposable container. Pour spaghetti sauce over meatballs, cover, and simmer, stirring from time to time, until meat balls are cooked through (about 15 to 20 minutes). Spoon the meatballs into the Italian bread loaf, cut into four sections, and serve.

Variation: Italian Sausage Heroes can be made the same way: substitute 1 pound of Italian sausage cut in 2- to 3-inch lengths for the meatballs and proceed as above.

*You can substitute 2 10-ounce refrigerated packages of bread dough, freshly baked

MAIN EVENTS

BBQ Spareribs

If you, like many Southwesterners, are occasionally overcome with an irresistible desire for barbecued ribs, sustain yourself with this simple recipe. (Not recommended for summertime in the desert.)

3 to 4 pounds of meaty spareribs, heavy bone or gristle section removed
1 cup barbecue sauce*

Preheat the oven to 375°. Cut the ribs into 3- or 4-rib sections. Rinse well and pat dry with paper towels. Arrange the ribs on a foil-lined baking sheet with a lip (a pizza pan will work). Roast for 30 minutes, turn ribs over and roast for another 30 minutes. Drain off as much of the excess fat as you can without getting burned (use a baster if you have one or dip it out with a spoon). Liberally paint the ribs on both sides with the barbecue sauce and return to the oven for another 10 to 15 minutes.

*We recommend one of the quality regional barbecue sauces, for example, *Bill Johnson's Famous Barbeque Sauce* from Phoenix, Arizona.

Ski Lodge Fondue

Along with other things Alpine, the Western ski country adopted fondue long ago; some credit the Unsinkable Mrs. Brown of Colorado with introducing fondue to the Rockies. This convivial dish continues to be a popular appetizer or light meal anytime. Prepared fondue is widely available in the refrigerator section of supermarkets, but if you want to make your own, this is a classic recipe.

8 ounces (about 2 cups) Swiss cheese, grated or shredded
1 tablespoon flour
1 clove garlic *or* garlic powder
1 cup dry white wine
Salt and pepper
Nutmeg
1 1½-ounce jigger kirsch (or substitute rum, brandy, or applejack)
1 loaf of crusty bread, cut in 1½-inch cubes (try to give each cube a bit of crust)

Mix cheese and flour. Rub a non-stick 2-quart saucepan with garlic clove, add wine, and heat. Just before wine comes to a boil, add cheese and stir until melted. Season to taste—light with the salt and garlic powder if you are using it, generous with the pepper and nutmeg. Add kirsch just before serving.

To serve put the pan on a hotpad on the table accompanied by the bowl of bread cubes, forks for dipping the bread cubes in the fondue, and generous glasses of white wine to wash it all down. If the cheese cools too much, put the fondue back on the heat for a few minutes. If you are having the fondue as the main event of a meal, plan to make seconds or even thirds of the recipe.

Fiesta Taco Salad

Our nomination for the ideal RV Mexican-style dinner, Taco Salad is a fast, cool, and delicious meal-in-a-bowl that can be easily expanded to feed a crowd in style.

1 pound lean ground beef
1 8-ounce bottle mild picante sauce
1 small head lettuce, washed, dried, and torn into bite-size pieces
2 tomatoes, diced
8 ounces (about 2 cups) Cheddar cheese, grated
1 8-ounce package tortilla chips, preferably nacho-flavored
½ cup black olives, sliced (optional)
1 avocado, peeled and sliced (optional)
1 8-ounce bottle Western or French dressing

Brown meat in a skillet over medium-high heat. Drain excess fat into a disposable heatproof container. Stir in picante sauce, heat through, and simmer for a few minutes. In your largest bowl (you may need 2), mix lettuce, tomatoes, cheese, and chips. Top with meat mixture and toss. Top with avocado and olives. Serve with Western dressing. All you need to complete your fiesta is a pitcher of sangria.

Variations: You can substitute a package of taco seasoning for the picante sauce. Many cooks like to add a 15-ounce can of drained kidney beans.

Tucson Sour Cream Enchiladas

"Do you want it smothered red or green?" is almost as common a question in the Southwest as whether you like your coffee with cream—red or green being chile sauces, of course. How hot either is depends on the cook not the color; green can be *very* hot or mild, red is more uniformly medium-hot. But this authentic and popular chicken enchilada recipe is ideal for the tender-mouth—the enchiladas are smothered in "white."

1 6½-ounce can boned chicken breast
6 small scallions (green onions) with tops, chopped (about 6 tablespoons)
1 12-ounce container sour cream with chives
1 10½-ounce can condensed cream of chicken soup
8 ounces (about 2 cups) Cheddar cheese, shredded or grated
8 corn tortillas

Preheat oven* to 375°. In a small bowl combine can of chicken and chopped scallions with ½ cup of sour cream, ½ cup of the condensed soup, and 1 cup of the grated cheese. Put ¼ cup of the mixture in the center of each tortilla and roll up. Arrange enchiladas seam down in a baking pan and cover tops with remaining condensed soup, sour cream, and grated cheese. Bake until cheese is melted and enchiladas are heated through (about 15 to 20 minutes).

*If you have a microwave oven, this recipe is ideal for the microwave; it will take about 10 minutes on high to melt the cheese and heat through—turn once during cooking.

Note: If you want to vary the number of enchiladas—the general proportions of the filling are 1 tablespoon each of soup, chicken, sour cream, scallions, and cheese.

Colorado Chile Rellenos

Stuffed chilies are a popular Hispanic dish from South America to Canada. This recipe for crispy wonton-wrapped rellenos, although ideal for the RV, is not our adapatation but the way many of the Colorado restaurants famed for their rellenos make them. The wonton skins or wrappers, readily available at supermarkets in the region, come in pound packages—15 or 16 wrappers. Double this recipe if you are serving the rellenos as the main dish of a dinner.

6 wonton skins (about 6-inch
   square eggroll wrappers)
6 1-ounce slices Cheddar cheese
1 7-ounce can whole green chilies
   (6 whole chilies)
½ cup oil
Green chile salsa or hot green
   chile

Heat oil in a skillet over medium to medium-high heat until a piece of eggroll wrapper browns easily without burning. On each wrapper center one whole chile. Fold cheese in half forming a rectangle about 4 inches by 2 inches, tuck cheese inside chile. Dampen edge of eggroll wrapper with water, fold bottom up, top down, and ends in, making a long neat package. Fry rellenos until slightly puffed and golden, turning once with a pancake turner. (You can use tongs though we find this tricky with the hot oil.) Serve with green chile salsa.

Note: Leftover wonton skins make delightful *Cinnamon Crisps*: Fry in oil (you can use the oil left in the skillet); then sprinkle with cinnamon sugar (½ cup sugar mixed with 1 teaspoon cinnamon).

 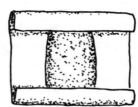 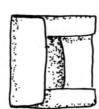 

Wyoming Porcupines

The fanciful name of these meatballs comes from the rice "quills" that appear as they cook.

1 pound lean ground beef
1 cup instant rice, uncooked
1 egg
1 tablespoon instant minced
   onion (optional)
1 teaspoon salt
Pepper
1 10½-ounce can condensed
   tomato soup

Mix beef, rice, egg, seasonings, and ¼ cup of the condensed soup thoroughly in a bowl. Shape into firm walnut-size meatballs. Brown meatballs in skillet over medium heat (you may need a little oil with lean meat). Pour off excess fat into disposable heatproof container. Stir remaining soup and ½ can of water into skillet. Cover and cook over low heat, stirring occasionally, until meatballs are cooked through (about 20 minutes).

Rocky Mountain Trout Baked in Cream

This pioneer recipe will do justice to your prized trout from the snow-fed streams of the Rocky Mountains.

For each 1 *pound of trout*:
1 cup prepared herbed bread-
crumb dressing (follow
package instructions)
Salt and pepper
Dried chervil or parsley (optional)
Flour
Butter
½ cup whipping cream

Preheat oven to 425°. Generously butter a baking pan large enough to hold the whole fish or fishes without overlapping (or shape a baking pan out of double layer of heavy-duty aluminum foil to fit fish, butter foil, and set foil-pan on baking sheet). Rinse dressed trout in cool water, and pat dry with paper towels. (You may use boned trout without any adjustments in the recipe; but leave the head on while cooking to keep fish moist.) Liberally salt and pepper both sides of trout and sprinkle with chervil. Roll trout in flour. Stuff trout with prepared dressing and lay in baking pan. Pour cream over trout. Bake until fish is tender. (The rule of thumb is 10 minutes per inch of thickness, but about 30 minutes is average.) Baste from time to time with pan juices (add more cream if pan juices bake away).

Lone Star Red Snapper

Red snapper cooked in a vibrant array of vegetables is the most famous Mexican-style fish dish south or north of the border. We have not experimented with a whole red snapper when we had the opportunity—the last time we saw one of these highly prized, colorful fish of the Gulf of Mexico in our local market it ran to about $40 for a meal-size fish! But, we have often prepared fillets of Gulf red snapper and its taste-alike, Pacific red snapper, in this popular spicy style (not recommended for tender-mouths).

1½ pounds fresh red snapper
fillets, cut into 4 pieces
1 8-ounce jar of *mild* picante
sauce*
½ cup black olives, sliced
1 4-ounce can sliced mushrooms,
drained (optional)

Put all ingredients into a skillet and bring to a boil. Reduce heat, cover, and simmer until the fish flakes easily (about 10 to 15 minutes). Serve with warm flour tortillas and rice.

Variations: Substitute 1 10-ounce can of chopped tomatoes and green chilies and 1 small thinly sliced onion for the picante sauce. Or substitute 1 cup of green chile salsa for the picante sauce.

**Pace Picante Sauce* from San Antonio is appropriate and good.

Texas Shrimp Boiled in Beer

The cry of "shrimp boats are a coming" echoing along the Gulf coastline is an image from American folklore that makes millions of seafood lovers want to put the pot on to boil—the large sweet shrimp caught in the Gulf of Mexico are perhaps America's favorite shellfish. And there are few more leisurely ways of enjoying fresh shrimp than to cook them in simmering spiced beer and wash them down with icy cold beer.

2 pounds unshelled large raw shrimp, deheaded
2 12-ounce cans of beer
2 tablespoons seafood seasoning *or* **2 tablespoons crab boil seasonings**

In large pot, bring beer to boil with spices. Stir in shrimp and cover. Return to boil and simmer for about 5 minutes. Turn off the heat and leave the shrimp in the hot beer for a few more minutes, until they are cooked through and bright pink. Drain shrimp and serve immediately on newspaper-covered table (preferably the camp table), letting everyone peel their own. Have on hand lemon wedges and cocktail sauce for dipping and a good supply of cold beer and paper towels.

Snowbird Shrimp

This is the kind of dish you were dreaming of when you left the snowshovel behind and headed out for a life of easy elegance.

1 pound large raw shrimp, peeled and cleaned*
½ cup (1 stick butter)
½ pound fresh mushrooms, sliced
1 cup sour cream
Salt
Chili con carne seasoning

Melt about ¼ cup of the butter in a skillet over medium heat (don't let butter brown). Fry shrimp just until they are tender and pink (about 5 minutes). Stir in remaining butter and mushrooms and fry just until mushrooms are cooked (about 5 minutes). Sprinkle shrimp with salt and chili seasoning (use like you would pepper). Stir in sour cream until smooth and heated through. Serve over rice with a substantial vegetable side dish or salad.

*Notes: If you can afford to, increase the amount of shrimp without altering the rest of the recipe (you may need a bit more butter). You'll enjoy the shrimp more if you do the shelling and deveining outside of your RV—that step tends to leave a lingering odor.

ASIDES

Green Chile Salsa

Green chile sauces and salsas are a prized ingredient in the cooking of the Southwest. Hot cooked green chile sauces (a kind of chile gravy) may include pork, tomatoes, or other ingredients according to local custom. (One of Loretta's claims to gastronomic fame was identifying the small placita a Denver restaurant cook came from by tasting her chile verde.) Green chile salsa is a "fresh" sauce that can be served cold or hot, as a dip with tortilla chips, or poured over tacos, tostadas, enchiladas, eggs, etc. Many excellent bottled salsas are available in the region, for example, *Territorial House Gourmet Green Chile Salsa* from Corrales, New Mexico. But if none is available where you are, this is a simple authentic recipe from Arizona.

1 16-ounce can whole tomatoes, drained
1 7-ounce can diced green chilies
2 scallions (green onions), chopped
1 teaspoon garlic salt

Mash drained tomatoes in a bowl. Mix well with green chilies, scallions, and garlic salt. Chill.

Chile con Queso

The Southwest's famous dip is available ready-made or in packaged mixes. But it is just as easy to make your own with this popular recipe.

1 8-ounce jar pasteurized process cheese spread *or* 8 ounces of pasteurized process cheese, cubed
½ cup picante sauce *or* ¼ cup chopped green chilies

In a small saucepan, heat cheese and picante sauce over low heat, stirring frequently, until the cheese is melted and smooth. Serve warm with tortilla chips or vegetable dippers as an appetizer or snack.

Note: To make *Easy Nachos*, pour the Chile con Queso over plates of tortilla chips. The authentic finishing touch is sliced jalapeño pepper—definitely not for the tender-mouth.

Crispy Quesadillas

Kind of a nippy Southwest version of the pizza, quesadillas are good as appetizers or as a meal if you pile on the toppings: sliced olives, mushrooms, and/or chopped onions can be added with the cheese before broiling; chopped lettuce, diced tomatoes, and/or guacamole can be added after broiling.

2 flour tortillas
Butter, softened
8 ounces (about 2 cups) Cheddar
   cheese *or* Monterey Jack
   cheese, shredded
1 4-ounce can chopped green
   chilies

Preheat oven to broil. Butter each tortilla and place on a baking sheet. (If your oven broiler won't take a baking sheet that will hold both, do one at a time in a pie pan or cake pan.) Broil until tortillas are lightly brown. Remove and sprinkle top with cheese and chilies. Broil until cheese is melted. To serve, cut in wedges (scissors work well).

Texas Caviar
(Black-eyed Peas Appetizer)

This whimsically named appetizer is fun to serve with Texas-size drinks—its usual role.

1 14½-ounce can fresh shelled
   black-eyed peas, drained,
   rinsed, and drained
½ medium onion, peeled, sliced
   crosswise in ⅛-inch rounds,
   and separated into rings
1 cup (8 ounces) bottled Italian
   dressing (zesty style is good
   with this)
Salt

Combine black-eyed peas, onion rings, and dressing in a 3- or 4-cup refrigerator container. Salt liberally and stir everying until the peas are well coated with dressing. Cover container and refrigerate overnight or longer (the classic recipe calls for 2 or 3 days). Stir occasionally. Drain off the excess marinade (save it for a salad) before serving the "caviar" with crackers.

Beer Bread

We were given this unbelievably easy recipe for Beer Bread by a couple from Amarillo who were our neighbors at the campground on the Santa Clara Pueblo Reservation in New Mexico. (We were regretting having finished off the last crumbs of the Pueblo Bread we had bought on the Santa Fe Plaza.) Beer Bread looks different than conventional kneaded breads, but its home-baked flavor will astonish you.

3 cups *self-rising* flour
3 tablespoons sugar
1 12-ounce can warm beer

Preheat oven to 350°. When the oven is ready, mix flour and sugar in a bowl and add beer, stirring until the flour is all mixed into the dough—a matter of seconds. Put dough into a buttered baking pan (a round or square cake pan) and bake for 1 hour. Beer Bread is usually eaten pulled apart rather than sliced and is good warm or cold.

Cherokee Strip Fry Bread

Our easy version of this traditional favorite of the Wichita Indians is from the folks at the Museum of the Cherokee Strip in Enid, Oklahoma, who have served fry bread to thousands of visitors to their regional Indian festival.

3 cups *self-rising* flour
1 heaping teaspoon sugar
1 cup lukewarm water
Cooking oil

Mix flour, sugar, and water well. Roll dough to ½ inch thick. Cut into squares or rectangles and cut a slit in the center of each square or rectangle. Fry in hot deep oil,* as you would doughnuts. Drain on paper towels. Serve with soup or stew, or cover with jelly for a dessert.

*This is a fun recipe to try, but it may be hazardous to your RV interior. We suggest you take your skillet or saucepan out to the campfire—which is more in the spirit of the recipe anyway.

Gold Nugget Stuffed Potatoes

Baked potatoes, fried potatoes, mashed potatoes, scalloped potatoes, hash brown potatoes.... Potatoes every which way 'til Sunday are eaten in the West which counts more than a few "just give me meat and potatoes" types among its citizens. When the potatoes are those handsome specimens for which Idaho is famous, it's not hard to understand why potatoes are an overwhelmingly popular "aside" in most of America.

In or out of the cool mountains of Idaho, your flavor buds will strike pay dirt with these golden delights, a pioneer favorite.

4 large Idaho baking potatoes
3 tablespoons butter
¼ cup milk
¼ cup whipping cream
1 egg
Salt and pepper
4 "nuggets" Cheddar cheese
   (each about a rounded
   teaspoonful)

Preheat oven to 400°. Bake potatoes for 1 hour. Remove from oven and let cool briefly. Reset oven temperature to 450°. Cut the tops off each potato lengthwise, scoop out centers with a spoon, leaving about a ¼-inch shell. In a bowl, mash removed potato and whip in butter, egg, milk, and cream until light and fluffy. Salt and pepper to taste. Spoon whipped potatoes into shells, burying a nugget of cheese in each. Bake until reheated through with the tops lightly golden (about 10 to 15 minutes).

Tip: To insure evenly baked potatoes, try the old household tip of baking the potatoes with a large clean nail or skewer piercing each potato through its short dimension.

The Baked Potato Bar

As restaurants devoted exclusively to stuffed baked potatoes spring up, delighted potato-lovers are discovering there is a whole world beyond butter, sour cream, and bacon bits. You can change the status of this perennial All-American favorite from side show to main event by topping Idaho potatoes (baked in a preheated 400° oven for 1 hour or over the coals) with your choice of toppings:

- Cooked packages of frozen dinners—creamed chipped beef, chicken a la king, barbecued beef
- Taco filling plus grated American or Cheddar cheese and chopped lettuce and tomato
- Browned ground beef heated in pizza sauce plus grated Mozzarella cheese
- Cooked packages of frozen vegetables in a sauce—broccoli in cheese, peas and onions in cream sauce
- Heated chili con carne plus grated American or Cheddar cheese

DESSERTS

Fiestaland Ambrosia

1 cup miniature multi-flavored
  marshmallows
1 cup shredded coconut
1 8-ounce can mandarin orange
  sections, drained
1 8-ounce container sour cream
  or 1 cup whipped cream
  topping
½ cup walnuts, broken into
  pieces

Mix everything in a serving bowl. Serve immediately or chill for later.

Snowballs

Your young travelers can make Snowballs on any cool day even if you are in the snowless Sunbelt.

½ cup (1 stick) butter
¼ cup sugar
1 cup flour
1 cup pecans, broken
1 teaspoon vanilla
Confectioners' sugar

Preheat oven to 350°. Mix butter and sugar in a bowl until smooth. Add flour, pecans, and vanilla and mix well. Shape the dough into 1-inch balls and arrange on a foil-lined baking sheet (leave 1 inch around the balls). Bake until set and light brown (about 12-17 minutes). Allow to cool for a few minutes then roll the balls in confectioners' sugar 1 or 2 times until nice and snowy.

Pecan Cookie Pie Shell

The Snowballs cookie recipe is closely related to a delicious shortbread pie crust.

½ cup (1 stick) butter
¼ cup sugar
1 cup flour
¼ cup finely chopped pecans*
1 teaspoon vanilla

Preheat oven to 400°. Mix butter and sugar in a bowl until smooth. Add flour, pecans, and vanilla and mix well. Press dough into a 9-inch pie pan. Bake for 15 to 18 minutes.

*Chop nuts easily by putting them into a sealable plastic bag and beating on them with the back of a heavy spoon.

Variation: Cut ¼ inch slices from a roll of refrigerated packaged cooky dough and press into pie shell. Bake according to package directions.

Fresh Peach Tart

1 9-inch pecan cookie pie shell, baked and cooled
6 fresh peaches (about 1½ to 2 pounds), peeled* and sliced
1 cup (1 12-ounce net weight jar) peach preserves (or substitute apricot or plum preserves), warmed

Arrange peach slices in decorative circles if you have the time or simply spoon in layers over the bottom of baked pie shell. Pour warm peach preserves over top of peaches and chill pie until preserves are set. Serve with whipped cream or ice cream.

*Peaches peel effortlessly if you dip them in boiling water for a few seconds.

Spirited Chocolate Fondue

Fondues are casual, convivial, and cosmopolitan—just the right combination for an evening with friends in the New West. In minutes you can put together this fun and flashy dessert with a tray of assorted dippers: pineapple chunks, banana chunks, apple wedges, maraschino cherries, fresh sweet cherries, fresh strawberries, poundcake cubes, doughnut wedges. Add coffee and/or liqueur and relax with your company.

2 ounces dark chocolate or ½ cup chocolate chips
1 tablespoon butter
1 7-ounce jar marshmallow creme (1¾ cups)
¼* to ½ cup Kahlua or other liqueur (Vandermint, Creme de Cacao, Sabra, Amaretto, etc.)
Assortment of dessert dippers

Melt butter, chocolate, and marshmallow creme in a small non-stick saucepan over medium-low heat, stirring until smooth and hot. Stir in liqueur and place on hot pad on table. Serve with a tray of dessert dippers, forks or toothpicks, and napkins.

*Miniature liqueur bottles usually hold about 50 milliliters (about ¼ cup). If you are pouring from a larger bottle, be more generous.

Colorado Cooler

Southwestern herbalists have been brewing tonics and teas since at least Spanish Colonial days, but in recent decades *Celestial Seasonings* of Boulder, Colorado, has made mixed herb teas popular refreshments. This herbal cooler brews with time rather than heat, but it's worth the wait.

1 32-ounce (1 quart) bottle apple juice
4 *Cinnamon Rose* tea bags

Open bottle and add tea bags. Recap and shake bottle. Chill in the refrigerator for a day.

Centennial Punch

In celebration of the Centennial State's Centennial—which, of course, coincided with the nation's Bicentennial—we refreshed hundreds and hundreds of people on behalf of the State of Colorado with this Victorian garden party punch. We mixed it in 10-gallon batches (and it was easy to do even on a mountain top), but you can make it for a more intimate gathering.

1 25-ounce bottle rose wine
1 6-ounce can frozen pink lemonade concentrate
1 32-ounce bottle club soda
1 lemon, thinly sliced

In a pitcher or bowl, dissolve lemonade concentrate in the wine. Add ice cubes and lemon slices. Pour in club soda just before serving.

Prairie Firewater

Slushes are a pleasant way of wetting your whistle, popular in the dry regions of the Southern Plains. They make long cooling drinks light in alcohol.

1 6-ounce can frozen lemonade or limeade concentrate
½ cup vodka or gin
Lemon-lime soda

Mix lemonade concentrate, 2 cups water, and vodka in a 1-quart refrigerator container and freeze (it won't get rock-hard), stirring from time to time. Spoon or fork mixture into 4 tall glasses and fill with lemon-lime soda.

Hot Buttered Rum by the Batch

Practically every American traveler where the temperature drops below freezing knows about the restorative powers of Hot Buttered Rum, one of America's oldest and most beloved chill-chasers.

In its original form, Hot Buttered Rum is basically just that—2 or 3 ounces of rum warmed with boiling water or sweet cider with a pat of butter set adrift. Most people added a little sugar and spice. Then along came ski-lodge hot-buttered-rum batter and prepared mixes, and Hot Buttered Rum became a different drink, a sort of warm nog. This recipe seemed to be everyone's cup of cheer in the High Country during a recent fierce winter. It will make enough batter to warm up a small group on a long cold night or to see you through a cold spell (it keeps in the freezer).

1 pint French vanilla ice cream, softened
1 cup (2 sticks) butter, softened
2 cups confectioners' sugar
1 cup brown sugar
2 teaspoons ground spice (this is where you get to be creative: mix any combination of cinnamon, nutmeg, and/or clove)
Dark rum

Mix everything but rum together. Freeze in a refrigerator container. To make a drink, use 1 heaping tablespoon in a mug with a jigger of dark rum. Fill mug with *boiling water* and stir. Makes about 15 to 20 drinks.

Note: If you are doubling this recipe use 1 pound confectioners' sugar and 1 pound brown sugar.

Margaritas

1½ cups tequila
½ cup lime juice
½ cup Triple Sec *or* Cointreau *or* curacao

Chill ingredients, if you can. Mix ingredients together, shake with ice cubes and strain into salt-rimmed glasses. To salt-rim glasses: Rub a wedge of lime around the rim of each glass (stemmed glasses if you have them along) and dip upside down in a saucer of salt.

Note: Some drink mixers omit the Triple Sec and substitute 4 teaspoons of sugar.

Hearty Fare

THE HEARTLAND

The Breadbasket, America's Dairyland, Fisherman's Paradise, Hog Capital of the World, the Cornbelt, America's Cherry Capital—the bill of fare of the Heartland is written in sobriquets across its map. But fertile lands and feed lots are only part of the story. The harvest table of Mid-America is laden with an international smorgasbord highly seasoned with the culinary heritage of the Old World—Cornish pasties and Swedish meatballs, German pork chops and Polish sausages, French cheeses and Danish pastries. And yet the hearty fare of the Heartland is as distinctively American as the skylines of its sprawling industrial cities and the still visible ruts carved into the land by the wagon wheels of the pioneers.

EYE OPENERS

Shaker Sausage in Cider

The culinary heritage of the Shakers has outlived the Shaker communities that thrived in nineteenth century Ohio and Indiana. Their simple and delicious recipes often used cooked-down apple cider as a sweetener.

1 12-ounce package pork
   sausage links
1 tablespoon flour
¼ teaspoon salt
1 cup apple cider *or* apple juice

If sausage links have casings, prick with fork. Cook sausages in ¼ cup water in covered skillet 5 minutes. Drain into a heatproof disposable container. Brown sausages in uncovered skillet. Remove sausages and pour off all but a film of fat (about 2 tablespoons). Stir in flour and salt. Add cider and cook and stir until sauce turns syrupy. Return sausage to skillet. Cover and heat through (about 5 to 10 minutes). Makes four servings of three sausages each. For a heartier breakfast increase amount of sausage.

Kansas Roadside Breakfast

The hospitable state of Kansas invites overnighters to more than 130 roadside rests. This delicious honey-glazed sausage and apple skillet will get your crew quickly and happily back on the road.

1 8-ounce package brown-and-
   serve sausage links
1 20-ounce can sliced apples,
   well drained
⅓ cup honey (or substitute ⅓ cup
   sugar)
¼ teaspoon cinnamon (optional)

In a skillet, brown sausages according to package instructions. Drain off fat into a heatproof disposable container. Stir in well-drained apple slices, honey, and cinnamon. Cook over high heat, stirring frequently, until liquid has boiled away and the apples are tender, glazed, and lightly browned.

Wagonwheel

This fun breakfast featuring two convenience foods will take the chill off a cool morning on the trail and start your family's day with a smile.

Pancake batter from mix for
   12-15 pancakes, made
   according to package
   directions
1 8-ounce package brown-and-
   serve sausage links

Preheat oven to 450°. Butter 14½-inch pizza pan with lip. Pour prepared batter into pizza pan. Arrange sausage links like spokes around a hub. Bake until pancake is cooked through (it will look more like cake than skillet pancakes) and the sausages are lightly browned (about 15-20 minutes). Serve with butter and syrup.

Coffee-Klatch Coffeecake

Sharing a cozy, congenial moment and something sweet and warm from the oven is a nostalgic tradition still enjoyed in some parts of the country, especially in the Heartland. What better time than vacation to trade a quick coffee-and-donut break for a leisurely coffee-klatch? It's one of the most relaxed ways to entertain friends or new "neighbors" in your RV. Many refrigerated rolls and frozen pastries would fit the bill, but with very little extra trouble or time your can bake this delicious homemade treat. And it's a delightful way to enjoy local specialty preserves and nuts.

2 cups buttermilk baking mix or buttermilk biscuit mix
1 3-ounce package cream cheese
¼ cup (½ stick) butter (preferably cold)
⅓ cup milk
Confectioners' sugar
½ cup preserves (blueberry, wild blackberry, currant)
½ cup nuts, whole, broken, or chopped (walnuts, almonds, pecans, hazelnuts)

Preheat oven to 425°. Blend baking mix, cream cheese, and butter in a 1½-quart bowl until the mixture is crumbly. (It is a little harder to work in the butter when it's cold, but if the butter is warm, the dough will be sticky.) Stir in milk to make a soft dough.

Line a baking sheet with aluminum foil. Spread a few tablespoons of confectioners' sugar on foil and put the dough on the sugar. Work the dough a bit to make it smoother using confectioners' sugar to "flour" your hand and the dough. Roll the dough out to a rectangle about 8 by 11 inches (the size of a sheet of typing paper)—you don't need a rolling pin, a glass or clean pop can will do.

Pour the preserves in a centered stripe down the length of the dough. Sprinkle the nuts on the preserves. Make a slit every inch along the dough on both sides from the edge almost to the preserves. Fold each strip carefully over the preserves (the strips don't have to overlap or touch). If your foil is messy, wipe it up a bit. Bake at 425° until coffeecake is golden (about 15 minutes). And put the coffee on.

Marzipan Crescents

Our preschoolers like to make these dainties at roadside rests, but they taste like the work of a pastry chef at Mackinac Island's Grand Hotel.

1 8-ounce can refrigerated crescent rolls
Marzipan or almond paste (available in cans or packages)

Preheat oven to 375°. Unroll dough and separate into 8 triangles. Make 1-inch balls of marzipan, flatten and roll into 2-inch long logs. Place a marzipan log at shortest side of each dough triangle and roll log and dough loosely to the opposite point. Pinch to seal roll on either side of marzipan log. Place crescent rolls on foil-lined baking sheet. Bake until golden brown (about 11 to 13 minutes).

SOUPS, SALADS, AND SANDWICHES

Noah's Ark Soup

Fresh vegetables go two by two into the pot in this soup inspired by an old Shaker recipe for spring vegetable soup.

2 tablespoons butter
2 leeks, top and root trimmed to about an 8-inch stalk, sliced (about 2 cups)
2 stalks celery, sliced
2 medium potatoes, peeled, halved, and sliced
2 carrots, peeled and sliced
2 quarts hot chicken broth (make with 10 bouillon cubes)
2 teaspoons dried parsley or chervil *or* 2 tablespoons chopped fresh parsley
Pepper to taste

Put 2 quarts of water on to boil in your kettle. Melt butter in large saucepan (4-quart). Add leeks and celery to saucepan and cook over medium heat—do not brown—while you get the potatoes and carrots ready. Add potatoes and carrots. Dissolve bullion cubes in boiling water. (It's easier to do this in small batches—don't worry if the cubes aren't completely dissolved.) Pour the hot broth over the vegetables and simmer covered for 20 minutes.

Note: You can also add 2 chopped parsley roots, 2 peas, 2 beans . . .

German Potato Salad

2 pounds (about 6) potatoes (preferably red)
2 tablespoons finely chopped onion (½ small onion or more to taste)
4 slices lean bacon
⅓ cup vinegar
¼ cup sugar
1 teaspoon salt
Pepper
¼ teaspoon celery seed (optional)

Boil potatoes until tender (about ½ hour). While potatoes are getting cool enough to handle, fry bacon until crisp (you may find this easier to do if you cut the bacon into pieces). Remove bacon pieces from skillet. Peel potatoes and slice into a 1½- or 2-quart bowl. Crumble bacon and add bacon and onion to bowl. In skillet, combine bacon drippings with vinegar, sugar, salt, celery seed, and pepper to taste (be especially generous with the pepper if you don't have celery seed). Heat and pour over potatoes. Stir everything together and serve warm.

Variations: Many cooks like to add a couple of sliced hard-boiled eggs and/or a sprinkling of parsley. A Canadian variation adds celery and a touch of mustard.

Calico Potato Salad

The faithful standby of family picnics, church suppers, potlucks, and countless summer meals, it is nigh onto impossible to grow up in America without eating potato salad. And it seems like almost everyone who cooks has a recipe for potato salad, a recipe just a little different from the next—bet you've been to picnics with half a dozen potato salads and no two alike. That's the American way, as American as potato salad. Here's a Midwestern favorite.

2 pounds (about 6) potatoes (preferably red)
1 teaspoon vinegar
1 teaspoon sugar
1 teaspoon salt
2 small scallions (green onions) including tops, sliced into small pieces (about ¼ cup)
4 hard-boiled eggs, diced
½ cup sweet pickle relish
¼ cup mayonnaise (more to taste or if other vegetables are added)
½ teaspoon prepared mustard (optional)

Boil potatoes until tender (about ½ hour). Drain and allow potatoes to get cool enough to handle comfortably. Peel potatoes and dice. Toss potato cubes in a 1½- or 2-quart bowl with vinegar, sugar, and salt. Stir in remaining ingredients. Allow flavors to mellow and serve at room temperature or chill and serve later.

Variations: And now the fun begins. Add ¼ to ½ cup of any of the following, singly or in combinations: diced cucumber; sliced celery; sliced black, green, or stuffed olives; sliced sweet pickles (substitute for pickle relish); chopped or sliced dill pickle (substitute for pickle relish); chopped onion or thin onion rings (substitute for scallions); sliced radishes; shredded carrot; diced red and/or green pepper; and/or your own favorite. Various seasonings can also be added, for example, celery seed, dill weed, or paprika. For *No-Cook Potato Salad*, substitute 2 1-pound cans of new potatoes for the raw potatoes.

Picnic Pasta

Pasta salads are almost as popular as potato salads and are made the same way. Follow the Calico Potato Salad recipe but substitute a 6- to 8-ounce package of pasta, cooked according to package directions, for the diced potatoes. Macaroni, seashells, spirals, small bow ties, or *Kraft* dinner (including the cheese packet) are all good.

Confetti Pea Salad

1 10-ounce package frozen petite
   peas, defrosted
3 ounces Cheddar cheese, cut in
   small pea-size dice (about ¾
   cup)
2 small scallions (green onions)
   including tops, sliced into small
   pieces (about ¼ cup)
2 hard-boiled eggs, sliced or
   diced
¼ cup mayonnaise or salad
   dressing

Drain defrosted peas and mix with remaining ingredients in a refrigerator container. Cover and let flavors blend in refrigerator for an hour to overnight.

Nebraska Grilled Reubens

The Reuben was born in Nebraska in 1956, the brainchild of an Omaha chef.

8 slices rye or pumpernickel
   bread
½ pound canned corned beef,
   sliced thin
4 slices Swiss cheese
½ cup sauerkraut, drained
Thousand Island dressing
Butter

Spread 1 side of each slice of bread with Thousand Island dressing. Fill each sandwich with a slice of Swiss cheese, a small mound of sauerkraut, and a couple of slices of corned beef. Butter the outside of sandwich and fry in buttered skillet over medium heat (as you would an ordinary grilled cheese sandwich) until cheese is melted and bread is toasted.

Variations: You can eat the sandwich cold without grilling. Or dip each sandwich in beaten egg and milk (about ¼ cup to each egg) before frying in butter. Or try toasting the Reubens in a long-handled campfire pie cooker over the coals. Make *Miniature Reubens* with party rye bread as an appetizer or snack. Make the sandwiches open-face ending with a small slice of cheese. Bake in a 350° oven until cheese melts.

Chicago Club Sandwiches

If you wheel into the heart of any of the Heartland's big cities, reward yourself with a stop at a delicatessen or a supermarket deli to pick up the makings of a nerve-soothing, soul-satisfying, mouth-watering triple-decker club sandwich. Compose your classy Dagwood of layers of cold cuts (roast beef, turkey, ham), cheeses (Cheddar, Muenster, Swiss, Provolone), and fresh vegetables (tomatoes, avocado, mushrooms, alfalfa sprouts, lettuce), all thinly sliced and sandwiched between three thin slices of good bread that have been spread with butter, mayonnaise, or Thousand Island dressing.

There's no rule against putting in a few adventurous slices of lunchmeats (Chicago, Milwaukee, and other big cities in the Heartland are famous for their selections of the world's finest sausages). Enjoy your creation at the nearest pleasant parking place and congratulate yourself on your good fortune at finding one of the best restaurants in town.

MAIN EVENTS

North Woods Savory Beef Pie

When your crew comes in with Paul Bunyon appetites, you can whip together this hearty meat pie in about half an hour.

1 9-inch refrigerated pie crust
3 hard-boiled eggs, chopped*
2 pounds lean ground beef
8 ounces (about 2 cups)
  Swiss cheese, grated or
  shredded
½ cup instant minced onion
1 teaspoon salt
Pepper to taste
1 teaspoon dried savory or
  mixed herbs (Herbs de
  Provence are good)
1 egg, beaten with a fork

Preheat the oven to 450°. While the oven is heating, brown the hamburger in a skillet over medium-high heat, stirring in the dried onion as you are browing the meat. When meat is cooked but not dry, pour off excess fat into a disposable heatproof container. Stir in chopped eggs, cheese, and seasonings. Transfer the mixture to a 9-inch pie pan or 9-inch cake pan. Top with pie crust, tucking in edge so it doesn't hang over the pan, but do not seal the pie crust to the pan edge. Brush the top of the pie crust with beaten egg (use a basting brush or piece of paper towel) and prick crust with a fork. Bake until golden (about 10-12 minutes).

A cool vegetable—cucumbers in sour cream, green beans or sliced beefsteak tomatoes in vinegar and oil—makes a satisfying complement to this filling pie.

*Tip: The chopped eggs can be hot, so if you don't happen to have hard-boiled eggs on hand put them on to boil while you are browning the meat and they'll be ready about the time you need them.

South Dakota Cornish Pasties

The pasty has a legendary status going back to the fourteenth century in the Old World and the mid-nineteenth century in the New. Even Shakespeare wrote about the hot pasty and so has almost every writer about regional foods in America. Introduced into America by immigrant Cornish miners, the hearty hand pie was reheated on a shovel with a candle, making a substantial warm lunch for the hard-working miner. The fame of the pasty spread wherever there were Cornish miners, notably in the iron and copper region of Michigan.

We were first introduced to pasties by a roommate from Deadwood, South Dakota. She'd fill our tiny apartment with their memorable aroma whenever the need for Heartland "soul food" hit her. They take more time than we like to spend cooking in the RV, but we just couldn't write about regional cooking in America and leave out pasties (we did make it a little easier).

1 pound tender boneless sirloin
  steak, trimmed and cut into
  ¼-inch cubes
2 small potatoes, peeled and cut
  into ¼-inch cubes
1 turnip, peeled and cut into
  ¼-inch cubes *or* 1 rutabaga,
  peeled and cut into ¼-inch
  cubes
½ large sweet onion, chopped
  or 3 tablespoons instant minced
  onion
½ teaspoon dried thyme (nice
  but not necessary)
½ teaspoon Worcestershire sauce
1 teaspoon salt
Generous sprinkling of pepper
1 17¼-ounce package frozen
  puff pastry

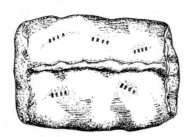

Preheat oven to 400°. Allow pastry to defrost enough to handle without cracking (about 20 minutes at room temperature). Combine diced meat and vegetables in a large bowl. Add seasonings and mix well. Cut each pastry sheet in half crosswise. Place a heaping cup of filling in the center of each pastry rectangle. (Depending on the size of your vegetables, you may have extra filling.) Bring up the two short sides of the pastry and pinch and seal together over the top of the filling. Fold over the other edges and seal firmly. (If you are having difficulty making the edges stick, dampen with water.) Prick pastry top with fork to allow steam to escape Bake on foil-lined baking sheet for 45 minutes. Check the pasties about half way through: if the pasties seem to be getting too brown, cover with aluminum foil. Serve pasties hot, warm, or re-warmed, accompanied with ketchup and dill pickles.

Notes: These pasties are untraditionally square (to save rolling and cutting). Usually pasties are made from 8- or 9-inch circles crimped along the top of the filling. We experimented with prepared pie crusts for the pastry, but they made a very fragile pastry—hard to get from pan to plate let alone survive a trip to the mine or the stream. If you are making your own pastry, we suggest you make it sturdier than usual and roll it out fairly thick.

Variation: An untraditional but tasty pasty can be made by substituing 3 cups of partially defrosted O'Brien potatoes for the diced vegetables in the above recipe.

Pork Chops Jubilee

Imported from the Black Forest of Europe to the Black Hills of America, chops with cherries is glamorous but easy-to-prepare fare fit for almost any occasion.

4 pork loin chops
2 tablespoons vegetable oil
1 ounce brandy, cherry brandy, kirsch, or other spirits (optional)
¼ cup beef broth (make a cup of broth with a bouillon cube and use the leftover broth in stovetop stuffing or rice)
1 17-ounce can pitted dark sweet cherries
½ teaspoon cinnamon
½ teaspoon chervil, parsley, or mixed salad herbs (optional)
2 tablespoons lemon juice
2 teaspoons cornstarch
½ cup broken walnuts
Salt and pepper

Salt and pepper chops generously. Heat oil in skillet over medium heat. Brown chops on both sides. Transfer chops to a plate and pour off fat from pan (use a disposable heatproof container: plastic may melt with hot oil). Return skillet to fire and pour in brandy and boil a moment. Add chops and beef broth. Cover and simmer over low heat for ½ hour to 1 hour depending on thickness of chops (1½-inch-thick chops take about an hour).

Drain syrup from cherries into a small saucepan. Add seasonings to syrup. In a small container mix lemon juice and cornstarch together (a paper cup is fine for this step). Slowly dribble lemon mixture into syrup mixture and cook over low heat stirring often until sauce is thick and shiny. If you happen to be using a fresh lemon for the lemon juice, grate a little of the lemon peel into the syrup while you are cooking the syrup. About 10 minutes before you think the chops are going to be done, pour syrup into skillet over the chops. When the chops are cooked, stir in the cherries and walnuts and heat for a few minutes until warm. Serve with stovetop stuffing or rice.

Smothered Supper Chops

If you've skipped onion-smothered pork chops because of residual atmospheric conditions, here's how to have the flavor without being reminded of it for the next week.

1½ pounds (6 to 8 chops) pork loin chops, trimmed of excess fat
1 tablespoon cooking oil
1 10¾-ounce can condensed French onion soup
Salt and pepper to taste
½ cup regular converted rice or 1 cup instant rice

Brown chops in oiled skillet over medium-high heat. (This may be easier to do in two or three batches; add more oil if needed.) Pour excess fat into a disposable heatproof container. Salt and pepper chops. Stir soup, regular converted rice, and ½ cup water into chops in skillet. (If you are using instant rice, add rice five minutes before chops are done.) Cover tightly and simmer, stirring occasionally, until chops are cooked through (about 30 minutes).

Swedish Meatballs

This enduring American favorite is just one of the many delicious Scandinavian foods that are familiar and welcome fare on Heartland tables. As is often the case with a dish of such widespread popularity, there are many variations of the recipe. The most frequent change is in that all-important dash of seasoning—caraway seed, Worcestershire sauce, paprika, dill weed, allspice, nutmeg, or combinations of spices. This is a classic and simple version of Swedish Meatballs that will brighten brunch, lunch, dinner, or drinks.

Meatballs:
1 pound ground beef
1 cup fine fresh bread crumbs
  (about 2 slices of bread)
¼ cup finely chopped onion
  or 4 teaspoons instant minced
  onion
½ cup milk
1 egg
1 teaspoon salt
Generous dash of pepper
Generous dash of nutmeg or
  allspice

Cream Sauce:
¼ cup butter
¼ cup flour
1 cup sour cream and 2 cups
  boiling water *or* 2½ cups milk
½ teaspoon salt
Generous dash of pepper
Generous dash of nutmeg or
  allspice

Combine meatball ingredients, mixing well. Shape into balls about the size of a walnut. Melt butter in skillet. Brown meatballs well. (This step may be easier in two batches if your skillet isn't large.) Remove meatballs from pan and stir flour into fat and pan juices. Stir in boiling water and sour cream (or milk) until sauce is smooth and beginning to simmer. Stir in seasonings. Return meatballs to sauce. Cover and cook 15 to 20 minutes over low heat until the meatballs are cooked through. (This makes a generous amount of sauce—even if you increase the meatball recipe by half or so, the sauce can stay the same.) Serve with lightly buttered noodles.

Farmhouse Chicken

2 pounds chicken parts
2 tablespoons butter
1 4-ounce can of sliced
  mushrooms, drained
1 10¾-ounce can condensed
  creamy chicken mushroom or
  cream of chicken soup
Hot cooked wide noodles or
  noodle dumplings

Rinse chicken pieces in cool water and pat dry. Skin pieces if desired and trim excess fat. In skillet brown chicken in butter over medium-high heat. Pour off fat into a disposable heatproof container. Add mushrooms and soup. Cover and cook over low heat, stirring occasionally, until chicken is cooked through (about 45 minutes). Serve over hot noodles.

Great Lakes Smelt Fry

Of the many traditional American seafood feasts that you may enjoy in your RV, high on the list of those *not to try* is Wisconsin's Door County Fish Boil. It's not so much that you need a couple hundred pounds of fish and potatoes, and a *very* big pot, it's the last step in the recipe you want to leave to expert hands: a gallon of kerosene flaming up in one whoosh. Far better to drive to one.

However, another Great Lakes tradition is ideal for the RV cook. If you happen to be in the Wisconsin-Michigan area in April, or, for that matter, wherever the smelt are running, get your skillet ready for the Great Lakes Smelt Fry.

In this neck of the woods, the littlest fish has the biggest tradition. A salt water fish originally imported to feed salmon, the smelt multiplied so well in the western Great Lakes that when in the dark of night in the early spring, they head into the streams to spawn, thousands of people with nets, buckets, and hands scoop out millions of the small silvery fish. If you happen to be there, you can get lots of advice from fellow fisherfolk on how best to fry them. If, however, you come by a catch of smelt in less crowded circumstances, this recipe is a popular one. It is easy to multiply to suit the supply and your appetite—it is not unusual for someone at a smelt fry to eat twenty-five.

1 pound smelt, cleaned and deheaded
1 cup pancake mix
¾ cup beer
Salt and pepper
Butter
Cooking oil

Heat ¼ cup butter and ¼ cup oil in a skillet over medium-high heat. In a bowl, stir beer into pancake mix. (If you are in a dry climate you may need more beer to make batter of normal pancake consistency.) Season batter to taste with salt and pepper. Dip smelt in batter and fry several at a time until golden (about 3 minutes on each side), adding more butter and oil as needed. The bones are so soft that those in the littlest can be eaten, while in the larger fish they are easily pulled out with the tail.

Brookside Trout

If trout sizzling in bacon isn't a marriage made in heaven, it is certainly a heavenly combination that has inspired many to head for the streams, brooks, and lakes of the Heartland and wherever else those beautiful silvery creatures reside. Ideally, the trout make the shortest trip possible from brook to pan, which accounts for the many simple campsite recipes. Bacon-sauteed trout is not only simple, but so mouth-watering that it is even popular for breakfast, although fish isn't usually considered morning fare in America.

4 to 8 pan-size rainbow or brook trout, cleaned
8 slices lean bacon
Milk
Flour
Salt and pepper
1 fresh lemon, cut in wedges (optional)

Fry the bacon over medium heat until it is crisp and brown. If you plan to serve the fish with large bacon bits, you can cut the bacon into short sections before frying to fit your pan more easily.) Remove the bacon and drain on a paper towel. Meanwhile, rinse the whole fish in cool water and pat dry inside and out. Sprinkle the cavities of the fish with salt and pepper. Dip each fish in milk (with a little juggling you can do this in a fairly small bowl) and roll each fish in flour (pour about ¼ cup of flour on waxed paper or foil). Fry the fish two or three at a time in the hot bacon fat for about 5 minutes on each side, turning the fish carefully with a large spatula or pancake turner. Don't be concerned if your trout are a little big for your skillet, just bend them a bit to get the head and tail in and shift them around slightly during the cooking to get them to cook evenly. When the trout is cooked—the flesh flakes easily with a fork—tuck a bacon strip in each fish or sprinkle large bacon bits on top and serve the fish hot from the skillet with wedges of lemon. Pour a fresh cup of coffee or drink for those still patiently waiting and cook the rest of the fish.

Variation: Dip the trout in cornmeal or a half-and-half mixture of cornmeal and flour instead of the flour and proceed as above.

Redcoat Trout

If you happen to have Canadian bacon rather than regular bacon, try this old English treat. It is a little more trouble than Brookside Trout but excellent.

4 to 8 pan-size rainbow or brook trout, cleaned
8 to 12 slices Canadian bacon
Milk
Flour
Salt and pepper
2 to 3 tablespoons butter
2 to 3 tablespoons oil
1 fresh lemon, cut in wedges (optional)

Rinse the whole fish in cool water and pat dry inside and out. Sprinkle the cavities of the fish with salt and pepper. Dip each fish in milk and roll in flour. Melt butter and oil in skillet over medium-high heat until it is foamy but not brown. Saute the fish two or three at a time for about 4 minutes on each side, turning the fish carefully with a large spatula or pancake turner. Repeat with additional batches of fish, adding more butter and oil if needed. Note: If you stop at this point you have the American classic *Pan-fried Trout*. Meanwhile, preheat the RV oven broiler. Transfer fish to a baking pan and peel the skin off the top sides. Lay a slice or two of Canadian bacon—depending on the size of the fish—on the exposed side of each fish, and broil until bacon is well browned. Serve the trout in its bacon-coat with lemon wedges.

Trout Amandine

This elegant star of fancy French restaurants is even better in your private dining room on wheels with nature providing the decor. And it is as easy to prepare as plain pan-fried trout. Simply follow the preparations and stovetop directions in the Redcoat Trout recipe, adding part of a 4-ounce package of sliced almonds to the skillet with each batch of trout. As the trout is cooking, stir the almonds now and then. Spoon the golden almonds over the cooked trout as you finish each batch and serve with lemon wedges.

Mississippi Valley Fried Catfish

The lazy Mississippi River, cane poles, barefoot Tom Sawyer and Huck Finn look-alikes, big smiles, and a string of big catfish—a nostalgic image, but these days it's more likely the ominous-looking fish came from a catfish farm. The tastiest, the spotted or fiddler cat, is still freshest in the Mississippi Valley, and here's an easy recipe for cooking up the mess of cats you talked Tom and Huck out of. (Although it's not *too* messy, in the spirit of the event, you might want to take your skillet outdoors to the grill.)

2 pounds catfish fillets
1 egg
1 cup cornmeal
Salt and pepper
1 cup cooking oil

Wipe catfish fillets with damp paper towels. Beat egg with 2 tablespoons of water in a flat bowl. Dip each fillet in egg then roll in cornmeal until well coated (T*ip*: Use a paper plate for the cornmeal.) Salt and pepper generously. Heat oil in skillet until it is hot enough to brown a cube of bread in 1 minute. Fry fillets in hot oil until they are crisp and golden brown (about 3 minutes on each side). Drain on paper towels and serve with hush puppies and coleslaw.

Easy Hush Puppies: Decrease the amount of liquid called for on a corn muffin or cornbread mix by a few tablespoons so that the batter is stiff. Stir in 1 or 2 tablespoons of minced dried onion. Drop batter by spoonfuls into the hot oil that the fish has been fried in and cook until crisp and brown.

ASIDES

America's Cheese Board

Before, during, or after a meal, few things are more appealing and appetizing than a platter of cheeses from the heart of America's dairylands. A sampling of Heartland cheeses with crackers and fresh crisp vegetables is an unbeatable way to stave off hunger and restore spirits when dinner is down the road. It's also a happy solution to what to nibble with drinks almost anytime. Add a loaf of bread or crusty rolls and you have lunch or a cool, easy supper. For a continental finale for a meal or a sumptuous snack, team a creamy Wisconsin brie or camembert, a potent Minnesota blue cheese, or a pungent Ohio Liederkranz with fruits and nuts from the region's orchards. And then there are cheese dips and spreads, all-American anytime favorites.

Blue Cheese Dip with Mackinac Miniatures

Mackinac Island was a summer home of the region's rich in days gone by. It still is a luxury summer resort area, but one of the few places in the country you can't enjoy in an RV—no motorized vehicles are allowed on the island. Michigan farmers along the coast specialized in growing tiny tender vegetables for the summer visitors. They still do. These delicate little miniatures—green beans, peas, zucchini—are delightful additions to a tray of fresh vegetable dippers. Other possibilities for your tray are: young asparagus stalks, whole or quartered mushrooms, small Brussels sprouts, carrot sticks, wedges of red or green peppers, cauliflower or broccoli florets, radishes, celery, tomato wedges, fennel, sliced kohlrabi or jicama, cucumber sticks or slices, and scallions.

1 4-ounce package blue cheese, crumbled
1 12-ounce carton sour cream with chives

Mix blue cheese and sour cream as smooth as desired (most people prefer the dip lumpy with blue cheese). Chill until serving time. Serve with an assortment of crisp vegetable dippers.

Wisconsin Beer Cheese

Wisconsin Statute No. 160,065: *Butter and Cheese to be served.* Every person, firm or corporation duly licensed to operate a hotel or restaurant shall serve with each meal for which a charge of twenty-five cents or more is made, at least two-thirds of an ounce of Wisconsin butter and two-thirds of an ounce of Wisconsin cheese.

Beer cheese is a particularly pleasant way to fulfill the spirit of the law in your restaurant on wheels, although the statute is no longer on the books.

1 10-ounce package Wisconsin Longhorn Cheddar cheese (or other Cheddar), grated (about 2½ to 3 cups)
2 teaspoons Worcestershire sauce
Beer (about ½ cup)
Garlic powder to taste (optional)

Beat the cheese with the seasonings and a little of the beer at a time until the spread is smooth. Serve the spread at RV temperature with crackers and ice-cold schooners of beer.

Note: If you omit the garlic powder, try adding prepared mustard to taste (about ½ teaspoon).

Perfect Corn on the Cob

Among the many tips for making perfect corn on the cob in Corn Country is one on which there is unanimous agreement: the fresher the corn the better.

1 RV
8 ears of fresh young corn on the
  cob
Butter
Salt

Find a cornfield with a sign that says Fresh Corn. Park. Get out your largest pot. Pick the corn and remove the husks and silk. Rinse corn in cold water. Meanwhile, bring 1-inch of water in the saucepan to a boil over medium heat. When the water is boiling, put the corn in the pot. When the water again starts to boil, cover the pot and cook the corn for 5 minutes. Turn off the heat and lift the ears out of the pan with tongs. Serve with butter and salt.

Tips: If your corn isn't quite this fresh or young you may have to cook it longer. If you are doing fewer ears of corn at a time because your pot is small, use the same amount of water. If you only have a small pot (2-quart), you can still cook a couple of ears by breaking the ears in half and standing them on end (be sure the lid fits). Or you can steam a couple of ears in a covered frying pan.

Poppy Seed Noodles

Their Eastern European heritage make poppy seed speckled noodles an appropriate accompaniment to Heartland favorites like wiener schnitzel (fried breaded veal cutlets) and grilled European sausages. They are also good with plain chops and steaks.

½ **pound wide egg noodles**
¼ **cup (½ stick) butter**
½ **cup sour cream (optional)**
2 **tablespoons poppy seed**
Salt and pepper

Cook noodles according to package directions. Toss noodles with butter and sour cream until the hot noodles melt the butter. (If you don't use sour cream add a little more butter.) Sprinkle with poppy seed and salt and pepper to taste. Toss again.

DESSERTS

Johnny Appleseed Apple Crisp

The apples you are using, especially if you are traveling in Pennsylvania, Ohio, or Indiana, may have come from a tree descended from a seed nurtured and carried west by the legendary barefoot, pot-hatted Johnny Appleseed. Born John Chapman in 1774, Johnny Appleseed devoted an eccentric lifetime to spreading seeds, trees, and his gospel that there was little on earth that equalled a good apple. Too bad Johnny didn't have an RV to help him do and enjoy the fruits of his work.

5 medium apples, peeled and
   sliced
1 tablespoon lemon juice
½ cup light brown sugar
½ teaspoon cinnamon

Streusel Topping:
¼ cup (½ stick) butter, softened
½ teaspoon cinnamon
½ cup light brown sugar
½ cup flour
½ cup nuts (walnuts, pecans,
   hazelnuts, etc.), chopped*

Slice apples into a large bowl. Sprinkle with lemon juice, brown sugar, and cinnamon, and stir to coat slices evenly. Transfer apples to a 9-inch baking pan (a cake pan). To make streusel topping, mix butter, cinnamon, brown sugar, and flour until it is crumbly. Mix in nuts. Cover apples with topping. Bake at 375 ° until top is lightly browned and apples are cooked through (about 30 minutes). Apple crisp is served warm and often topped with cream.

*Tip: Put nuts in a sealable plastic bag and tap on them with the back of a heavy spoon.

Grand Traverse Bay Cherry Pie

It's the cherries that count! And nowhere do they count more than in the hundreds of orchards of America's cherry capital and at the week-long National Cherry Festival at Traverse City, Michigan. The festival celebrating the incomparable juicy Montmorency cherries has been held for well over sixty years. If you are among the more than half a million celebrants at the July festival, you could collect thousands of inventive recipes for cherries—in drinks, main courses, preserves, tarts, sundaes, cakes, cookies, candy, and, of course, imaginative pies. But to our mind it's hard to beat the simple, perfect, old-fashioned cherry pie wherever or whenever you happen on a quart of beautiful fresh red cherries (if you have an oven).

1 quart of Montmorency cherries
   (or other sour red cherries),
   rinsed and pitted
1 cup sugar
1 tablespoon flour
Salt
1 15-ounce package refrigerated
   pie crusts (2 9-inch pie crusts)

Preheat oven to 425° (to avoid sweltering, open the RV windows and go out to the camp table to do the cherry pitting and preparation). In a bowl mix pitted cherries, sugar, flour, and a dash of salt. Line a 9-inch pie pan with pie crust. Heap the cherries into the pie shell. Cover with second pie crust, fluting edges to seal well. Cut slits in the top and bake for 40 minutes.

Tip: We like to brush the top crust with milk and dust with a bit of sugar before baking.

Cherry Supreme Waffles

A fluffy cream sauce and canned cherry pie filling transform frozen waffles into a company-special showy dessert.

8 frozen waffles (a 10 or 11-ounce package)
1 21-ounce can cherry fruit filling
1 4-ounce package whipped cream cheese
¼ cup confectioners' sugar
1 4-ounce container whipped topping, defrosted

Preheat oven to 400°. Place waffles on baking sheet and bake until crisp and hot (about 5 minutes). Meanwhile, in a bowl whip together cream cheese, confectioners' sugar, and, finally, whipped topping until smooth and fluffy. In a small saucepan, heat cherry pie filling, stirring occasionally. (If you happen to have almond extract on hand, put a few drops in the cherry pie filling.) Stack two waffles for each serving, topping both waffles generously with cream sauce and cherry filling.

Variation: For an easier version, substitute plain whipped topping or a cup of sour cream for the cream cheese sauce.

Strawberry Tallcake

Although America's local bakeries provide a never ending array of goodies mirroring the tastes and ethnic richness of the country, there is one bakery's products that seem to match the national taste. Like millions of other Americans, we are unabashed fans of *Sara Lee*. We have yet to encounter an occasion at home or on the road that was too special for *Sara Lee* to come to the rescue. We have decorated their fancy cakes for birthday parties and built our wedding cake, a towering, tiered Italian cassata, out of split and filled *Sara Lee* pound cakes. Paying the ultimate tribute to this phenomenally successful Deerfield, Illinois, company, a great number of Americans now make the quintessential American dessert, strawberry shortcake, with *Sara Lee* pound cake. This is a show-off version fit for a celebration.

1 1-pound pound cake
1 quart fresh ripe strawberries,* sliced and sugared
1 4-ounce carton whipped cream topping, thawed, *or* 1 6½-ounce can whipped cream topping

Slice the pound cake into horizontal slabs about ½ inch thick (this is easy to do while the cake is still frozen); layer the slabs with thick layers of whipped cream and sliced strawberries; press gently on the top so everything sticks together. Decorate the top with more whipped cream and whole strawberries. To serve, slice vertically into 1-inch-thick slices and top with vanilla ice cream and more sliced, sugared strawberries.

*Reserve several of the prettiest strawberries whole for the top of the cake.

Ohio Buckeyes

If your walk in the woods gets rained out, put your gnomes to work on these.

½ cup (1 stick) butter, softened
1 cup peanut butter
1½ cup confectioners' sugar
½ tablespoon vanilla
1 6-ounce package chocolate chips

Mix butter, peanut butter, sugar, and vanilla. Shape into small balls and chill. Melt chocolate over low heat in a small saucepan. Using a toothpick to hold balls, dip each in chocolate leaving a small space on top free of chocolate so it resembles a buckeye nut. Makes about 50 buckeyes (which disappear very quickly). Keep chilled.

Note: Without the chocolate, this no-cook peanut butter candy is known as *Peanut Butter Clay* in other parts of the country.

CHEERS

Mocha Cooler

This refresher from America's Dairyland is for those who like their coffee light and luscious.

1 quart chocolate milk
2 cups cold strong coffee

Pour 2 cups of chocolate milk into ice-cube trays and freeze. For each serving, fill large glass or mug with chocolate-milk cubes. Mix remaining milk and coffee (you can do it in the milk carton). Pour coffee-milk mixture over cubes in each glass.

Variation: For a *Spirited Mocha Cooler*, add a full or half jigger of brandy or bourbon to each glass before pouring in coffee-milk mixture.

Autumn Cider

Russet leaves, crisp air, and steamy mugs of spiced cider are high on the list of the joys of fall travel.

1 quart (32 ounces) apple cider
1 tablespoon lemon juice
1 cinnamon stick
1 teaspoon whole cloves
(or ⅛ teaspoon of ground cloves)

Simmer all ingredients in a saucepan until as spicy as desired (about five minutes). Fish out the whole spices. Serve cider very hot.

Variations: Some people like to put a few lemon slices in with the simmering cider; if you do, insert the cloves into the lemon slices. In a pinch, you can substitute ground mixed spices to taste (about ½ teaspoon) for the whole spices but the cider will be muddy.

Open House Eggnog

This effortless rich creamy eggnog is too good to reserve for the holidays. Mix up a batch for four to forty in a minute. Fill a tray with samplings of the Heartland's fine baked goods and you have festive refreshments for any fall or winter open "house."

1 quart French vanilla ice cream
1 pint (2 cups) bourbon or rum
Grated nutmeg

In your nicest bowl or pitcher, stir ice cream and liquor together until well mixed and smooth. Sprinkle nutmeg on top. Makes about 12 4-ounce servings.

Port and Starboard

This pretty pousse-cafe is popular with boating RVers. You do need small clear glasses for the effect. For each drink:

½ jigger (¾ ounce) grenadine
½ jigger (¾ ounce) creme de menthe

Pour grenadine in glass first. Carefully pour creme de menthe on top.

Grand Occasion Punch

Glad tidings from the folks at home? Announcing an engagement or celebrating your seventh or seventy-seventh anniversary? Won the fishing contest with a record-breaking catch or a million in the lottery? This elegant brew will rise to the occasion.

1 25-ounce bottle domestic champagne, well-chilled
1 pint lemon sherbet
½ cup brandy or Grand Marnier

Put scoops of sherbet into a pitcher or bowl. Pour brandy over sherbet and stir gently. Pour champagne over sherbet and serve immediately to four well-wishers or two celebrants.

Cosmopolitan Cuisine

CRADLE OF LIBERTY

Cranberries and cod, pumpkins and poultry, squash and shellfish—the bounty of the native tables of the Northeast is written indelibly on the menu of America.

As each ship arrived, new dishes came with it. Not surprisingly, much of the historic cooking of New England and the Middle Colonies—Pennsylvania, New Jersey, and Delaware—is kin to the cooking of the Mother Country with a decidedly Yankee accent. But there are also the unforgetta-

ble contributions of Dutch and German settlers and, as time went by, the wonderful, tantalizing aromas and flavors of the foods of dozens of other cuisines in America's Melting Pot—African, Arabian, Austrian, Belgian, Bulgarian, Carribean, Chinese, Czech, Danish, Egyptian, Ecuadorian, Finnish, French, Greek, Hungarian, Indian, Indonesian, Irish, Italian, Jewish, Khmer, Laotian, Latvian, Mexican, Mongolian, Morrocan—enjoyed by people of every ethnic background.

EYE OPENERS

All recipes serve four unless otherwise stated.

A Pancake Tour of the Northeast

One could easily take a cook's tour of the cosmopolitan cuisine of the Atlantic North simply by sampling the pancakes of the region.

The oldest are, no doubt, corn griddlecakes. *Rhode Island Johnnycakes*, thin corncakes made from almost equal parts of salted white cornmeal (1 teaspoon salt to 1 cup cornmeal) and boiling water, are still popular today, though they date back to early Colonial times and were probably originally an Indian food. Johnnycakes, also called journey cakes, were long considered a traveler's friend. (We found them fun to try, but so slow cooking—4 to 6 minutes a side for each pancake— that we can't recommend them for modern hungry travelers.)

The Dutch, who settled in the New World in what is now New York in the seventeenth century, introduced the more familiar pancakes and waffles. You can easily enjoy modern versions of these ageless favorites with any pancake mix or baking mix pancake or waffle recipe. Unless you are among the waffle fans who have them almost daily, it would be better to leave your waffle iron home and get frozen waffles.

Add blueberries to your pancake batter (about 1 cup berries to 2 cups mix) for that old New England standby, *Blueberry Pancakes* (also available in mixes).

In Pennsylvania Dutch country, *Funnel Cakes* are the traditional treats. You can make them from special funnel cake mix which is widely available, especially around the holidays (or substitute regular pancake mix flavored with a few drops of vanilla). Funnel Cakes are cooked in hot oil ½ inch deep. When a drop of batter browns in 5 seconds, you pour or squeeze a thin stream of batter in an interlocking design—a spiral, star, or web. When the edges brown (about ½ minute), turn with tongs and continue cooking until brown (about another ½ minute). Dust the funnel cakes with confectioners' sugar. Traditionally, the batter is poured through a funnel or pitcher, but what works better is a plastic squeeze jar like a ketchup or honey dispenser.

Then there are all the other ethnic pancakes from delicate Russian blini with sour cream and caviar to crispy German potato pancakes with sour cream and applesauce. Two international favorites born abroad have almost become naturalized Americans—the French crepe and the Dutch or German puffed pancake. We find we tend to make both of them when either we want something special or when the cupboard's bare—a combination which makes them handy recipes to have on hand. Though both take a little effort, they are wonderfully versatile.

Crepes Marshall

Crepes are a family specialty with us—we won the James Beard/Woman's Day Creative Cookery Contest, taking First Prize in the Crepe Division; won a Fourth Prize in the Bertolli Italian Recipe Contest with a crepe recipe; and started our married life by serving them at our wedding breakfast. Quite an accomplishment for a few eggs and a cup of flour!

3 eggs
1 cup flour (preferably instant flour)
⅛ teaspoon salt
1 cup milk
¼ cup water
Melted butter

Beat eggs in a small bowl with a fork. Add the flour and salt and continue beating until batter is smooth. Gradually add milk and water and continue beating until batter is smooth. (Note: Altitude and lack of humidity do strange things to crepes, but this recipe works well under most circumstances especially if the batter is left to sit awhile.) Cook the crepes in a medium-hot skillet brushed with melted butter using your most successful method. Ours is: Pour about ¼ cup of batter in the skillet and tilt it until there is a thin even layer over the bottom; cook crepe until it is bubbly all over and lightly browned on the bottom (about 1 minute); turn crepe and cook another ½ minute on the other side. This recipe should make 16 to 17 perfect 7-inch crepes. If it doesn't, enjoy the "mistakes" and make some more. (You can store well-wrapped crepes, separated by pieces of foil or waxed paper, in the refrigerator or freezer for later use.)

The crepes are now ready to fill. A filling we find irresistible is fresh strawberries or blueberries folded into whipped cream. Or, try hot creamed chicken, seafood Newburg, or beef Burgundy (all available as frozen entrees). Or fill with warmed apple, cherry, or blueberry pie filling (the last two are good with sour cream). Or try baking crepes that have been lined with thin slices of ham and filled and topped with grated cheese in a 350° oven until the cheese is melted. In most cases, it's nice to also top the crepes with some of the filling or sauce.

New Amsterdam Puffed Pancake

This giant popover-like pancake, sometimes called a Dutch Baby or a Pannekoek, will make you feel like a real gourmet-on-the-go chef.

The ingredients are simple and inexpensive, so if your first doesn't puff up, eat it, and try again. It *should* have high sides and, usually, a wavy, airy bottom. (The most likely mistake is that the oven wasn't hot enough at the beginning.) Once you get it right, you'll make these simple show-offs any time it's cool.

2 eggs
½ cup flour
½ cup light cream
¼ teaspoon salt
1 tablespoon butter

Preheat oven to 450°. Heat a 9-inch baking pan in the oven until very hot. Meanwhile, beat eggs, flour, salt, and cream until smooth. Carefully, remove hot pan from the oven, add butter, and swirl butter around until pan is coated. Immediately pour batter in hot pan. Bake for ten minutes; lower heat to 350° and bake until golden (about 10 to 15 minutes). The pancake is delicious by itself with melted butter and confectioners' sugar or filled with almost anything. Cut into wedges to serve.

Fillings: Fresh or cooked fruits or vegetables are traditional fillings For example, mix 2 cups of bite-size fresh fruit (green grapes, peach slices, strawberries) with fruit yogurt. Or prepare a 10-ounce package of frozen mixed vegetables and toss with about a cup of mild shredded cheese (Cheddar, Swiss, Monterey Jack). Or fill with a baked 12-ounce package frozen escalloped apples (start baking the apples about ten minutes before the pancake goes in the oven). Or use the pancake as a boat for a chicken or seafood salad or . . .

Pennsylvania Dutch Scrapple and Red Eggs

Scrapple, a kind of pork sausage and corn meal mixture originally devised as a thrifty way of using scraps of pork, teams up with another Pennsylvania Dutch specialty for an unusual but traditional regional breakfast. You might enjoy this more as a lunch or supper.

1 16-ounce package frozen
Country Style Scrapple
4 to 6 hard-boiled eggs
1 16-ounce jar sliced sweet
***pickled* beets**

The night before you plan to have this breakfast, transfer the frozen scrapple to the refrigerator and prepare the eggs: Shell and cool the hard-boiled eggs; put the eggs in a 1-quart refrigerator container and pour the beets and all the juice over them; cover and chill until breakfast, turning the eggs from time to time if they are peeking out of the juice. At breakfast time, slice and cook scrapple according to package instructions. (From experience, we suggest reading the directions *before* slicing on the guidelines.) Remove the eggs from the bowl of beets, pat dry with a paper towel, and slice lengthwise into halves. Arrange the red egg halves around the browned scrapple slices and serve with the beets as a side dish. Traditionally, biscuits with apple butter round out the meal.

Eggs Benedict

This all-American fancy breakfast favorite may be easier to do in your RV than at home since the trick is getting everything done, assembled, and served while still warm. With the breakfasters within arm's reach, the juggling is simpler, and any mistakes can be chalked up to the adventure of playing roadside gourmet chef.

The basic recipe for this classic is simple:

**8 English muffin halves, toasted
and lightly buttered
8 to 16 small thin slices of fully
cooked ham,* warmed
8 eggs, poached or boiled for
5 minutes
Hollandaise Sauce**

Arrange 2 warm buttered muffin halves on each plate. Top each with 1 or 2 slices of warm ham, 1 egg, and 1 or 2 tablespoons of Hollandaise Sauce. Serve immediately.

Now let's take the steps one at a time. To toast the muffins use your toaster if you have one. Or warm the oven at 425° for awhile, and then toast all the muffins, cut side up, until lightly brown (about five minutes). Butter the muffins.

To cook the eggs, you can poach them as is usually called for. But an easier method for this recipe, especially when doing this large number of eggs, is to do *Five-Minute Eggs*.(what the French call *Ouefs Mollets*): Lower unshelled eggs into a saucepan of boiling water to cover; cook for 5 minutes from when they return to boil; immediately turn off the heat and drain off the hot water; replace the hot water with cold water; tap the eggs all over and shell. They'll stay warm for several minutes (long enough to get the rest of this recipe ready), but if sometime you want to keep Five-Minute eggs warm longer, put them in warm water. The ham can be warmed in the oven along with the toast or in a skillet.

Last and most challenging is the Hollandaise Sauce. Classic hollandaise has a reputation for being tricky which has spawned all sorts of *Easy Hollandaise* recipes which range from gently warmed mayonnaise with lemon juice (1 cup to 2 tablespoons) on down to elaborate concoctions and packaged mixes and bottled sauces. True, almost all of us that make hollandaise today make Blender Hollandaise and, by all means, if you have a blender do that foolproof version. But, don't pass up real Eggs Benedict just because you don't have a blender on board. We've tried this traditional version under trying circumstances and even when it "failed" it worked.

*Sometimes Canadian bacon is used instead of ham (cook in skillet). We like to use finely shaved ham sort of piled on as a nest for the Five-Minute Eggs.

Hollandaise Sauce

2 egg yolks
2 tablespoons lemon juice
½ cup (1 stick) butter,
   cut in pieces

Over *low* heat in a small saucepan, combine eggs, lemon juice, and about ⅓ of the butter. Don't be in any hurry. Let the butter melt slowly as you stir from time to time (and do the other things to be done). When it's melted, add the rest of the butter a little at a time and continue cooking and stirring until the sauce is smooth and slightly thickened. That's it.

If the sauce should happen to separate, remove from heat and whisk until smooth again. If that doesn't do it, try adding a little cold water and whisk again.

Blender Hollandaise

4 egg yolks
2 tablespoons lemon juice
½ cup (1 stick) butter

Heat butter until bubbling (but not browned). In blender, mix egg yolks and lemon juice on high. Then with blender going, slowly pour in bubbling hot butter.

SOUPS, SALADS, AND SANDWICHES

Bay Scallop Bisque

This sumptuous delicate bisque is the kind of dish that makes a restaurant's or a cook's reputation. Serve it to start your most elegant dinner or as a luncheon feature with a cool, crisp salad.

1 pound scallops, cleaned and
   picked over
4 tablespoons (½ stick) butter
½ teaspoon tarragon *or* dill weed
   or mixed herbs
2 cups (1 pint) white wine *or*
   clam juice
2 cups (1 pint) light cream

Cook scallops gently in butter in a skillet over medium heat until opaque (about 4 minutes). Stir in tarragon and cook for a moment more. Stir in wine and cream, turn up heat, and warm just until it comes to a simmer.

New England Clam Chowder

Perhaps the most traditional of all American soups is clam chowder, popular from coast to coast. You'll have no trouble finding a good clam chowder already made. There are several widely available canned brands that are tried-and-true favorites (*Snow's* from New England, *Jake's* from the Pacific Coast) plus restaurant take-home canned chowders, frozen chowders, and readymade hot chowders sold in super-market delis. And for people who are digging clams, add to those the chowder mixes and starters available along the coast.

Practically no one we have met in an RV, including those who were at the seashore especially for clam digging, makes chowder from scratch. Most start with a favorite canned chowder (or potato soup) and add chopped fresh clams. However, if you'd like to try homemade clam chowder, this is a classic recipe.

1 quart clams in their shells *or*
   2 cups (1 pint) shucked clams
2 slices bacon, cut in small pieces
2 potatoes, peeled and diced
**1 tablespoon instant minced
   onion**
2 cups (1 pint) light cream
Salt and pepper
Paprika (optional)

If you are using clams in their shells, you can open them by steaming briefly; then clean and chop unless they are tiny. (Chop very fine if they are one of the less tender varieties—see *Clams in Living on the Land*.) If you are using shucked clams, chop unless they are tiny. Save the liquid in either case.*

In a small saucepan, boil potatoes and onions in about 1 cup of water, covered, until tender (about 15 minutes). In a 2-quart sauce-pan, fry bacon pieces until crisp. Add a cup of liquid made from the reserved clam juice and the potato water. Then stir in the drained potatoes and onions. Simmer, covered, for 5 minutes. Stir in light cream and heat just until simmering. Stir in clams and heat for about 4 or 5 minutes more. Season to taste with salt and pepper. Sprinkle with paprika and serve.

*Note: If the clam juice is sandy, it should be strained. If you don't have cheesecloth, try a tea strainer, coffee filter, cloth handkerchief, or a sterile gauze pad.

Variation: To make a *Manhattan Clam Chowder*, substitute tomato juice for the light cream. (This variation is considered such heresy in most parts of New England, that the Maine legislature once attempted to outlaw the mixing of clams and tomatoes.)

Cape Cod Chowder

Fish chowders are as traditional as clam chowders, and this simple version is the best of both.

1 pound cod or haddock fillets
1 15-ounce can condensed New England clam chowder
1 cup milk
1 cup light cream
Sherry or marsala (optional)

Rinse fish with cold water; pat dry with paper towels. Cut fillets into ½-inch cubes. In a 2-quart saucepan, heat the fish cubes and milk over medium heat to a low simmer; cook fish gently until fish is opaque and flakes easily (about 5 minutes). Stir in condensed clam chowder and light cream and heat until just beginning to simmer. Season chowder to taste—some people like more salt and pepper, a pinch of thyme or chives, and/or a pat of butter. We like to add a couple tablespoons of marsala.

Note: If you like a thicker chowder, stir in instant mashed potato flakes to thicken to taste.

Waldorf Salad

Simplicity is the hallmark of this high-born American classic created by Oscar of the Waldorf, maitre d' of New York's celebrated Waldorf Astoria—proof that you can have the best with ease.

3 red apples, diced (about 2 cups)
1 cup thinly sliced celery (about 2 stalks)
½ cup mayonnaise or salad dressing
½ cup walnuts, coarsely chopped or broken
Several washed lettuce leaves (optional)

If you are preparing the salad ahead of time, toss the apple cubes with 1 tablespoon of lemon juice (to prevent discoloration) before mixing the apple cubes with the other ingredients. Combine apple cubes and celery slices with mayonnaise and walnuts. Spoon salad into lettuce cups to serve.

Variation: Waldorf salads in gelatin are almost as popular as the original. To make a Waldorf Jewel Salad: Prepare a 3-ounce package of strawberry gelatin as directed on package and allow to chill until thickened. Add about ½ of the diced apple (1 apple), sliced celery (1 stalk celery), and broken walnuts called for in the above recipe. Chill until set.

Catskill Salad

1 16-ounce carton cottage cheese with chives
8 radishes, trimmed
4 small scallions (green onions) including part of the tops, trimmed and sliced
1 tomato, diced
1 cucumber, peeled and diced
Sour cream

Make 4 radish roses (see index) and slice remaining 4 radishes. Mix sliced radishes and scallions and diced cucumbers and tomatoes. On each plate, mound about ½ cup of cheese and top with ¼ of the mixed vegetables. Top with a dollop of sour cream and a radish rose. Serve with buttered rye bread.

All-American Chef Salad

It wasn't all that long ago that a chef salad was a bowl of iceberg lettuce with maybe a sliced tomato or two and strips of cheese, ham, and chicken or turkey. Chefs have become more imaginative, eaters more cosmopolitan, and chef salads more of an adventure. You can still start with a bowl of iceberg lettuce, but then it's no holds barred. Even a few creative additions will take your salad out of the ordinary.

4 cups salad greens (iceberg, leaf, romaine, butter-head lettuce; spinach; watercress; rugala)

4 cups mixed fresh garden vegetables (broccoli and cauliflower florets; bean, alfalfa, and wheat sprouts; tiny whole vegetables; petit peas and snow peas; sliced avocado, carrots, celery, cucumber, jicama, kohlrabi, mushrooms, scallions, sweet onion rings, green pepper, radishes, tomatoes, zucchini)

½ to 1 pound cheese and fully cooked meat (Cheddar, mozzarella, provolone, Swiss, Monterery Jack, Muenster, American cheese; ham, turkey, chicken, roast beef, leftover steak or pork loin, lunchmeats, pepperoni)

1 8-ounce bottle of your favorite salad dressing

Garnishes: Sliced hard-boiled eggs; shelled sunflower seeds, piñon nuts, pistachios, almonds, pecans; grated Parmesan or Cheddar cheese; toasted soybeans; sesame seeds; black or green olives; drained garbanzo beans; drained quartered marinated artichoke hearts (use the marinade as part of the salad dressing); pickled peppers or pepper rings; and/or croutons.

Have all salad greens washed, dried, crisp, and torn into bite-size pieces. Toss with fresh vegetables in your largest bowl or arrange in 4 serving bowls or plates. Cut all cheeses and meats into thin strips or thin slices. Scatter strips over top of the salad. Pour dressing over salad or salads (or pass dressing at the table). Top with choice of garnishes.

All-American Heroes

In parts of New England they're called submarines; in Philadelphia, hoagies; in New Jersey, grinders; and elsewhere, poor boys. Whatever you call these giant savory sandwiches, they are among America's favorites. Whether you build your hero out of one long loaf of bread split in half lengthwise or on individual Italian sandwich loaves, try to get the best bread available—crusty Italian or French bread, possibly sprinkled with sesame seeds, is traditional. Our hero is modeled on the winners of the totally unofficial First Annual New York Hero Sandwich Competition of *New York Magazine* which rated the city's best restaurant heroes.

1 loaf Italian bread *or*
  4 sandwich loaves, split
  lengthwise
1 pound sliced meats—salami,
  prosciutto, ham, mortadella,
  bologna
4 ounces sliced provolone cheese
8 to 10 ounces Italian marinated
  mixed vegetable salad*
  (cauliflower, onions, peppers,
  etc.) *or* **marinated red pepper**
  salad *or* **marinated pickled**
  mushrooms, drained

Layer ingredients in any order you wish between the bread halves; cut into 4 sandwiches and serve. For a hot hero, wrap the sandwich in foil and warm in a 250° oven for about 10 minutes.

Variations: Hero sandwiches like their human counterparts are highly individual. The most usual variation is to substitute lettuce and sliced tomatoes for the marinated salads. Others add sliced onions, sliced hot peppers, a sprinkle of oregano or chopped parsley, capocollo, anchovies, etc.

*Marinated salads can be found in jars in the Italian specialties section of the market and in some deli sections.

Maine Lobster Roll

At one time the world was young and lobsters were plentiful and inexpensive. When lobsters were used in prodigious amounts for stews, salads, croquettes, and endless other casual and complex everyday recipes, a lobster roll was as ordinary as a tunafish sandwich. But today it seems almost sacriligious to pile lobster meat into a hamburger roll. At the very least, we think you ought to find quality French or "home-made" bakery white rolls for this famous traditional sandwich.

2 cups cooked chilled Maine
  lobster meat
2 tablespoons mayonnaise
¼ cup finely diced celery
4 white rolls
Butter

Mix lobster meat with mayonnaise and celery and refrigerate until ready to use. Split and toast rolls spread with butter in a 425° oven until lightly browned. (You don't have to completely preheat the oven, just let it get warm for a while.) Fill rolls with lobster and serve.

Variations: You can surround the lobster rolls, as restaurants do, with a variety of garnishes—tomato, cut in slices or wedges; cucumber sticks; black olives; radish roses; hard-boiled egg, cut in slices or wedges—to make this more of an event. To make a classic *Maine Lobster Salad*: Double the filling ingredients and serve in scoops on crisp lettuce leaves or in an avocado half or in a tomato, cut into wedges almost to the bottom. For a gourmet touch, sprinkle with capers and surround with hard-boiled egg wedges.

MAIN EVENTS

Hundreds, perhaps thousands, of international restaurants that add spice to our country's metropolises have an almost irresistible allure. Take in the big city sights, a concert, or an exhibit, but save your nerves and your money and eat in on one of these dining-out classics.

Coquilles St. Jacques

Coquilles St. Jacques is the French name for scallops, not the manner in which they are prepared, but when the name appears on American menus it brings to many minds the mouth-watering French recipe for scallops and mushrooms baked in a rich cheese sauce. Coquilles St. Jacques prepared in the French manner are usually baked in individual baking dishes or scallop shells. Use them if, by luck, you have them. Otherwise, use a pie pan.

1 pound bay scallops
½ pound fresh mushrooms,
 cleaned and sliced
¼ cup (½ stick) butter
6 ounces Swiss cheese,
 shredded or grated
 (about 1½ cups)
1 cup mayonnaise
¾ cup white wine
Pepper
Tarragon, dill weed, or mixed
 herbs (optional)
1 slice white bread, grated (½
 cup crumbs)

Preheat oven to 450°. (If using large sea scallops, cut the scallops into quarters. In a large bowl, combine the shredded cheese and mayonnaise. In a skillet, cook the sliced mushrooms in the butter until they are soft. Add the mushrooms to the cheese mixture in the bowl. In the skillet, heat the wine and scallops to simmering over medium heat and cook just until opaque (about 2 minutes). Spoon out about ½ cup of the wine and discard or use for another purpose. Add the remaining wine and scallops to the bowl and combine gently. Pepper to taste and sprinkle with herbs to taste. Spread scallop-mushroom-cheese mixture in a pie or individual baking shells. Sprinkle with bread crumbs. Bake the scallops until the crumbs are browned and the dish is hot and bubbly (about 5 to 10 minutes). Serve at once. (This is very rich—make the rest of the meal simple.)

Sole Veronique

A perennial favorite at French restaurants is Sole Veronique, featuring one of the East's most popular fish.

2 pounds sole or flounder fillets (thawed if frozen)
1 cup (¼ pound) white or green seedless grapes
1 cup dry white wine
2 tablespoons lemon juice
2 teaspoons salt
¼ teaspoon mixed herbs
¼ cup (½ stick) butter
2 tablespoons flour

Arrange sole fillets in a skillet in layers and scatter grapes over the top. Combine wine, lemon juice, salt, and herbs. Pour over sole and grapes and heat to simmering. Cook gently, covered, for about 5 minutes or until fish flakes easily when tested with a fork. As soon as the sole is cooked, turn off heat. Meanwhile, in a separate small saucepan, melt butter and blend in flour. When the sole is cooked, spoon and/or pour the poaching wine from the skillet a little at a time into the sauce, until all the liquid from the skillet has been drained off (put the cover back on the skillet to keep the sole warm). Continue stirring the sauce and cooking until thick and smooth; the sauce should be light. Pour sauce over sole and grapes and serve.

Beef Stroganoff

This is one of those great recipes that is easiest when done authentically and far better than the pale imitations full of secret ingredients.

1½ to 2 pounds fillet of beef
1 cup (2 sticks) butter
½ to 1 pound fresh mushrooms, cleaned and sliced
Salt and pepper, preferably freshly ground
2 cups (1 pint) sour cream
Shoestring potatoes or cooked rice or cooked noodles

Trim beef of all fat; slice into thin slices (¼ inch); and slice again into thin strips (¼ inch). In a skillet melt 1 stick of butter over medium-high heat and brown the beef strips in several batches. (As each batch is lightly browned, transfer to a bowl.) When all the meat is browned, add more butter to the skillet and cook all the mushrooms until they are soft. Stir the beef back into the skillet and warm for a few moments. Salt and pepper generously to taste. Stir in the sour cream a little at a time, reduce the heat to low, cover the skillet, and simmer for 2 or 3 minutes. Serve with shoestring potatoes scattered on top or over hot rice or noodles.

Variation: If stroganoff doesn't seem like stroganoff to you without onions: finely slice 1 large onion and separate into rings; while you are cooking the stroganoff, cook the onions with 1 tablespoon of butter in a small covered saucepan over low heat, stirring from time to time, until they are soft; add the onions to the skillet when you combine the beef strips and the mushrooms.

Note: When you get to the part where everything gets combined in the skillet, you may find your skillet isn't large enough. If so, juggle the meat and mushrooms between the bowl and the skillet until you have a fair amount of both in the skillet with the drippings; stir in the sour cream and cook as above; then combine with the rest of the ingredients.

Sukiyaki

Sukiyaki, one of the most popular Japanese dishes in Japan and America, is traditionally cooked in one pan right at the table, which makes it a natural for the RV's intimate eating and cooking area. Since no two Sukiyaki recipes seem to call for exactly the same ingredients, you have a lot of leeway in which vegetables to use. The ones suggested here may seem like a small mountain as you prepare them but won't be that much after they are cooked. This is a particularly nice meal to share with friends—kick off your shoes, put some Japanese beer in to chill, and slide open the windows of your tearoom.

1 pound boneless lean beef, preferably tenderloin or sirloin

1 8-ounce can sliced bamboo shoots, drained

½ pound fresh mushrooms, cleaned and sliced

1 medium-sized sweet onion (Spanish onion, Bermuda ónion), peeled and sliced

8 scallions (green onions) with part of the tops, trimmed and cut into 1-inch pieces

½ pound fresh spinach leaves, Chinese cabbage, and/or watercress, washed, trimmed, and sliced if large

Fresh tofu (cakes of soybean curd often sold in the specialty section of the produce department or with the cheese), drained and cut into 1-inch cubes (optional)

½ to 1 cup bottled teriyaki sauce

½ to 1 cup sake (rice wine) or white wine

Put the meat in the freezer for about 30 minutes to make it easier to slice. Cut the meat against the grain into ⅛-inch slices. Arrange the meat and vegetables in bands on a large platter or your cutting board. Call everyone to dinner.

Heat your skillet for several minutes. Put at least a half a dozen slices of meat in the skillet and pour ¼ cup of teriyaki sauce over them; cook for 1 minute and push to the side of the pan, rare side down. Add about ⅓ of each of the vegetables and tofu to the skillet and sprinkle them with ¼ cup of wine; cook for about 4 to 5 minutes. Serve in individual serving plates or bowls. Repeat process in two or more batches.

To round out your Japanese tearoom meal, add a pot of hot rice and finish up with sherbet and green tea.

Variations: Some other vegetables used in Sukiyaki are green pepper, kohlrabi, carrots, leeks, and endive—all thinly sliced; drained sliced water chestnuts; diagonally sliced celery pieces; and florets of cauliflower and broccoli. Often each diner is given a bowl with a whole beaten egg or egg yolk for dipping.

Fettucine Alfredo

The pride-and-joy specialty of fine Italian restaurants is the internationally popular Fettucine Alfredo prepared with a flourish at the guest's table. It takes to roadside cooking so naturally, you'd suspect it had been invented for the RV instead of for a famous Roman restaurant. You can use packaged dried fettucine, but for the full treatment get frozen fettucine. Judging from the unlikely places we have found frozen noodles from coast to coast, you have a pretty good chance of buying them almost anywhere. An 11-ounce package will serve four if you are also having some other substantial course—an antipasto tray or a large salad. If Fettucine Alfredo is really the main event, allow a pound of noodles for four and double the rest of the ingredients.

1 11-ounce package frozen fettucine
¼ cup sour cream or whipping cream
¼ cup (½ stick) butter, softened
½ cup grated Parmesan cheese
Pepper, preferably freshly ground
Extra Parmesan cheese

Cook the noodles according to package instructions in salted water until they are *al dente* (firm but cooked). Drain off all the water. Toss the fettucine with cream, butter, and cheese until every noodle is coated. (Don't forget the flourish.) Generously grind black pepper over the fettucine and serve. Pass additional Parmesan cheese in a small bowl.

Variations: For extravagant *Fettucine Newport*, add the cooked meat of 1 lobster warmed in a little butter.

For *Fetucine alla Papalina* add 2 cups of thinly sliced cooked ham strips.

Or make *Pasta al Burro* with any hard pasta using the same recipe; it makes an easy meal-in-minutes anywhere. If you don't have cream on hand, just use a little more butter.

For *Spaghetti Carbonara*, substitute spaghetti for the fettucine and add ¼ pound of bacon, cooked crisp, drained and crumbled. Many people like to also add 1 beaten egg to the hot spaghetti.

Or you can add freshly cooked vegetables for *Pasta Primavera*.

Or toss in toasted chopped hazelnuts, or fresh chopped basil and piñon nuts, or . . .

Fourth of July Salmon

Poaching salmon is a classic and cool way to prepare New England's traditional Independence Day dish. Whole salmon and large pieces generally require a fish poacher—a piece of equipment not many RVers travel with, at least not any we have met. But serving-size pieces can easily be done in a covered skillet.

4 salmon steaks, about 1-inch thick
1 46-ounce can mixed vegetable juice

Rinse salmon steaks and pat dry with paper towels. Arrange salmon steaks in a skillet (you may have to do this in two batches depending on the size of your steaks and skillet). Pour juice over steaks so they are just covered and bring to a simmer over medium heat. When it begins to simmer, lower the heat, and cover. Simmer the salmon gently until it flakes easily (about 10 minutes). Lift the steaks out carefully with a spatula and let them drain on paper towels. Serve warm or cold (chill for a few hours) with *Caper Mayonnaise* or sour cream. To traditionally round out this Fourth of July fest, add new peas, new potatoes, and hard-boiled eggs.

Grossinger's Seafood Newburg

The kosher cuisine of a number of America's fine resort hotels has introduced the delights of Jewish cooking to Americans of diverse ethnic backgrounds. Many of the dishes associated with Jewish-American cookery have far-flung roots—gefilte fish from Germany, pirogen from Poland, borscht from Russia. But this dish, credited to Jennie Grossinger, is a delicious kosher kin of an American classic, Lobster Newburg.

1½ cups cubed cooked salmon (about ¾ pound)
1½ cups cubed cooked halibut (about ¾ pound)
4 tablespoons butter
3 tablespoons instant flour (or substitute all-purpose flour)
2 cups light cream
¼ cup sherry
2 egg yolks, beaten with a fork
Paprika
Salt

In a 2-quart saucepan, combine butter, flour, and cream. Heat over medium heat, stirring constantly, until the sauce is smooth and thick and is just beginnning to simmer. Stir in sherry and eggs. Season to taste with paprika (about ⅛ teaspoon) and salt (up to 1 teaspoon). Stir in salmon and halibut cubes and heat over very low heat just until fish is warm. Serve on toast.

Note: A simple way of cooking the salmon and halibut is to poach it in white wine (about a cup) until the fish is opaque and flakes easily (about 5 to 10 minutes). If you cook the cubed fish while you are making the sauce, they will both be ready at about the same time. (Drain the fish cubes before adding them to the sauce.)

Maine Boiled Lobster

In one of the most charming verdicts in American history, an early nineteenth-century arbiter ruled against the party in a wager who could not come up with an example (out of season) of the 30-pound lobsters that he claimed inhabited American waters, though he had produced several eye-witness accounts. "Depositions are not lobsters," said the arbiter, and the luckless admiral paid up.

Today's lobsters may be runts by comparison, but they still are considered by many to be the king of the shellfish. Whole boiled American lobster with melted butter is one of the simplest and most popular shellfish dinners in the country.

Many places that sell live lobsters will cook them for you, and they need only to be rewarmed (or serve cool with mayonnaise). But if you've decided to prepare this American classic yourself, you need a fairly large pan and a fair amount of courage—you may find it unnerving to have dinner underfoot in the close confines of an RV.*

4 1- to 2-pound live lobsters
Melted butter

If you have a very large pan (7 or 8 quarts) you can do the lobsters all at once: Bring 4 quarts of salted water (add about 3 tablespoons of salt) to boiling. Plunge the lobsters, head first, into the rapidly boiling water and boil immersed, covered, until lobster meat is opaque and firm (from when the water resumes boiling, allow 12 to 15 minutes for 1-pound lobsters; 15 to 20 minutes for 1½- to 2-pound lobsters). In the likelihood that you don't have an extremely large pan, you may have to do the lobsters 1 or 2 at a time—just so they are submerged. Allow 1 tablespoon of salt for each quart of water. Continue as above. Drain the cooked lobsters immediately and serve with melted butter or a sauce of capers and butter.

Everything in an American lobster is edible except the shell structure, the small crop or craw in the head of the lobster, and the dark vein runnning down the back of the body meat into the tail. To eat a cooked whole lobster, you need a nutcracker, a pair of pliers, or a hammer. Twist off the claws, crack them with whichever tool you have, and pick out the delicate meat. Twist off the tail, break off the flippers, and push the choice succulent tail meat out the large end. On small lobsters, many people stop at this point. Or you can press on: Unhinge the back from the body section, remove the stomach or craw located behind the eyes and the dark vein and discard. All the rest is eatable. Pick out whatever else you like—bits of meat; the green tomalley or liver, which many people consider very choice; and/or the red or dark coral found in female lobsters and also considered good eating. There are also delicate morsels in each of the small legs if you can get them out.

Note: Live spiny lobsters can be cooked the same way, but generally only the tail portion is eaten.

*Don't keep your live lobsters in water—it will kill them. Keep them in a cool place in a brown paper bag. They'll keep for up to 24 hours.

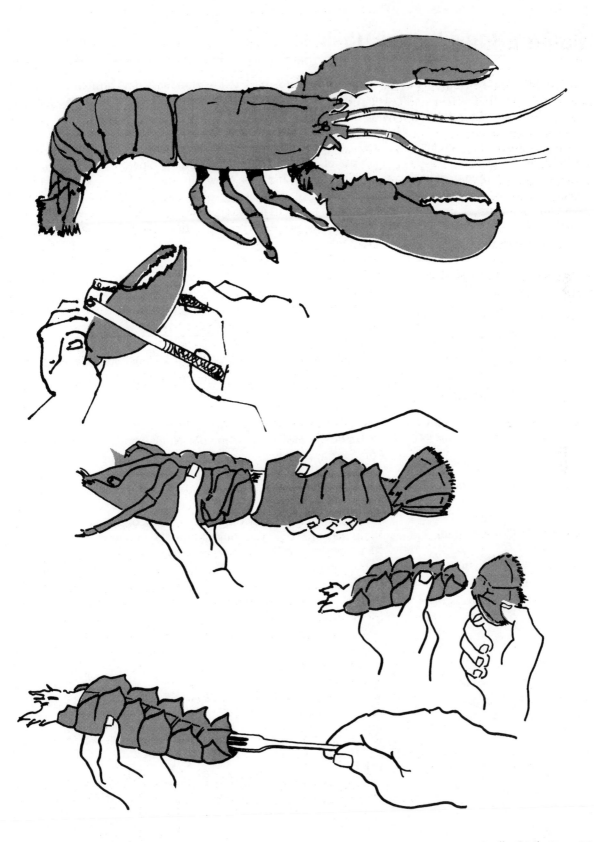

Yankee Red-Flannel Hash

There are many versions of this old favorite that dates back to Revolutionary days and about as many versions of how it originated. Early fans of red-flannel hash were Ethan Allen and his brave men from the Green Mountains, where according to Vermont lore this hearty dish began.

1 1-pound can julienne beets, drained
2 1-pound cans corned beef hash
2 tablespoons instant minced onion
Tabasco sauce or other hot pepper sauce (optional)

Mix well-drained beets with corned beef hash and onion. Add a couple of drops of hot sauce to taste. Spread hash over bottom of skillet, cover, and cook slowly until crusty-brown on both sides—check after 10 minutes or so on one side to see if it is crusty enough to turn (cut into large wedges with your turner). Serve with poached eggs or eggs boiled in their shells for 5 minutes for an old Yankee touch.

Schnitz-Un-Gnepp

Roughly translated, this Pennsylvania Dutch dish is cut apples and dumplings. Although old-time recipes using uncooked ham and dried apples often take more than 3 hours to prepare, this tasty version will be on the table in minutes.

2 apples, washed, cored, and thinly sliced (don't bother to peel the apples)
1 1-pound fully cooked smoked ham slice (about ½-inch thick)
1½ cups apple juice
1 cup buttermilk baking mix
½ cup milk
2 tablespoons brown sugar

In a skillet brown ham lightly over high heat (about 2 minutes on each side). Remove ham. Wipe out skillet if it has any burned bits. Combine apple slices and apple juice in skillet and cook over medium heat, covered, for 5 minutes. Meanwhile, make dumpling dough from baking mix and milk and cut ham into bite-size squares. Stir ham and brown sugar into cooked apples. Drop dumpling dough by heaping spoonfuls on top. Cover and cook until dumplings are cooked through (about 10 minutes).

ASIDES

Oyster House Oysters

Countless American recipes begin with a plate or a peck of freshly shucked oysters or clams—including an all-time national favorite, fresh raw oysters on the half shell. In a New England oyster house, you can still sit down to this simple delicacy at a shucking stone dramatically gouged by centuries of service as deft shuckers opened mountains of the storied oysters. But today your RV is the oyster house, and you are the one confronting a pile of crusty, gray, knobby, mostly randomly-shaped, uncooperative oysters, holed up in their shells. Take heart. With a little muscle, a dollop of ingenuity, and a generous portion of persistence you can triumphantly end up with a tray of fresh oysters on the half shell.

24 very cold oysters in their shells
Fresh lemon wedges
Seafood cocktail sauce

To begin, throw out any which are open and won't close when tapped, they are no longer living and worthy. Scrub the oysters vigorously under cold running water. To open the oysters you will need an oyster knife (which you probably don't have) or a screwdriver and a sharp knife. Hold the oyster down on a nonslip surface (stone or rough cloth) with the flattest shell up, the deeper, cupped shell down. Work the tip of the screwdriver in between the shell halves at the oyster's hinge and twist to open the shells. Slide the sharp knife in and cut along the top, flatter, shell. Throw away the top shell. Slip the blade under the oyster and cut it free from the lower shell. Look for a pearl (and, incidentally, any broken shell pieces). Serve immediately with lemon wedges and a cup of seafood cocktail sauce.

Note: Shucked oysters called for in other recipes are done exactly the same way. If you aren't preparing them immediately, pour the oysters and their liquor (liquid in the shell) into a covered refrigerator container and keep refrigerated (try to use within a day).

Atlantic Steamers

Whether you dig your own or buy them at the market, tender clams are a snap to prepare by steaming for either a traditional, luxurious meal-starter or a seashore snack. See Clams in Living on the Land for which clams are good steamers and for cleaning tips.

48 fresh clams, cleaned
1 cup (2 sticks) butter, melted
Fresh lime or lemon wedges
** (optional)**

Put the clams in your largest pot with a cup of water, cover, and boil until the clams open (about 5 to 10 minutes). Discard any clams that don't open. Serve with bowls of broth from the pan and melted butter. To eat, pull each clam out of its shell by its neck, dip it in broth and butter, and then bite it off at the base of the neck.

Note: Mussels can be prepared the same way.

Clams on the Half Shell

Another oyster bar and seashore special is an icy platter of small clams, like cherrystones and littlenecks, served raw on the half shell.

24 to 36 very cold small hard-shell clams
Fresh lemon or lime wedges
Seafood cocktail sauce

Clean the clams as described in Living on the Land. To open clams, use a heavy-bladed knife. Slip the knife between the shell halves opposite the hinge and twist the blade to pry apart the halves enough to run the knife along the upper shell to cut the muscle. Discard the top shell. Slip the blade under the clam and cut it loose from the other shell half. Serve immediately with lemon or lime wedges and seafood cocktail sauce.

Note: Shucked clams called for in other recipes are done exactly the same way. Refrigerate, tightly covered, and use as quickly as possible.

Beachcomber's Mussels

All those pretty blue-black shells on the seashore that you may be passing by might be the makings of a gourmet treat if the season is right. Though most Americans walk right over the mussels, many Europeans consider them a delicacy, especially when prepared as *Moules Mariniere*, sailor's mussels. See *Mussels* in Living on the Land for information and tips on cleaning. (Caution: Mussels are subject to "red tide" contamination; check before collecting.)

36 mussels, cleaned
1 cup white wine
¼ cup chopped shallots or onions (or substitute 1 tablespoon instant minced onion)
¼ cup (½ stick) butter
2 tablespoons dried parsley or chervil
Pepper
Thyme (optional)

Rinse the mussels again just before you cook them and pull off their beards. Combine the wine, shallots, butter, parsley, a generous sprinkling of pepper, and a pinch of thyme in your largest pan and bring to a boil. Put in the mussels, cover, and simmer gently until mussels open (about 5 minutes). Discard any that don't open. Serve the mussels in bowls with the broth accompanied by more melted butter and French bread.

Variation: Sometimes more butter and parsley are added to the broth after the mussels are cooked.

Oysters Florentine

Usually oysters baked on the half shell are done in pie pans filled with rock salt to hold the shells steady. But since several pie pans won't fit in an RV oven and we don't usually have rock salt around, we find it more convenient to arrange the oysters on a large baking pan—a pizza pan, for example—which has been covered with aluminum foil crumpled into hills and dales to hold the oyster shells level.

24 live oysters, well scrubbed
1 12-ounce package frozen
   spinach souffle, defrosted
1 small shallot, peeled and finely
   chopped (optional)
Grated Parmesan cheese

Preheat the oven to 475°. Open the oysters as described for Oyster House Oysters, leaving each resting on its lower shell (discard the upper shells). Mix chopped shallot into spinach souffle. Arrange oysters on crumpled foil on a large baking pan. Spread about a tablespoon of the spinach souffle over each oyster. Sprinkle with Parmesan cheese. Bake the oysters until the oysters and spinach are heated through and the top is lightly brown (about 5 minutes).

Stuffed Pennsylvania Mushrooms

Although wild mushrooms are greatly admired by connoisseurs, we suggest you do your mushroom hunting in the market rather than the woods. Wild mushrooms can be deceptive and deadly. On the other hand, plump fresh market mushrooms, most of which come from Pennyslvania, are a special treat, too. When choosing market mushrooms look for fresh unblemished mushrooms with the caps closed. Ideally, to clean the mushrooms you wipe them with a dampened paper towel because mushrooms soak up water like sponges. If you do rinse them, do it quickly.

16 large mushrooms, cleaned
½ cup seasoned bread crumbs
   (use crushed herb-seasoned
   stuffing or croutons or grated
   bread with your choice of
   seasonings)
2 tablespoons water or wine
   (optional)
Salt and pepper
Butter

Preheat the oven to 350°. Remove the stems from the mushrooms, trim the stems, and chop them fine. Mix chopped stems and bread crumbs (if you are using dry crumbs, add a little water or wine). Salt and pepper to taste. Fill caps with mixture and dot each with butter. Bake on a foil-lined baking sheet until mushrooms are soft and tops are lightly browned (about 20 minutes).

Fresh Mushrooms Boursin

16 large mushrooms, cleaned
1 4-ounce package Boursin or
   other herb-and-garlic
   triple-cream cheese

Remove the mushrooms stems. Fill the caps with cheese and serve.

Variations: Various cheese spreads are good in mushrooms—cream cheese and chives, cheddar and bacon, olive and pimento cheese spread.

Shallot-Stuffed Mushrooms

16 large mushrooms, cleaned
2 shallots, peeled and chopped
(about ½ cup)
2 tablespoons fresh parsley,
chopped, or 2 teaspoons dried
parsley or chervil
3 tablespoons butter
Salt and pepper

Preheat the oven to 350°. Remove the stems from the mushrooms trim the stems, and chop them fine. In a skillet melt the butter; add the chopped stems, shallots, and parsley; and cook a few minutes, stirring frequently. Salt and pepper to taste. Fill caps with mixture and bake on a foil-lined baking sheet until mushrooms are soft (about 20 minutes).

Stuffed Mushrooms Florentine

16 large mushrooms, cleaned
1 12-ounce package frozen
spinach souffle, partially
defrosted
Grated Parmesan cheese
(optional)

Preheat oven to 400°. Remove the mushroom stems and discard or save for another dish. Spoon the spinach souffle into the mushroom caps. Sprinkle with Parmesan cheese. Bake on a foil-lined baking sheet until mushrooms are soft and filling is cooked (about 15 to 20 minutes).

Tip: The leftover souffle can be saved in the refrigerator for a day or two. Add it to breakfast scrambled eggs or make *Tomatoes Florentine*: Fill slightly hollowed tomato halves with spinach souffle, sprinkle with Parmesan cheese, and bake as above—it may take longer than the mushrooms.

Pilgrim's Pride

The brilliant little berries that grow along our country's northeast shore were adding sparkle to meals long before that first Thanksgiving and have been ever since. Cranberries are often considered a fitting symbol for the cuisine of New England and, certainly, no cook's tour of the country would be complete without a few cranberry recipes. This one, delicious any time, doesn't even need to be accompanied by a slice of turkey. This sweet fruit salad easily doubles as dessert, preserves, or sauce.

1 1-pound can whole cranberry
sauce
1 10-ounce package frozen
sliced strawberries, defrosted
1 3-ounce package raspberry or
strawberry gelatin
½ cup walnuts, broken

Add 1 cup boiling water to gelatin in a refrigerator container, stirring until dissolved. Add the strawberries and cranberry sauce, continuing to stir until sauce is well mixed with gelatin. Stir in nuts. Refrigerate until set.

Note: This makes less than a quart of salad, but it is easier to make in a 6-cup container because of the stirring required to break up the cranberry sauce.

Vermont Maple Baked Squash

It's almost impossible to envision New England in its gorgeous fall colors without also envisioning its equally colorful stands of squashes. If you'd like to enjoy baked winter squash as generations of New Englanders have before you, try this old recipe.

2 to 2½ pounds butternut or
   acorn squash (or other winter
   squash like Hubbard
   or buttercup)
¼ cup pure maple syrup
¼ cup (½ stick) butter
Salt and pepper
Nutmeg (optional)

Preheat oven to 350°. Slice squash in 1-inch thick slices (circles or wedges). Remove seeds. Arrange the squash slices in a large foil-lined baking pan. Bake covered with foil until squash is almost tender, about an hour. Meanwhile, heat syrup, butter, a generous dash of salt, and a sprinkling of pepper in a small saucepan until bubbly; cook for a minute or two, stirring frequently. Spoon sauce over squash. Continue baking, uncovered, until squash is tender, basting from time to time with sauce. Sprinkle grated nutmeg over squash before serving.

Delaware Succotash

The cooks of the Northeast were mixing up beans and corn with a bit of this or that long before the Pilgrims arrived and adopted the recipe. There are many variations of this still popular combination—summer succotashes, winter succotashes, succotashes that are more like hearty stews, and succotashes that are plain and simple.

2 thin slices lean bacon, cut in
   squares
1 10-ounce package frozen
   succotash (lima beans and
   corn)
1 small tomato, cubed
Salt and pepper
Nutmeg (optional)

In a saucepan, cook bacon until done but not crisp. Add frozen succotash, cubed tomato, and a generous sprinkling of salt and pepper. Cook according to package instructions. Sprinkle lightly with nutmeg and serve with butter.

DESSERTS

Country Inn Coeur à la Crème

Cheesecakes have long been popular in this cosmopolitan region and, happily, several of the old favorites are available in the market (bless you, Sara Lee). One that is currently in vogue is the fresh, simple, French classic, Coeur à la Crème, which has long been a favorite of ours—we made it for our wedding breakfast among other happy occasions. Coeur à la Crème is equally delightful for a romantic breakfast for two served with fresh strawberries and croissants or as a company-special dessert surrounded with a garland of berries, mandarin orange sections, green grapes, and almonds.

1 cup (8 ounces) sour cream
4 ounces whipped cream cheese
1 cup ricotta cheese, drained of
   any excess fluid
Scant ½ cup sugar
¼ teaspoon vanilla
Cheesecloth
Fresh berries

Line a colander or a disposable foil cake pan punched with holes at 1-inch intervals with a double layer of cheesecloth that has been dipped in cold water and wrung out. If you are using a perforated cake pan as a mold, be sure that the cheesecloth extends over the sides. Stir the sugar and the vanilla into the sour cream in a medium-size bowl (at least 6-cup). Fold in the ricotta and whip until fairly smooth. Gently fold in the whipped cream cheese until well blended. Spoon the mixture into the cheesecloth-lined mold or colander and fold the cheesecloth over the top. Set the mold on a plate or shallow bowl and refrigerate. Let the Coeur à la Crème drain for at least several hours.

To unmold, fold back the cheesecloth and invert on a plate. If you want to be traditional, you can shape the dessert at this point into a heart with your hands. Peel off the cheesecloth. Surround the Coeur à la Crème with fresh strawberries or raspberries and serve.

Note: If you like a smoother Coeur à la Crème and have an electric mixer, beat the ricotta until smooth before folding with the other ingredients.

Massachusetts Cranberry Mousse

As New Englanders will assure you, cranberries are far too good to reserve for an occasional holiday turkey dinner side dish; they have hundreds of traditional cranberry recipes dating back to colonial times. This is a new one, but it is so refreshing and so simple, we expect it will be around a long time, too.

1 1-pound can cranberry sauce or
   orange-cranberry sauce
1 8-ounce or 9-ounce tub
   whipped topping, thawed
2 to 3 tablespoons orange or
   cranberry liqueur or orange
   brandy (optional)

Stir liqueur into cranberry sauce (dip a little of the sauce out of the can so you can do this without making a mess). Gently combine the sauce and whipped topping in a refrigerator container. Freeze for at least an hour.

Chocolatetown Cloud

This wonderfully rich, light-as-air chocolate cream started out as an on-the-road substitute for our favorite company-special mousse which requires a food processor. But this shortcut turned out to be a chocolate lover's dream, good enough to serve to a visiting head of state.

1 10-ounce tub whipped cream topping, thawed
1 16-ounce can (about 1 ¾ cups) chocolate-flavor Hershey's Syrup
1 jigger (about 3 tablespoons) Amaretto liqueur (or substitute other liqueur of your choice or rum)

In a 6-cup refrigerator container, combine whipped cream topping, chocolate syrup, and liqueur, mixing until evenly colored. Cover and freeze until firm (several hours). Spoon into serving dishes to serve. For a fancy finish, top with chocolate curls (run your vegetable peeler over the flat side of a Hershey bar). This recipe makes about a quart—enough for generous second helpings. Or save in the freezer.

Variation: Spoon the desert into a chocolate-cookie crumb crust (see Mississippi Mud Pie) or a graham cracker crust for an effortless French Chocolate Silk Pie.

Maple Snow

Sugaring-off parties, a charming part of Americana (and Canadiana), feature bowls of clean fresh snow topped with pure maple syrup. Today the former is harder to come by than the latter, but you can make your snow by mashing ice cubes by whatever means you usually use to make cracked ice—hammer, blender, etc. And you don't have to wait for tree-tapping time, since maple syrup is available all year. You can make Maple Snow in one of two ways. The first is a fun and simple do-it-yourself treat for children, a sort of maple snow cone.

4 small paper cups filled with snow or crushed ice
½ cup pure maple syrup

Pour 1 or 2 tablespoons of syrup over each cup of snow and eat immediately.

The second method is more of a production—you cook the maple syrup until it spins a thread when dropped in cold water (the syrup would register 232° on a candy thermometer if you had one). When the hot syrup is spooned on bowls of snow, it turns into a sweet taffy candy (recommended only for those with good teeth).

2 to 4 flat bowls or plates of snow
1 cup maple syrup

In a small saucepan, cook syrup over medium-high heat until it comes to a boil. Boil just until it reaches the thread stage (about 1 or 2 minutes). Spoon onto the snow. To clean your pan and spoon, pour boiling water into the pan and let them soak. Complete your sugaring-off party with cake doughnuts and apple cider.

Cobblestones

Like most RVers, we usually get our cookie supply prebaked or at least premixed. But if you or yours feel like baking cookies from scratch someday, these very old cookies from New Jersey are worth the effort. In their eighteenth-century version, people would have used cracked chocolate since chocolate drops were an innovation of the region in the mid-twentieth century. You'll recognize these cookies as forebearers of that all-American favorite, the chocolate chip cooky.

1 cup brown sugar
½ cup butter, (1 stick)
  slightly softened
1 teaspoon vanilla
1½ cups flour
½ teaspoon baking soda
½ cup chocolate chips

Preheat oven to 375°. Mix the sugar and butter until smooth. Stir in egg and vanilla. Stir in flour and soda and beat well. Fold in chocolate chips. Drop batter in heaping tablespoons 3 inches apart onto a greased foil-lined baking pan (a pizza pan will work). Bake for 12 to 15 minutes. This makes about 2 dozen 3-inch cookies (2 batches).

Fresh Plum Kuchen

Make this old-fashioned kuchen on some cool late-summer day when you have a dozen or more Damson, greengage, or Italian prune plums.

1 8-ounce package buttermilk
  baking mix (about 2 cups)
⅓ cup sugar
1 egg
¾ cup milk
12+ plums, halved
¼ cup (½ stick) butter
½ cup brown sugar
¼ cup flour
½ teaspoon cinnamon

Preheat oven to 400°. Mix baking mix, sugar, egg, and milk well. Pour batter into a 9-inch round pan that has been well-greased and floured. Cover the top with halved plums, cut side down. In a small bowl, mix butter, brown sugar, flour, and cinnamon until crumbly. Sprinkle over top. Bake until cake layer is done (about 30 minutes).

CHEERS

New Jersey Stone Fence Punch

Americans have been drinking Stone Fence Punch since the eighteenth century. Several other North-eastern states claim this invigorating libation. It's said that "two cups and a man can leap a stone fence."

1 pint *Laird's** Applejack or other applejack brandy
1 pint apple juice
1 pint club soda

Pour everything over ice cubes in a pitcher and stir. Drink in *small* cupfuls.

Laird's, America's Oldest Brandy Distillers, has been making applejack in New Jersey since 1780.

Fish House Punch

Born in the eighteenth century, this punch gets its fame and name from an exclusive Philadelphia fishing and social club. In early days Philadelphia punches were served in prodigious amounts: one visitor in 1744 reported being greeted by a bowl of punch large enough to have "swimm'd half a dozen young geese." Our recipe makes a considerably smaller, and lighter, punch than the colonial versions.

1 6-ounce can frozen lemonade concentrate
1 pint 100-proof Jamaica rum (or 80-proof light or dark rum)
1 cup cognac or brandy
2 tablespoons peach brandy (optional)

Mix all ingredients and dilute with 2 cups of water. Allow to "ripen" at room temperature for an hour or more. Serve over ice cubes or add a tray of ice cubes to the pitcher.

Tip: An old Philadelphia trick is to make the ice cubes out of tea.

Cape Codder

This Northern cousin of the Scarlett O'Hara is one of those anytime drinks, as appropriate for the First of January as the Fourth of July, before breakfast as before dinner.

2 cups cranberry juice
6 ounces (¾ cup) vodka or rum
1 fresh lime, quartered

For each drink, fill a tall glass with ice cubes and add 1 jigger (1½ ounces) of vodka and ½ cup of cranberry juice. Squeeze in a bit of lime juice and toss in the wedge. Or, mix all ingredients in a pitcher and serve over ice cubes in any glass.

Variations: For a *Bog Fog*, substitute 1 cup of orange juice for 1 cup of the cranberry juice. For a *Cape Cod Cooler*, top off a Cape Codder with a little club soda.

Ivy League Mulled Wine

Hot mugs of mulled wine or glühwein are classic chill-chasers after sports and sporting events. Like many RVers, we usually take advantage of the hot spiced wine mixes that are available, since they make preparing a panful of mulled wine as easy as instant coffee. To dress for company, you can add lemon or orange rings and/or cinnamon sticks. Or you can make this traditional mulled wine from scratch.

1 quart (or 1 25-ounce bottle) hearty red wine
1 orange
1 lemon
1 cup sugar (or less)
1 teaspoon whole cloves
1 long cinnamon stick, broken into 4 pieces

Slice 4 slices from the center of the orange and 4 slices from the center of the lemon. Cut the flesh from the center of the slices to make lemon and orange rind rings. In a large saucepan, bring wine to a very slow simmer. Squeeze juice from remaining parts of the orange and lemon into the wine. Stir in sugar, cloves, and cinnamon sticks; until sugar dissolves. Add lemon and orange rings and heat over low heat (do *not* boil) for about 10 minutes. Serve in mugs with a piece of cinnamon stick in each.

Manhattans To Go

As you'd expect, Manhattans began in Manhattan. The sweet Manhattan was named for the Manhattan Club; the dry Manhattan originated in an Eastside speakeasy. If Manhattans are your cocktail—sweet, dry, or perfect—premix a bottle to suit your preference before you leave home.

1 32-ounce (1 quart or 1 liter) bottle blended whiskey
1 cup vermouth (sweet for sweet Manhattan; dry for dry Manhattan; ½ cup of each for perfect Manhattan)
Bitters
Maraschino cherries (for sweet Manhattan)
1 fresh lemon (for dry or perfect Manhattan)

Pour out 1 cup of whiskey from the bottle and reserve for another use. Replace with 1 cup of vermouth. If you are making dry or perfect Manhattans, peel the lemon in a long continuous spiral and add the lemon peel to the bottle before recapping. You can either chill the whole bottle in your refrigerator or stir each drink with ice cubes at cocktail time and strain into a glass. When serving, add a dash of bitters to each glass. If it's a sweet Manhattan, add a maraschino cherry too.

Boston Tea Party

No trip to New England would be complete without a cup of the brew that set off the most famous "party" in American history. The Cradle of Liberty still imports most of America's favorite teas. Bigelow's *Constant Comment*, an orange-spice tea, is the basis for this old-fashioned tea punch that is simple enough to enjoy anytime you want a real thirst quencher.

3 *Constant Comment* tea bags
1 quart cranberry juice cocktail
1 12-ounce can lemon-lime soda
1 lemon, thinly sliced

Place tea bags in a 2-quart heat-resistant container. Pour 2½ cups of boiling water over tea bags and steep 5 minutes. Remove bags. Add cranberry juice cocktail. Chill thoroughly. Just before serving, pour over ice in a punch bowl or pitcher and add lemon-lime soda and lemon slices. (Makes about 2 quarts.)

Southern Delights

DIXIE

Southern style cooking. It's a phrase that instantly conjures up some mouth-watering image for almost everyone. But the culinary delights of Dixie that come to mind can be vastly different—succulent hams and crispy chicken, delicate seafood bisques and spicy jambalayas, rum-laced fruits and molasses-glazed yams, rich warm pecan pies and cool lime ones. There are many cooking heritages of the Southland: colonial, plantation, country-style, soul food, Creole, fine French, Old World Spanish, and the international cuisine of the big cities and resorts, to name just a few. But they do have something in common beyond being south of the Mason-Dixon line: each is steeped in tradition and lore. Tradition is as much an ingredient in the recipes of the South as anything that comes out of a market.

EYE OPENERS

Plantation Ham in Cream

Traditional Southern breakfasts can be overwhelmingly opulent feasts for those of us unaccustomed to beginning the day with a several course meal. We found we enjoyed these perennial ham-and-biscuit breakfast favorites more when they starred on their own accompanied only by coffee or tea and a fresh fruit course like ambrosia, a bowl of peaches and cream, or wedges of cool melon and pineapple.

4 cups (1 quart) whipping cream
2 cups cubed Virginia ham
(fully cooked)

Heat cream in a skillet until it just begins to simmer. Stir in ham and gently simmer uncovered for 30 minutes. Serve with freshly baked hot biscuits.

Jefferson Biscuits

2 packages (10 biscuits each)
refrigerated biscuits
½ to 1 pound shaved (very thinly
sliced) Smithfield or other
Southern ham that has been
fully cooked
Butter

Bake the biscuits according to package directions. Serve piping hot from the oven, split, buttered, and piled with cool sliced ham. You will also want to put out jelly, jam, or preserves for some of the biscuits.

Ham with Red-Eye Gravy

4 slices country ham *or* fully
cooked ham (either 2 ½-inch-
thick ham steaks cut into 4
servings or 4 ¼-inch-thick
whole slices of ham)
½ cup very hot coffee

Fry ham in a hot skillet until both sides are browned. For ½-inch thick slices it will take about 5 minutes on each side. Remove ham from skillet and stir in coffee. Stir all the little dark bits from the pan bottom into the gravy—they are the "red eyes"; and bring mixture to a boil. Serve ham with gravy and hot biscuits.

Derby Day Turkey Hash

Perhaps the most famous breakfasts in the South are those served on Kentucky Derby Day to lucky guests—lucky enough to be invited to one of these elaborate brunches, that is. Turkey Hash accompanied by batty cakes (lacy corn pancakes) is a traditional feature of these feasts. But this version is too simple and too good to save for one day a year or even for your trip to Kentucky. You'll enjoy it as a hearty breakfast or lunch whenever you have a couple of cups of cooked turkey (or chicken) on hand. It may be difficult for Yankees to distinguish southern turkey or chicken hash from creamed turkey or chicken—unless, of course, you accompany the hash with a Mint Julep.

1 10 ¾-ounce can condensed cream of chicken or cream of mushroom soup
¼ cup dry sherry (or ¼ cup milk)
2 cups diced cooked turkey
1 4-ounce can sliced mushrooms, drained
1 to 2 teaspoons dried chopped fine herbs—chives, chervil, and/or parsley (optional)
Salt and pepper

Heat soup, sherry or milk, and mushrooms over medium heat, stirring until sauce is smooth and barely simmering. Stir in turkey, heat through, and season to taste. If the hash is too thick, thin with a little milk. Good with cornbread or biscuits as well as batty cakes.

Appalachian Apples and Chops

In striking contrast to the elegant Derby buffets are the equally appetizing hearty family breakfasts enjoyed in much of the South. Regional breakfast standbys are hot biscuits and gravy, boiled or fried grits (a cereal made from white hominy), and main dishes that seem more like dinner in other parts of the country—ham steaks, fried fish, grilled country sausage patties, fried chicken livers, and pan-fried pork chops. Apple rings are a pleasing accompaniment to breakfast chops. They can be fried—Southerners often enjoy fried bananas, peaches, yams, or tropical fruits with breakfast—or glazed as in this recipe.

2 large firm cooking apples
½ cup maple syrup
2 tablespoons apple cider or apple juice or cider vinegar
¼ teaspoon salt
¼ teaspoon cinnamon
4 small pork chops (for example, 5-ounce pork loin butterfly chops)
Flour
Salt and pepper
2 tablespoons cooking oil

Wash and core apples. Cut unpeeled apples in ½-inch rings. Mix syrup, cider, salt, and cinnamon in a saucepan and bring to a boil. Add apple rings and cook, turning rings from time to time, until the apple rings are tender and beginning to be transparent.

Meanwhile, dip the chops in flour and lightly season with salt and pepper. Heat cooking oil in a skillet over medium-high heat. Cook chops, turning as needed to cook evenly (you'll have a crowded skillet), until they are browned and meat near bone is no longer pink, about 7 minutes on each side. Top with glazed apple rings and sauce and serve.

Kentucky Scramble

8 slices lean bacon
1 tablespoon butter
1 12-ounce can Mexican-style
   corn (whole kernel corn with
   red and green sweet peppers),
   drained
6 eggs
1 teaspoon salt
Pepper

Cut bacon into quarters and fry in a skillet over medium heat until the pieces are crisp and brown. Transfer the bacon to paper towels to drain. Pour off all but 3 tablespoons of the bacon fat into a heatproof disposable container. Add the butter to the fat in the skillet and stir in the corn, cooking for several minutes until the corn is heated through but not browned. In a small bowl beat eggs, salt, and a generous sprinkling of pepper. (The eggs need only to be slightly beaten—you can use a fork.) Pour the eggs into the skillet and cook over low heat, scrambling the eggs a little as they are cooking with a spatula. When the eggs are set but still moist, arrange the bacon slices on top and serve at once.

New Orleans Pain Perdu

Breakfast in New Orleans is justifiably legendary. Contributing to the fame of the French Quarter are the breakfast specialties of fine restaurants and fancy sweet pastries like Beignets (square French doughnuts) and Little Ears (deep-fried Acadian confections with praline sauce). One traditional favorite is a natural for the RV cook—Pain Perdu ("lost bread"), a regional version of French toast sparkled with a little bit of lemon peel.

2 eggs
2 tablespoons confectioners'
   sugar
¾ cup milk
Grated rind of half a lemon
   (about 1 teaspoon)
8 1-inch-thick slices French bread
Butter
Maple syrup

Beat eggs, sugar, milk, and lemon rind in a fairly flat-bottomed bowl. Dip bread in mixture (the bread shouldn't be too fresh), and fry in butter over low heat until crisp and golden brown on both sides. Serve with syrup and butter.

SOUPS, SALADS, AND SANDWICHES

Black Bean Soup

This velvety classic American soup has long had an international reputation. (It was the soup that Wallis Simpson served at the "traditional American dinner" on the Fourth of July, 1932, that first charmed the Prince of Wales.) But making it is a tedious production unsuited to the RV kitchen. Despair not. Do what many fine Southern cooks do: gussy-up a good canned soup with a lacing of sherry and a flourish of garnishes.

2 11-ounce cans condensed
    black bean soup
2 cubes beef bouillon
1 can boiling water
½ cup sherry or madeira
    or ¼ cup dark rum
Thin lemon slices
2 hard-boiled eggs, coarsely
    chopped

Empty black bean soup into saucepan. Dissolve bouillon cubes in can with boiling water. Add hot bouillon to bean soup a little at a time, stirring until smooth as you heat soup to simmering. Stir in sherry just before serving. Garnish with lemon slices and chopped egg. You can also offer some finely chopped ham or a dollop of sour cream if you have either on hand.

Charleston She-Crab Soup

On our first visit to Charleston, South Carolina, it seemed that everywhere we went someone mentioned she-crab soup. When we finally tasted this delicate, creamy bisque, we understood why it is the pride of the Low Country. Our recipe was given to us by a cook at one of the history-rich plantations along the Ashley River, where the cultural and botanical heritage of the area is being preserved at two of America's oldest and most beautiful gardens.

2 cups crab and roe*
1 quart milk
½ cup (1 stick) butter
1 tablespoon flour
Several drops onion juice*
½ teaspoon Worcestershire sauce
½ teaspoon salt
Mace to taste*
Pepper to taste
4 tablespoons sherry, warmed
    (optional)

Heat milk, butter, and flour over very low heat, stirring until smooth. Add crab, roe, and all seasonings except sherry. Continue heating and stirring constantly for about 20 minutes. To serve, top each serving with a tablespoon of warm sherry. If you have whipped cream on hand, put a little dollop on each serving.

*Tips: In the likelihood that you don't have roe, the soup is still very good. As a substitute for roe, Charleston cooks sometimes add a little crumbled egg yolk to each bowl when the soup is served. Nutmeg is from the same plant as mace and makes a passable substitute. A small amount of finely minced fresh or dry onion can be substitued for the onion juice.

Sunbird Salad

Almost any of the beautiful familiar and unfamiliar fruits that are found in the markets of the Deep South can go into this glorified fruit cocktail long enjoyed in the region.

4 cups mixed fruit (oranges, grapefruit, peaches, pineapple, mangoes, guavas, bananas, carambolas), cut in bite-size pieces
1 cup rum
1 cup sugar

Heat the rum and sugar together just till boiling, stirring continuously. Pour syrup over the fruit and stir to coat the fruit. Cover bowl and chill several hours.

Tip: To avoid heating up your refrigerator, wait a little while before putting the fruit in the refrigerator.

St. Augustine Ensalada

This hearty vegetable and sausage salad from the Southland's Spanish past will serve four as a light lunch or as a substantial salad course to go with a simple main dish such as grilled meat or fish.

¼ to ½ pound chorizo or other Spanish or Italian sausage
1 10-ounce package frozen mixed vegetables
1 small head romaine or the inner leaves of a large head, washed, dried, and torn into bite-size pieces
1 tomato, sliced
1 or 2 scallions with tops, chopped (optional)
¼ cup pitted black olives, sliced (optional)
½ cup Italian dressing

Cook sausage in a covered skillet (to keep down spattering) with about a ¼ cup of water for 10 minutes. Pour off accumulated oil (use a heatproof container; the hot oil can melt plastic), and continue frying sausage over medium heat until brown and cooked through. Drain sausage and cut into ¾-inch slices. Meanwhile, cook mixed vegetables as directed on package except reduce cooking time to 5 minutes. Drain. Toss romaine, tomato, olives, mixed vegetables, green onions, and sausage in a large bowl. Pour dressing over salad and cover. Chill at least 1 hour before serving if you can.

Monticello Salad

The Southern taste for salads goes back to at least the beginning of recorded history, and the salad fixings at the great houses of Early America would make a dazzling salad bar even today. Thomas Jefferson's garden at Monticello included nineteen varieties of lettuce alone. Jefferson was also largely responsible for introducing sesame seed oil to American salad bowls. For a centuries old treat that will please your guests as much as it did Jefferson's guests at Monticello, dress a bowl of cool crisp mixed greens—lettuces, endive, chicory, spinach, watercress—with a zesty garlic dressing (crush a garlic clove in a vinaigrette made with sesame seed oil or use bottled garlic dressing).

St. Augustine Empanadas De Camarones

Traditionally, these individual shrimp pies are made as small round pastries, a time-consuming process. Our shortcuts, including making them as wedge-shaped turnovers with ready-made pie crust, cut kitchen time to almost nothing.

½ **pound cooked shrimp, chopped**
⅓ **cup chopped black olives (10 or 12 large olives)**
⅓ **cup mild chile salsa or picante sauce**
½ **teaspoon salt**
1 **15-ounce package (2 crusts) refrigerated pie crusts**

Preheat oven to 400°. Mix shrimp, olives, salsa, and salt (if salsa is very liquid try to use mostly the solid part of the salsa). Cut each pie crust in quarters (along the fold lines). Off-center on each wedge of pastry, mound about ⅛ of the shrimp mixture (a scant ¼ cup). Dampen the edges of the pastry with a little water and fold the pastry over, crimping and sealing the edges together securely. Arrange turnovers on a foil-lined baking sheet (a 15-inch pizza pan will hold all 8). Bake until light brown (about 20 minutes).

New Orleans Oyster Loaf

New Orleans sandwiches, like everything else in that fabled city, are a special case. The Poor Boy sandwich was born on the wharves of New Orleans as a filling lunch for longshoremen. The individual loaves of French bread can be piled with sliced meats, cheese, or seafood—Shrimp Poor Boys used to be especially popular back when you could buy shrimp for pennies a pound. Another old favorite currently in fashion is the Muffuletta, a plump round loaf of bread filled with salami, ham, Swiss cheese, and olive salad.

But of all the sandwiches, the New Orleans Oyster Loaf is in a class by itself. Now in its second century of popularity, the oyster loaf was known in the nineteenth century as La Médiatrice or the Mediator, since they were often brought home after an evening in the French Quarter as a peace offering.

4 **individual French bread loaves** *or* 1 **medium loaf French, Italian, or home-style bread, unsliced**
1 **pint shucked oysters, drained**
Butter
Salt and pepper
Tabasco **(optional)**

Slice off the top of the bread and scoop out the center of the loaf leaving a ½-inch shell. Brush the cut side of the lid and the scooped out center with melted butter. Toast bread—tops and shells—in a 425° oven until lightly brown. (You don't really need to have the oven completely preheated.) Meanwhile, fry the oysters in plenty of butter (up to a ½ cup) until their edges curl and they are plump. Sprinkle with salt and pepper to taste and add a dash or two of hot sauce if you like it. As soon as the bread is toasted, fill the bread cases with the oysters, top with lids, and serve immediately. Traditionally, oysters loaves are served with ketchup though some of the chic restaurants now mix the oysters with a seasoned mayonnaise.

Variations: Some people prefer the oysters rolled in flour, dipped in batter, or coated with crumbs before they are fried. You can also give the same presentation to other seafood, for example, French-fried shrimp stuffed in the bread case (good with a creamy dressing like Thousand Island).

MAIN EVENTS

Southern Fried Chicken

We spent a lot of time and trouble on one recipe that didn't end up in this book. In our quest for *the* Southern Fried Chicken recipe, we found so many different recipes, all accompanied by adamant insistence that this was *the* way, that we felt like saying "will the real Southern Fried Chicken please stand up." Actually, there are many quite different historic ways of frying chicken in the South, with new traditions being created every day. In the interests of peace we are inclined to take the advice of one astute writer on Southern cooking who cautioned that "any attempt to prescribe the best way to prepare fried chicken is likely to start the Civil War all over again."

If that dilemma wasn't enough, what we really had difficulty with was the point that most agreed upon: frying the chicken in a goodly amount of hot fat. Even when we used a lid for part of the cooking—which is a definite no-no to many Southern cooks—we couldn't avoid some grease popping. Now that may be no big deal in an ordinary kitchen, but when your kitchen is literally in your living room and bedroom, it can be an unpleasant and even expensive disaster. Our recommendation is if you don't already have a way of doing fried chicken that's not particularly messy, your RV is not the place to experiment. Fortunately, if you get the urge for crispy chicken there are fried chicken take-out places all over America. Or try baking a batch of this crusty savory oven-fried chicken.

Oven-Fried Deli Chicken

2½ to 3 pounds of chicken parts (preferably white meat—split breasts, thighs)
½ cup (1 stick) butter, melted, *or* cooking oil
1 cup herb-seasoned stuffing or or croutons, crushed to fine crumbs*
½ cup grated Parmesan cheese

Skin chicken if desired and trim off excess fat. Rinse chicken pieces in cool water and pat dry with paper towels. Mix crumbs and cheese. Dip each piece of chicken in butter then roll in crumb mixture until the chicken is heavily coated on all sides. Arrange chicken, meaty side up, on a foil-lined baking sheet or pan (the pan should have a lip—a pizza pan works well). Drizzle any leftover melted butter on the chicken. Have your oven preheated to 450°, put the chicken in, turn the oven down to 325°, and bake until crispy, brown, and tender (about 45 minutes to 1 hour—ovens and altitudes effect cooking time, so it may take longer).

Variations: Substitute crushed crispy rice cereal or corn flakes for the stuffing-cheese mixture, sprinkle with paprika or chicken seasoning, and proceed as above.

Tip: Put the stuffing or croutons in a sealable plastic bag and mash with anything heavy or tap with the back of a heavy spoon.

Chicken Jack Daniel's

The spirits of the South range from firey moonshines to the finest of America's whiskeys made at world famous distilleries in Kentucky and Tennessee. In Lynchburg, Tennessee, at the oldest registered distillery in America, Jack Daniel's creates the sparkle for this recipe featuring two of the South's other most prized products—chicken and oranges.

2 pounds (about 8 split breasts) boned chicken breasts, skinned
¼ cup (½ stick) butter
1 12-ounce can frozen orange juice concentrate, defrosted
1 teaspoon salt
Pepper, preferably fresh ground
¼ cup* Tennessee sour-mash whiskey (or bourbon)

Trim any excess fat off chicken, rinse in cool water, and pat dry with paper towels. Tuck thin pieces in to make a fairly neat package that will cook more evenly. Melt the butter in a skillet and brown chicken on both sides over medium heat. Pour orange juice concentrate over chicken, sprinkle with salt and a generous dusting of pepper, and bring to a boil. Cover skillet, reduce heat to low, and cook just until chicken is tender and done (about 10 minutes). While the chicken is cooking, spoon the sauce in the skillet over it a few times. When the chicken is done, remove the chicken pieces to a serving dish or dishes, turn the heat up, and cook and stir the sauce in the skillet until it is thick and golden brown. Stir in the whiskey and immediately pour the sauce over chicken. Garnish with orange slices if you want to be extra fancy.

*A miniature 50 milliliter bottle will do just fine, but then you'll miss having to deal with the "leftovers."

Mississippi Red Beans and Rice

For many years in parts of the Deep South, Monday meant Red Beans and Rice for dinner. In some parts it still does. Our quick and easy family supper recipe comes from Pearlington near the Gulf.

1 pound smoked sausage
1 27-ounce can red kidney beans
½ teaspoon crushed red pepper (optional)
Boiled rice

Cut smoked sausage in ½-inch chunks and heat with the kidney beans—and red pepper if you have it and like it—in a covered saucepan until boiling. Reduce heat and simmer for ½ hour or so, stirring occasionally. Serve beans over hot rice. The usual asides are cornbread and boiled greens.

V.I.P. Ham

You want something especially impressive or especially festive or both. Maybe it is for a Very Important Person or for a Very Important Occasion or both. Well, how about one of those glamorous hams in pastry crust that star on Southern buffet tables? Wait, don't turn the page—you don't have to be a chef to do this one. It took us less than 10 minutes to get the ham into the oven when we tested this in our RV oven. On other occasions our little children have helped with the decorating—that did take a bit longer. Incidentally, a variation of this recipe won us a prize in the Chun King Swing American recipe contest.

1 3-pound fully-cooked boneless ham*
1 17¼-ounce package (2 sheets) frozen puff pastry (or substitute 1 15-ounce package refrigerated pie crusts)
Orange marmalade
1 egg

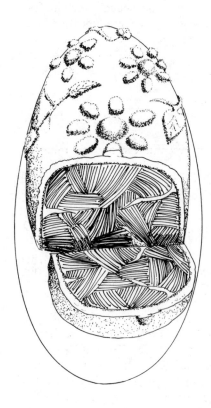

Take pastry out of freezer and allow to get pliable (about 20 minutes at room temperature). Skin ham if it has one. Drain off excess juice. Use heavy-duty foil or 2 layers of regular aluminum foil to line a baking sheet with a lip (a pizza pan will work fine). Place ham in center of baking sheet. Slather top and sides of ham with orange marmalade (about ½ cup will do it). In a small disposable cup make a simple egg wash by mixing egg with a half eggshell of cold water (about 1 tablespoon).

Wrap top and sides of ham in 1 sheet of puff pastry, using egg wash to make the corners stick—don't worry about the pastry overlapping. (If you are using pie crusts, extra overhanging pastry can be trimmed off.) Give the pastry an overall coat of egg wash, using a basting brush or a piece of paper towel. (Preheat the oven to 350° at this point.)

From second sheet of pastry, use scissors, a small knife, or cookie cutters to make flowers, leaves, winding stems, abstract shapes, or whatever you fancy. (You will probably use about ¼ of the sheet, put the rest back in the freezer for another time.) Dip each cutout in the egg wash and arrange attractively on the ham. If there is a gap in the pastry wrap at the front or back of the ham, patch the space with a decorative shape. You can shape leaves and roll up little flower buds with your fingers, add vein marks to leaves or print a message on a banner of pastry with the edge of a table knife: Have fun.

Give the whole crust and decorations another light going over with the egg wash. Wipe up the marmalade and egg wash that has dribbled on to the foil. Put the ham in the oven so that the sides of the ham are parallel to the sides of the oven. (It seems to brown more evenly in a small oven this way.) Bake at 350° for 1 hour. Allow ham to rest for 10 minutes or so and transfer to a cutting board or platter to serve.

Tips: To be at its best the pastry shouldn't get too warm while you're working with it. You can take your time cutting out the trims if you do that step while the pastry is still quite cold. By the time the other sheet is defrosted enough to wrap the ham, you'll be all set. The juices that dribble out as the ham is baking tend to make a mess out of the baking pan and burn. If you would like to bake whole yams alongside the ham on the baking sheet, wrap them in foil as you would for outdoor baking and be sure they don't touch the pastry.

*RV ovens are usually quite shallow. Measure the clearance space in yours and measure the ham when you buy it. Allowing for the pan, the crust (which will puff), and a little air space, you will need about 2 inches more than the actual ham. A canned ham, which works fine in this recipe, measures about 3 inches—just right for most RV ovens.

Jamboree Jambalaya

The mere mention of bayou country brings to mind the mouth-watering refrain "... jambalaya, codfish pie, filé gumbo ...," and no tour of the cuisine of the South would be complete without at least one of these Creole classics. Since the late 1700s, jambalaya has been a New Orleans favorite. Some say that its name derived from the Spanish word for ham, *jamon*; some say it comes from the French *jambon*. Almost everyone agrees that when this savory stew got into the creative hands of Cajun-Creole cooks, its appeal became international. Jambalaya can be made with a variety of vegetables, meats, shellfish, and seasonings. Our streamlined version has all the flavor of more time-consuming recipes and features the original ham and the most popular Creole addition, Gulf shrimp.

1 pound shrimp, fresh or frozen in shells or shelled
1 teaspoon salt
1 teaspoon seafood seasoning (optional)
½ pound ham (fully cooked), cut in ½-inch cubes
2 tablespoons butter
1 cup sliced mushrooms (less if using canned)
1 15½-ounce jar chunky garden-style spaghetti sauce with green peppers and mushrooms
Several dashes bottled hot pepper sauce (*Tabasco* and *RedHot! Sauce* are Louisiana favorites)
Creole seasoning (optional)*
Hot boiled rice

To cook raw shrimp in shells, boil a quart of water, stir in salt and seafood seasoning if you have it, and throw in a handful of celery leaves if you happen to have those. Add shrimp (they should be deheaded) and return water to boiling. Simmer about 3 minutes or until shrimp turn pink. Drain and peel shrimp, removing back vein. Meanwhile, in a 2-quart saucepan melt butter over medium-high heat and stir in mushrooms and ham cubes, cooking them just until the mushrooms begin to change color. Stir in spaghetti sauce and heat to simmering (use a lid to keep stove top clean). Stir in cleaned shrimp. (If you are using precooked shrimp, simmer in sauce until they are heated through.) Season with hot sauce and, if you have it, sprinkle on creole seasoning to taste (or salt and pepper to taste). Serve over boiled rice.

Tips: If on the off chance you have filé powder (dried and powdered sassafras leaves) along, stir in 1 teaspoon just before serving—don't boil it or the jambalaya will get stringy. This recipe is very easy to multiply to serve larger numbers, and, except for the shrimp peeling, there is no additional time or trouble involved—just the thing for when you feel like throwing your own jamboree.

*Creole seasoning is a combination of salt and spices—red and black pepper, chili powder, garlic—used liberally by Creole cooks to flavor everything from soups to salads. A popular brand is *Tony Chachere's Creole Seasoning* from Opelousas, Louisiana.

Mardi Gras Pompano

4 (each about 8 ounces) skinless pompano fillets (or substitute halibut fillets)
2 cups pecans, finely chopped*
6 tablespoons flour
1 teaspoon salt
Pepper
Maple syrup
Cooking oil

Rinse fillets in cool water and pat dry with paper towels. Mix chopped pecans, flour, salt, and a generous sprinkling of pepper on a flat plate. Using a basting brush if you have one, paint each fish fillet with maple syrup (pour a little syrup in a disposable cup as you need it); then dip each fillet in pecan mixture coating both sides well. (It is less messy if you do one side at a time.) Fry the fillets two at a time over medium heat in a couple of tablespoons of heated oil, adding more oil as needed. Turn the fillets halfway through cooking—it will only take a few minutes on each side, no more than 10 minutes total cooking time. Watch the fillets carefully to keep the pecan coating from scorching—blackened fish is in vogue in New Orleans now, but not desirable with this recipe, it should be crispy golden outside and flaky and white inside.

*Tip: Put nuts in a sealable plastic bag and tap on them with the back of a heavy spoon. If you are using a small sandwich bag do about a ¼ cup at a time.

"Fare Thee Well" Shrimp

A charmingly named example of Southern hospitality that will send you cheerily on your way in anticipation of an opulent roadside lunch or supper—a great antidote for last-day-of-vacation blues.

2 pounds medium cooked shrimp, peeled and cleaned*
1 medium red onion, thinly sliced
2 small lemons, thinly sliced
½ cup black olives, sliced
1 cup bottled Italian dressing
1 teaspoon salad herbs (optional)

Arrange shrimp, onion slices, lemon slices, and black olives in several layers in a refrigerator container. Mix herbs and Italian dressing and pour over the top. Cover and chill, preferably for 4 hours or more. Serve over avocado halves or in lettuce cups.

*We suggest doing this step out on the camp table to avoid lingering odors in the RV.

ASIDES

Cream Cheese and . . .

The trick of combining spicy and creamy has many tasty variations throughout the South. In Georgia they frost a package of cream cheese with green pepper jelly; in Washington, D.C., the topping might be caviar; and around the Gulf you are likely to find shrimp cocktail (small shrimp in sauce) atop the cream cheese.

Eastern Shore Crab Appetizer

Super simple and stylish, a platter of this appetizer surrounded by your favorite crackers makes a great first course or snack with something tall and cool to drink.

1 8-ounce package cream cheese, softened (leave it at room temperature for awhile)
1 8-ounce bottle seafood cocktail sauce
½ pound fresh cooked crabmeat *or* 1 6-ounce can crabmeat *or* ½ pound frozen crabmeat, defrosted

On a flat surface—a cutting board, tray, platter, or dishes—spread a layer of cream cheese. Top with a thin layer of cocktail sauce and then a layer of crab (make sure the crab is well drained to avoid getting the sauce watery). Serve immediately or chill.

Tip: We think this tastes best if the sauce and crab are cold, but the cheese easily spreadable—put the jar of sauce and the can of crab in the refrigerator for a few hours before assembling.

Florida Stone Crab Claws

This delicacy comes packaged by nature in one of the hardest shells around. Whether the claws you buy (only the claws are sold) are cooked or uncooked, it will take some time to warm them through and you'll need a hammer or nutcracker to get to the sweet meat. Allow 3 or 4 for an appetizer serving, 6 to 8 for a main event serving.

12 to 16 stone crab claws
Lemon or lime wedges
Creole Butter:
½ cup butter, melted
1 teaspoon creole seasoning

Garlic Butter:
½ cup butter, melted
Garlic powder to taste *or*
  1 crushed garlic clove

Caper Mayonnaise:
½ cup mayonnaise
2 teaspoons capers
Pepper to taste

Mustard Sauce:
1 tablespoon prepared mustard, preferably *Dijon*
¼ cup mayonnaise
¼ cup yogurt (or another ¼ cup mayonnaise)

Boil claws for 20 minutes in salted water (about 1 teaspoon to 1 quart of water). Serve hot or cold with lemon or lime wedges and a choice of sauces.

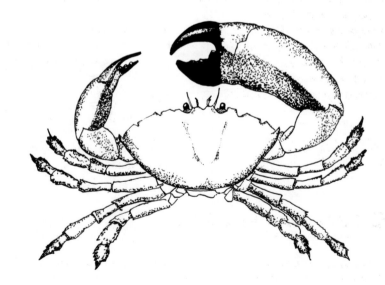

Carolina Pistachio Rice

It takes only a few minutes to make this version of a Carolina classic that goes back to colonial times when traders introduced a rice dish known as pilau from the Orient.

3 to 4 cups hot cooked rice (prepare 2 cups instant rice *or* 1 cup regular converted rice according to package directions)
¼ cup pistachio nuts, shelled and skinned
¼ cup pine nuts (also called pignon nuts or pignolia), shelled*
¼ cup (½ stick) butter, melted
Mace to taste (or use nutmeg)

While rice is cooking, stir nuts and butter together. (Some cooks like to slightly toast the nuts in the butter.) Stir in about ½ teaspoon of powdered mace. Mix seasoned butter-nut sauce into rice, add more mace if desired, and serve.

*We have tried for years to find an easy way of shelling pine nuts—to no avail. If at all possible buy already shelled pine nuts. In the event you can't find pine nuts at all, double the amount of the pistachio nuts.

Molasses Glazed Pan Yams

You probably already have a family recipe for baked candied yams that you dig out around the holidays. But in the South yams are an everyday staple served at most any meal and in every imaginable way; there are at least as many recipes for yams or sweet potatoes as there are for white potatoes in other parts of the country.

4 to 6 medium yams, scrubbed
Salt
3 tablespoons butter
Molasses

Put the scrubbed yams in a saucepan with salted water (about 1 teaspoon salt) to cover. Bring the water to a boil, cover, and simmer the yams until tender (about 20-25 minutes). Drain and peel yams. In a skillet melt butter and transfer the yams to the skillet. Turn the yams to coat with butter. Add molasses to depth of about 1 inch. Cook over low heat, turning frequently until yams are heavily glazed.

Variations: You can cut the yams into chunks, halves, or quarters before glazing if desired. Or you can substitute canned yams. For a richer dish, stir in ½ cup of broken pecans while the yams are being glazed.

Hoppin' Fast Hoppin' John

If you should find yourself in the Southland some New Year's Day, a dish of Hopping John is a necessity—guaranteed to ward off bad luck throughout the year. And it's a tasty way of enjoying black-eyed peas anytime. Although old recipes often take several hours of preparation, our hopping-fast version makes it to the table in half an hour.

3 slices bacon, cut into squares
1 teaspoon salt
1 10-ounce package frozen
   black-eyed peas
1 cup regular converted rice
1 tablespoon instant minced
   onion (optional)
Hot sauce (Tabasco or other
   Southern pepper sauce)

Fry bacon in 2-quart saucepan until done but not crisp. Turn off heat and allow to cool slightly to avoid spattering hot fat. Add 3 cups of water and salt to pan and bring to a full boil. Stir in black-eyed peas and return to boil. Stir in rice and onion, cover tightly, and simmer until all the water is absorbed (about 20 to 30 minutes). Add a dash or two of hot sauce to taste. According to custom, any children about must hop around the table before the dish is served.

DESSERTS

Ambrosia for Purists

At its simplest Ambrosia is sweetened oranges and coconut and is the classic Southern Christmas dessert as well as year-round "food for the gods" that can be served at almost any meal.

4 large seedless oranges
2 cups shredded coconut
¼ cup sugar or to taste

Slice oranges crosswise in thin rounds and run the tip of a paring knife between peel and orange removing all of the white pith. (Or peel oranges first, carefully removing all the pith; then slice.) In a large serving bowl arrange the slices in layers, sprinkling with sugar and coconut as you go. Cover and chill for preferably 2 hours or more before serving.

Ambrosia for Non-Purists

Add to the above recipe any of the following singly or in combinations:

Fresh or drained canned
   pineapple slices or chunks
   (add more sugar to taste if
   using fresh)
Fresh or drained canned
   grapefruit sections (add
   more sugar to taste if using
   fresh)

1 or 2 sliced bananas
1 pint fresh strawberries, washed,
   hulled, and lightly sugared
¼ cup sherry
¼ cup Grand Marnier

Ambrosia in the Wilderness

1 16-ounce can mandarin orange
   sections, drained
1 16-ounce can grapefruit
   sections drained
½ cup confectioners' sugar
1 cup shredded coconut
¼ cup *Grand Marnier* (optional)

Gently mix all ingredients in a bowl. Cover and chill, preferably for a couple of hours.

Tip: If you have the space, store the canned fruit in the refrigerator before making this ambrosia and even if it's mixed up on the spur of the moment, it will be delicious.

Georgia Pecan Pie

The pie of the South, especially in Georgia and Louisiana, this is one dessert worth having on the hips for a lifetime.

1 9-inch pie shell, unbaked
3 eggs
2 tablespoons flour
2 tablespoons sugar
1 teaspoon vanilla
Salt
1 pint (2 cups) dark corn syrup
1½ cups whole Georgia pecan
   halves (though pecans grown
   elsewhere *could* be used)

Preheat the oven to 400°. Beat the eggs until they are light-colored and foamy (3-5 minutes of vigorous hand whipping). Stir in the flour, sugar, vanilla, and a generous dash of salt until well mixed. Pour in corn syrup (use straight out of the bottle and save one sticky wash-up) and beat until batter is evenly colored and smooth. Stir in pecans. Pour pecan mixture into pie shell and bake at 400° for 35-40 minutes or until a knife inserted half way between center and edge comes out clean. Cool before serving. This heavenly pie is best served a little warm and with a swirl of whipped cream.

Gold Coast Bananas

Flaming bananas are a fitting finale for a special dinner.

4 firm ripe bananas, cut in ½-inch
   thick slices (keep each banana
   on part of its peel until you are
   ready for it)
4 tablespoons (½ stick) butter
4 tablespoons (¼ cup) sugar
4 tablespoons (¼ cup) Grand
   Marnier or brandy
Vanilla ice cream

This dish is easier to do in two batches: Melt 2 tablespoons butter in skillet over medium heat. Put 2 sliced bananas in skillet and sprinkle with 2 tablespoons sugar. Cook, stirring gently, until the slices are golden. Carefully add 2 tablespoons Grand Marnier to skillet and warm for a bit. Carefully light the liquor. (Turn off the range-hood fan to avoid sucking flames into the hood; use a long match if you have one and stand back when you light the liquor.) When the flame subsides, spoon bananas over dishes of ice cream and serve with fanfare. Repeat with remaining ingredients.

Key Lime Pie

Many new popular American recipes have been inspired by convenience foods, and we are used to finding easier ways of cooking old recipes with new products. We were, however, surprised to learn that condensed milk was an original ingredient and the inspiration for this classic Florida recipe—condensed milk was first manufactured in 1858.

1 6-ounce ready-made graham cracker crust *or* 1 8-inch home-made graham cracker crust
3 egg yolks
½ cup fresh Key lime juice (about 3 limes*; if Key limes aren't available use other fresh limes)
1 14-ounce can sweetened condensed milk
1 8-ounce or 9-ounce tub whipped topping, thawed, *or* 1 can whipped cream topping

In a 1-quart bowl, beat the egg yolks until they are very thick. (You can do this by hand with a whisk but it takes a very vigorous 5 or 6 minutes of beating.) Add the sweetened condensed milk and the lime juice and continue beating until smooth. Pour the filling into the pie crust; cover with plastic wrap, wax paper, or oil; and chill the pie in the refrigerator until the filling is firm (about 4 or 5 hours). Just before serving, spread the top of the pie with deep drifts of whipped topping and garnish with lime slices. (If you are not planning to eat the pie in one sitting, cut the pie into servings and put topping on the pieces as they are served—the pie keeps better and is easier to store without the topping.)

*Before you squeeze the limes, slice a few very thin slices out of the center and reserve for a garnish in a plastic bag.

Mississippi Mud Pie

As easy to make as the dirt variety and considerably better tasting, this ice cream pie is especially fun for children to make.

6 ounces (16 cookies) O*reos*
¼ cup (½ stick) butter, melted
1 quart ice cream (praline, butter brickle, chocolate chip, mint chocolate chip, coffee, Rocky Road, Tin Roof, etc.)
1 cup (½ 16-ounce container) ready-to-spread chocolate creamy frosting

Take the ice cream out of the freezer and allow it to get soft. Crush cookies. (Put them in a sealable plastic bag and mash with something hard until it looks like dark coarse sand.) Mix melted butter and crumbs. Press mixture into a 9-inch pie pan. Pour or spoon softened ice cream into the shell and freeze. (How long this will take depends on how cold your freezer is.) Melt the frosting in a small saucepan over low heat stirring constantly (or do it in a microwave oven if you have one). Now—and this is the only tricky part—you want the frosting to be warm enough to pour but not hot enough to melt the ice cream. Pour the frosting on the top of the pie completely covering the ice cream. Try not to use any tool on the pie or you may stir the ice cream into the frosting. Refreeze the pie until serving time. If you have a very efficient freezer and the pie is hard to cut, just let it sit at room temperature for awhile. Cover any leftover pie with foil and keep in the freezer.

Tip: If your freezer is too narrow for a pie pan—ours is—you can use a metal freezer tray (an ice cube tray with detachable divider) or make individual tarts in *Solo Cozy* cups.

Watermelon with a Secret

Just the thing for a party if you can make room in your refrigerator or a cooler for a whole watermelon—it doesn't have to be a big one. This R-rated dessert has been known to inspire some quite spectacular seed-spitting contests among dignified adults.

1 whole ripe watermelon
Light rum, white wine, or
  inexpensive champagne

The day before you plan to serve it, cut a 2-inch square plug out of the watermelon. Pour rum or wine slowly into the watermelon until it won't hold any more. Put the plug back in and seal with masking tape or other heavy sticky tape. Chill the watermelon, turning it now and then, until serving time. Slice as usual.

Sugar n' Spice Pecans

1 egg white
1 cup pecan halves
¼ cup sugar
1 teaspoon cinnamon
½ teaspoon ground nutmeg
⅛ teaspoon ground cloves
  (optional)

Use two bowls. In first bowl, mix egg white and pecan halves until well coated. In second bowl, mix sugar and spices. Transfer egg-coated pecans to the second bowl and stir until they are well coated with sugar and spice. Arrange on oiled aluminum-foil-lined baking sheet. Bake at 375° until almost dry and golden (10-15 minutes). Allow to cool for a minute before removing from foil.

Variation: Substitute 1½ teaspoons of apple-pie spice for the cinnamon, nutmeg, and cloves.

CHEERS

New Orleans Milk Punch

In a French Quarter nightclub this punch goes down as smooth as the music. For the full effect, put a jazz cassette in your tape player and lean back.

6 ounces bourbon
1½ cups half-and-half (light
  cream)
2 tablespoons simple syrup (or
  substitute sugar)
6 drops vanilla
Nutmeg (optional)

Combine everything but nutmeg in your shaker with several ice cubes. Shake hard and strain into the nearest thing you have to old-fashioned glasses. Sprinkle with grated nutmeg.

Fresh Lemonade

It would be practically un-American not to like lemonade, but just about everyone does, and just about everyone makes this all-time favorite cooler with a can of frozen lemonade concentrate or a package. But for the day you find yourself with a surfeit of fresh lemons and a powerful thirst, this is how we used to make it in the old days.

2 cups lemon juice
2 cups sugar
6 to 8 cups water

Shake lemon juice and sugar together until sugar dissolves. (This syrup will keep in the refrigerator.) For each glass of lemonade, mix ¼ to ⅓ cup water. Aaaah!

Ramos Gin Fizz

This cocktail is sometimes called a Silver Fizz and is good throughout the day, especially as an eye-opener with brunch. The fizz was devised almost a hundred years ago by Henry C. Ramos, the owner of a New Orleans drinking establishment, the Imperial Cabinet. Mr. Ramos believed the success of the drink depended on the shaking and employed young boys who stood behind the bar doing nothing but shaking the Gin Fizzes—it is said that during the 1915 Mardi Gras the Imperial Cabinet used 35 boys to keep up with the orders for this delightful drink. The fizz shouldn't be made in big batches, although you can make 2 at once. The recipe is for one drink.

2 tablespoons lemon juice,
  preferably fresh
2 ounces (⅛ cup) gin
1 teaspoon confectioners' sugar
1 egg white
2 tablespoons whipping cream
2 ounces (⅛ cup)
  cold club soda

Combine the lemon juice, gin, and sugar in a mixing glass and stir until the sugar is dissolved. Add the egg white, cream, and 4 or 5 ice cubes. Shake vigorously. (Mr. Ramos's shakers kept at it for 5 minutes.) Strain into a glass. Rinse the shaker with cold club soda and pour into the drink.

Variations: If you happen to have some cold champagne about, you can make a *French 75*, named for a powerful World War I gun. Substitute champagne for the soda and sip one of the world's finest drinks. If you use the entire egg in the Ramos Fizz, you have a *Golden Fizz*. Omit the egg altogether and the club soda; add a dash of grenadine and you have a *Magnolia Blossom*.

Scarlett O'Hara

This easy oldie, featuring Dixie's own *Southern Comfort*, is custom-made for sipping on the veranda—or any shady reasonable facsimile.

6 ounces *Southern Comfort*
6 ounces cranberry juice
1 fresh lime, quartered

Pour equal parts (a jigger of each) over ice cubes in 4 old-fashioned glasses or whatever you have. Stir, squeeze a little lime in and then toss in the lime wedge, and serve.

Daiquiris by the Pitcher

Rum has been the companionable drink of travelers since Spanish galleons sailed the Southern coasts. Daiquiris, now the reigning favorite rum drinks, originated in Cuba, the invention of American engineers there after the Spanish-American War.

A sparkle of fresh juice gives this easy daiquiri recipe distinction. Daquiris vary in serving size from a standard 4-ounce cocktail on up to giant party-sized drinks popular in bars with a Carribean motif. Accordingly, this recipe makes anywhere from 1 to 10 drinks.

1 6-ounce container of frozen limeade concentrate
18 ounces light rum (use the empty concentrate container as a measure—3 cans of rum)
1 fresh lemon

In a large (2-quart) pitcher, mix limeade concentrate and rum. Squeeze the fresh lemon into the pitcher. Add ice cubes to fill the pitcher and stir thoroughly until the daiquiris are icy cold.

Derby Day Julep

If there were a mint blight, it is entirely possible that the Kentucky Derby would have to be postponed, so integral is the mint julep to the proper celebration of the occasion. But the mint julep is something of an event itself: it looks good, smells better, and tastes wonderfully fresh anywhere the ingredients are available on a hot summer day. Here's what you need to build 1 perfect julep*:

1 or 2 teaspoons confectioners' sugar
Several sprigs of fresh mint
2 jiggers (3 ounces) Kentucky bourbon
Fine crushed ice (try using a mouli grater, if you have one)

In a tall glass mix confectioners' sugar and a splash of cold water (about 1 tablespoon). Add all but a couple of the sprigs of fresh mint and, with a muddler or spoon, crush the mint into the sugar and water to make a syrup. Pack the glass firmly to the top with fine ice. Pour in bourbon and stir gently. To serve, add more crushed ice to bring the julep up to the top of the glass and insert 2 sprigs of mint and straws.

Note: Traditionally, a carefully made julep is served in a silver mug or crystal glass, either iced before the julep is mixed or afterwards (by placing the julep in the freezer for about 20 to 30 minutes). These and other niceties to prepare and preserve a frosty flawless haze on the serving glass seem to be more trouble than they're worth in an RV situation.

*Be advised that there is no part of a julep recipe not subject to controversy.

LIVING
ON
THE LAND

The Best and Freshest
of Each Region

FRUITS
OF THE LAND

Sampling the marvelous and often unfamiliar fruits of land and sea discovered en route can be one of the easiest and most delightful ways of adding a dimension of adventure to your travels.

To help you take advantage of the moveable feasting that can be yours, we have put together this roadside guide. Unless your memory is a whole lot better than ours, we don't expect you to remember all this advice your next time to the market or roadside stand. But we have compiled here, mostly from United States federal government publications, a wealth of information that may sometime be useful to have with you, along with some tips on what to do with just about anything that doesn't come with a label once you get it back to the RV.

Delicious any time of day, needing little or no preparation, and offering a grand tour of eating adventures, nothing symbolizes the advantages of the RV life better than a bowl of luscious fresh fruit. It may be only hours from the tree, bush, or vine, the best and freshest the area has to offer. It may be from far off lands and now at its peak, waiting to be enjoyed in a remote wilderness region. Fruits are living on the land at its best.

Here are some tips on selecting and serving some of the familiar and unfamiliar fruits of the land that you may encounter in our country's fruit stands. But they are by no means all. Just about the time you think you've tried everything, you'll discover some new variety or old little-known exotic, many of which are grown in America.

Apples

For good eating as fresh fruit, the commonly available varieties are: Delicious, McIntosh, Stayman, Golden Delicious, Jonathan, and Winesap. For making pies, use tart or slightly acid varieties such as Gravenstein, Grimes Golden, Jonathan, and Newtown. For baking, the firmer-fleshed varieties—Rome Beauty, Northern Spy, Rhode Island Greening, Winesap, and York Imperial—are usually used. Look for firm, crisp, well-colored apples.

Apricots

Most fresh apricots are marketed in June and July, but a limited supply are available in the larger cities during December and January. Domestic apricots are grown principally in California, Washington, and Utah.

Choose apricots that are plump and juicy looking, with a uniform, golden-orange color. Apricots should be mature when picked. As they ripen they will yield to gentle pressure on the skin.

Avocados

Avocados—grown in California and Florida—are available all year. Two general types and a number of varieties of each are grown. Depending upon type and variety, avocados vary greatly in shape, size, and color. Most tend to be pear shaped, but some are almost spherical. Fruits weighing under ½ pound are most commonly available. Some have a rough or leathery-textured skin, while others have a smooth skin. The skin color of most varieties is some shade of green, but certain varieties turn maroon, brown, or purplish-black as they ripen. None of these variations affect flavor.

For immediate use look for avocados which yield to a gentle pressure on the skin. Firm fruits

that do not yield to the squeeze test should be left at room temperature to ripen. Avoid avocados with dark sunken spots or cracked or broken surfaces.

Peeled avocados can be eaten plain, lightly dressed with lemon or lime and salt, mashed for dips and guacamoles, sliced into fruit or vegetable salads, or as half shells for salads and creamed dishes.

Bananas

Unlike most other fruits, bananas develop their best eating quality after they are harvested. This allows them to be shipped great distances, and almost our entire supply of bananas—available the year round—is imported from Central and South America. Bananas are sensitive to cold: don't refrigerate. Best eating bananas are solid yellow specked with brown, but slightly greener bananas are better for cooking.

Berries

Blueberries

Fresh blueberries are on the market from May through September. Generally, the large berries are cultivated varieties, and the smaller berries are the wild varieties.

Look for a dark blue color with a silvery bloom, your best indication of quality. This silvery bloom is a natural, protective waxy coating. Pick blueberries that are plump and firm.

There are a number of delightful ways of sweetening a bowl of fresh blueberries: cream and sugar, Marsala and confectioners' sugar, softened pineapple sherbet, and brown sugar and sour cream (a New England favorite).

Cranberries

A number of varieties of fresh cranberries are marketed in large volume from September through January. They differ considerably in size and color but are not identified by variety names in most markets and do not differ much in flavor. Cranberries, which grow in bogs, can be found growing in the wild in several parts of the country, notably the New England seashore and the Northwest.

Look for plump, firm berries with a luscious color. Discard soft, spongy, or leaky berries.

Although cranberries are usually cooked before eating, a sprightly *Fresh Cranberry-Orange Relish* can be made by finely chopping 2 cups of fresh cranberries and 1 unpeeled orange and mixing them with about a cup of sugar.

To make a simple cooked *Cranberry Sauce*: Combine 2 cups of cranberries, 1 cup sugar, and ½ cup of water in a saucepan and bring to a boil. Reduce heat and simmer uncovered for 4 or 5 minutes, stirring now and then, until the cranberries begin to pop. Spoon into a refrigerator container and chill for 2 or 3 hours until firm and cool.

Raspberries, Blackberries, and Kin

Most of the common raspberry-like berries, though they differ from one another in shape and color, are selected and used similarly. These popular berries include raspberries, luscious berries that are characteristically red, but also available in other colors; blackberries, large black or dark-purple berries; boysenberries, a very large black berry that is a cross between a blackberry and a raspberry; dewberries, a variety of blackberry; loganberries, a red berry that is like a cross between a dewberry and a raspberry; and youngberries, a large reddish-black berry that is a cross between a blackberry and a southern dewberry. They are all available in the summer.

Look for bright, clean berries with uniform good color for the species. Berries should be plump and tender but not mushy or leaky. Look for berries that are fully ripe, with no attached stem caps. If you are picking these berries, the ripe ones almost fall in your hand, if you have to tug, they aren't ready.

Incidentally, mulberries, a berrylike purplish-red fruit that grows on mulberry trees, can be used like blackberries.

Strawberries

First shipments of strawberries come from southern Florida in January, and then production increases, gradually spreading north and west into many parts of the country before tapering off in the fall. Strawberries are in best supply in May and June.

Wild strawberries, unlike many other wild berry counterparts, are often better than cultivated berries—fragrant and tender. Look for berries with a full, red color and a bright luster, firm flesh, and the cap stem still attached.

Strawberries are such an all-American favorite that their arrival at the local market is cause for an occasion— strawberry socials, an old American tradition, are among the more formal recognitions of the strawberry's popularity; having a few friends over for shortcake is one of the most relaxed. Sugared strawberries and a little cream sandwiched between hot biscuits make *Camper's Shortcake*. A few strawberries dropped in a couple of glasses of champagne make a *Honeymoon Duet* for romantic interludes. But it's hard to improve on a perfect strawberry dipped in sugar.

A Note on Wild Berries

Sooner or later there are going to be some berries right outside your window just beckoning to be picked. We wish we could tell you whether you should, and what to do with them if they are good ones, but that is beyond the scope of this book. Our best advice is to inquire locally, securing permission and guidance at the same time. Park rangers and camp hosts make it a point to know about the local plants, and often there are local publications. One such leaflet on the Principal Berries of Provincial Parks in British Columbia gives some useful cautions:

> Berries are not always either edible or poisonous. Many fall somewhere between, being either disagreeable in taste or containing substances which make some people ill.... It is impossible to make absolute distinctions, because what tastes good to one person may taste horrible to another.... No native berry is known to be highly poisonous. The same cannot be said of garden berries, and we emphasize that some garden kinds are poisonous. It is reasonably safe to say that native berries that taste pleasant will also prove non-toxic. The doubtful or poisonous kinds are distasteful to most people.

Once you know what you are dealing with, fill your pail and have fun. Choose and use the ordinary recognizable sweet wild berries—strawberries, blueberries, blackberries, raspberries—as you would their cultivated counterparts. Huckleberries are used like blueberries. Tart wild berries like the small red currants and large green gooseberries—and their cultivated counterparts—can be used like cranberries.

If you want to, you can use the beach plum *Beach Jam* recipe for most wild berries. Though some don't quite jell, they will make a nice fruit sauce. Some berries will need more sugar.

Carambolas

Carambolas are among the exotic fruits grown in Florida that are good eaten plain and fresh. Carambolas are available during the early fall and winter. Look for carambolas that are bright yellow.

To eat carambolas, simply wash and slice. They make beautiful stars when cut crosswise and are very decorative in fruit salads and trays. The whole carambola is eaten, including skin and seeds.

Cherimoyas

Sometimes called "sherbet fruit" because of its texture when chilled, the cherimoya is a tropical fruit available from midwinter to spring. It is an unusual looking fruit with a thick green armored skin and a custard-soft creamy flesh that resembles a mixture of banana and pineapple.

Look for large olive-colored cherimoyas. They are ripe when they yield to gentle pressure; eat as soon as possible. To remove the peel from a cherimoya, halve and scoop out the flesh with a spoon. Or serve on the half or quarter shell with a spoon. Discard the seeds as you are eating.

Cherries

Excellent as dessert fruit, most sweet cherries found in the markets are produced in our Western states and are available from May through August. Bing, Black Tartarian, Schmidt, Chapman, and Republican varieties range from deep maroon or mahogany red to black. Lambert cherries are dark red. For cooking, the tart, lighter red pie cherries, Kentish and Montmorency, are used fresh, frozen, or canned. Most of the Montmorency red cherries come from Michigan. Look for bright, glossy, plump-looking surfaces, fresh-looking stems, and good color.

For a delicious old-fashioned treat made with fresh sweet cherries, try *Shaker Sweet Cherry Sandwiches* made with white bread spread with a mixture of crushed pitted cherries, chopped almonds, sugar, and a bit of lemon juice.

Dates

The ancient fruit of the date palm tree, dates have been grown in America since the 1890s. California is the main source of the dates available in the market. Most of the packaged dates you find in stores are fresh, not dried fruit—they are picked in a fully ripe, almost candied stage. Depending on the variety, dates can be gold to black. The most common varieties are Deglet Noor, Halawy, Black Abbada, Zahidi, and Medjhool—all originally from the Middle East and North Africa. Dates are available all year. Look for dates that are soft, plump, and shiny. Keep them in the refrigerator.

Dates are good as a natural candy, plain or stuffed; cut up into fruit salads; or added to sweet potatoes or baked goods. If you have a blender, try making a *Date Shake*, a Southern California treat: Use about a cup of pitted dates, a cup of milk, and a pint of vanilla ice cream. (Blend the dates and part of the milk until they are fairly smooth before adding the rest of the milk and ice cream.)

Figs

Fresh figs are very perishable and difficult to transport but are sometimes available in California, where they are grown, and in some other markets from June to October. Fresh ripe figs range in color from yellow to purple or black depending on the variety—Calimyrna, greenish-yellow; Black

Mission, almost black; Kadota, light yellow; Brown Turkey, reddish-brown; and Adriatic, yellow or greenish.

Look for figs that are firm but that yield slightly to pressure and are the correct ripe color for the variety. Avoid figs with a sour odor: they are overripe. Keep fresh figs refrigerated.

Fresh figs are eaten entirely, including the skin and seeds. If you prefer to peel figs, make a small cut in the skin near the stem and pull the skin away in strips. Fresh figs are such a delicacy, they are seldom cooked. Figs are good sliced with sweet or sour cream or with lemon or lime juice. Or serve chilled figs wrapped in thin slices of prosciutto or other ham as an appetizer. Another tasty appetizer is broiled bacon-wrapped figs, though we feel better about doing that to canned Kadota figs than to fresh ones.

Grapefruit

Grapefruit is available all year, with most abundant supplies from January through May. While Florida is the major source of fresh grapefruit, there also is substantial production in Texas, California, and Arizona. Several varieties are marketed, but the principal distinction at retail is between those which are "seedless" (having few or no seeds) and the "seeded" type. Another distinction is color of flesh; white-fleshed fruit is most common, but pink or red-fleshed varieties are becoming increasingly available.

Grapefruit is picked "tree ripe" and is always ready to eat when you buy it in the store. Look for firm, well-shaped fruits, heavy for their size; these are usually the best eating.

Grapes

Most table grapes available in the market are of the European type, grown principally in California. Only small quantities of Eastern-grown American-type grapes are sold for table use. Common varieties of European types are Thompson seedless (an early green grape), Tokay and Cardinal (early bright-red grapes), and Emperor (a late deep-red grape). These are all excellent grapes for your fruit bowl. American-type grapes are softer and juicier. The outstanding variety, for flavor, of the American-type is the Concord, which is blue-black when fully matured. Delaware and Catawba are also popular.

Look for well-colored, plump grapes that are firmly attached to the stem. White or green grapes are sweetest when the color has a yellowish cast or straw color, with a tinge of amber. Red varieties are better when good red predominates on all or most of the berries.

Guavas

A tropical fruit that grows in Hawaii, Florida, and Southern California, guavas are used extensively to make jams, jellies, and juice. But guavas are also good as a fresh eating fruit when they are available. There are several varieties, which range from green to yellow-red and can be various shapes from round to pear-shaped. Some varieties are known by their flavor resemblance to other fruits—strawberry guava, pineapple guava.

Look for firm, unblemished fruit. Guavas are ripe for eating fresh when they yield to gentle pressure. To prepare guavas for eating plain or in fruit salads, peel and discard seeds.

Kiwi Fruit

A New Zealand fruit covered with a fuzzy brown skin like its namesake, it has a bright green flesh that tastes a little like strawberry. It is available almost year round in some markets.

Look for firm unblemished fruit. Ripe kiwis yield to gentle pressure; they will ripen at room temperature. Refrigerate when ripe.

To serve kiwis, peel and slice horizontally. The ring of tiny edible black seeds make the kiwi slices decorative additions to fruit salads. Kiwis seem to be especially compatible with strawberries. Try mixing the two with a little sugar and lime or lemon juice for a brunch fruit dish.

Kumquats

Kumquats are small citrus fruits originally grown in China and Japan, available fresh in the winter. Look for perfect fruit, since kumquats are eaten whole. The skin is sweet, the flesh tart. These "miniature oranges" make pretty garnishes and delightful additions to a Christmas fruit wreath.

Lemons

Most of the country's commercial lemon supply comes from California and Arizona and is available the year round. Look for lemons with a rich yellow color, fairly smooth-textured skin with a light gloss, and those which are firm and heavy.

If you want to do something impressive and easy with whole lemons—and happen to have a jar of caviar (don't you always?)—make *Caviar Lemons*: Slice a little piece off the bottom of each lemon so it will stand, slice the top off, and slightly hollow the lemon. Fill lemons with caviar and serve with club crackers.

Somewhat more pedestrian uses for fresh lemons ideal for the RV's close quarters are as a pleasant air freshener and, reputedly, an effective insect repellent: just leave freshly cut lemon peel exposed to the air.

Limes

Most green limes sold in markets (sometimes called Persian or Tahitian limes) are produced in Florida. The smaller yellow (or Key) limes, which are juicier, tarter, and more acid, are also grown in Florida but seldom shipped elsewhere. Look for limes with glossy skin and heavy weight for the size.

Limes can be used interchangeably with lemons in many beverages, desserts, and seafood dishes that call for wedges or slices of either. Limes are especially nice for adding sparkle to Gulf shellfish, melons, avocados, and tropical fruit salads.

Lime juice, which is also available in plastic containers and bottles, can be used like lemon juice to protect bananas and other cut fruits from discoloration.

Mangoes

Mangoes are a versatile tropical fruit that are sometimes compared to cling peaches, though they are much larger. They are grown in Florida and Hawaii and are available on the market throughout the summer.

Look for mangoes with a smooth skin even though they may still be green. The shape and size vary widely but larger mangoes are more delicate. Mangoes ripen at room temperature to yellowish or reddish and may have speckles; when they yield to gentle pressure they are ripe and ideal for eating raw.

Mangoes may be used in most peach recipes but are good plain. To serve, peel the mango lengthwise and cut lengthwise away from the pit. They are very juicy—there's an old saying that the best way to eat a mango is over the sink.

Melons

According to the United States Department of Agriculture, "Selection of melons for quality and flavor is difficult—challenging the skill of even the most experienced buyer. No absolute formula exists . . ." Now doesn't that make you feel better? Maybe you thought you were the only one who didn't know the magic secrets of the thumping and sniffing that goes on around the melon stands. The following tips *might* help you pick the best of the most common melons.

Cantaloupes

Cantaloupes, generally available from May through September, are produced principally in California, Arizona, and Texas, and some are imported early in the season.

Look for the three major signs of full maturity: the stem should be gone, leaving a smooth, sunken stem end; the netting, or veining, should be thick, coarse, and corky; and the color between the netting should have changed to a yellowish rather than greenish color. A *ripe* cantaloupe will have a pleasant odor and will yield slightly when pressed on the blossom end.

Seeded cantaloupe halves are good for stuffing with main course salads, fruit salads, or a scoop of cottage cheese or ice cream. Wedges are good anytime by themselves or as dippers with fruit dips.

Casabas

This sweet, juicy melon is normally pumpkin-shaped with a tendency to be pointed at the stem end. It is not netted but has shallow irregular furrows running from stem end toward the blossom end. The rind is hard with a light green or yellow color. The stem does not separate from the melon and must be cut at harvest. The casaba melon season is from July to November; they are produced in California and Arizona.

Look for ripe melons with a gold yellow rind color and a slight softening at the blossom end. Casabas have no odor or aroma. Serve like other melons.

Honey Balls

The honey ball melon is very similar to the honey dew melon, except that it is much smaller, very round, and slightly and irregularly netted over the surface. Select as you would a honey dew melon.

Honey Dews

The outstanding flavor of honey dews makes them highly prized as a dessert fruit. The melon is large (4 to 8 pounds), bluntly oval in shape, and generally very smooth with only occasional traces of netting. The rind is firm and ranges from creamy white to creamy yellow, depending on the stage of ripeness. The stem does not separate from the fruit and must be cut at harvest.

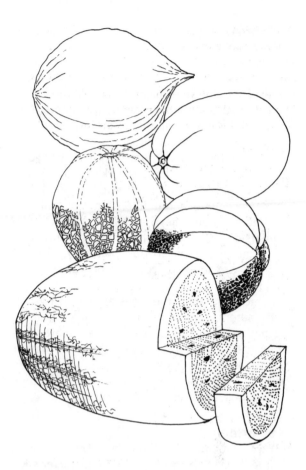

Honey dews are available to some extent almost all year round, due in part to imports. Chief sources, however, are California, Arizona, and Texas—with the most abundant supplies available from July through October. Look for maturity, shown by a soft, velvety feel, and for ripeness, shown by a slight softening at the blossom end, a faint pleasant aroma, and a yellowish-white to creamy rind color.

Honey dew wedges are good alone, sprinkled with lime, or topped with berries. A particularly elegant appetizer is chilled honey dew wedges wrapped in thinly sliced prosciutto (Italian ham).

Persian Melons

Persian melons resemble cantaloupes but are more nearly round, have finer netting, and are about the same size as honey dews. The flesh is thick, fine-textured, and orange-colored. Grown primarily in California, they are available in fair supply in August and September. Look for the same signs of quality and ripeness as described for cantaloupes.

Watermelons

Although watermelons are available from early May through September, they are *the* summertime fruit. Judging the quality of a watermelon is very difficult unless it is cut in half.

In cut melons, look for firm, juicy flesh with good red color and seeds that are dark brown or black. In uncut melons, look for a watermelon that is relatively smooth and neither shiny nor dull, and the melon should have a creamy-colored belly (underside). Go ahead and thump if you like, a ripe one is supposed to "plunk" instead of "plink"—provided, of course, you can tell the difference.

Some less common melons are fun to try too: baby watermelons seem sized for an RV; yellow-fleshed watermelons taste the same but are visually exciting; and, to celebrate the 212th day of Christmas, Santa Claus melons are ideal. (They used to be available only in the winter, but we have run across them in midsummer.)

Nectarines

This fruit, available from June through September from California, combines characteristics of both the peach and the plum and can be used like either.

Look for rich color and plumpness and a slight softening along the "seam" of the nectarine. Most varieties have an orange-yellow color (ground color) between the red areas, but some varieties have a greenish ground color. Bright-looking fruits which are firm to moderately hard will probably ripen normally within two to three days at room temperature.

Oranges

California, Florida, Texas, and Arizona produce our year-round supply of oranges. Leading varieties from California and Arizona are the Navel and the Valencia. The Navel orange has a thicker, easier-to-peel skin than the Valencia, and the segments separate easily. It is ideally suited for eating whole or as segments in salads. The western Valencia orange is excellent either for juicing or for slicing in salads.

Florida and Texas crops include the Valencia, Parson Brown, Hamlin, and the Pineapple Orange, a high-quality orange good for eating whole. The Florida Temple orange, like the Navel, peels easily, separates into segments readily, and has excellent flavor. Look for firm and heavy oranges with fresh bright-looking skin which is reasonably smooth for the variety. Skin color is unimportant to flavor.

Papayas

Sometimes called a tropical papaw, sometimes called a tree melon, the papaya is actually a berry, though it resembles a pear-shaped melon more in size, flavor, use, and character. The papayas on the market are grown mostly in Hawaii and Florida and are available all year. Look for a soft, medium-sized, smooth papaya. The skin will be predominately yellow when it is ripe, and it will yield to gentle pressure.

To serve a papaya, peel, halve, and scrape the seeds out. Eat papayas plain with a squeeze of lemon or lime, fill them with salads (especially good with seafood salads), or cut in chunks or balls to add to fruit salads.

Peaches

A great many varieties of peaches are grown, but only an expert can distinguish one from another. They fall into two general types: free-stone (flesh readily separates from the pit) and clingstone (flesh clings tightly to the pit). Free-stones are usually preferred for eating fresh or for freezing, while clingstones are used primarily for canning.

Look for peaches which are fairly firm or becoming a trifle soft. The skin color between the red areas (ground color) should be yellow or at least creamy.

It's hard to improve on a fresh peach, though countless recipes for cobblers, pies, and compotes try. Some simple classics to try if you have a windfall are *Peaches in Cream* made with softened vanilla ice cream and peeled sliced peaches; *Champagne Peach Bowl* made by pricking a perfect peach several times and putting it into a goblet with enough chilled champagne to cover (in lieu of a goblet, which we seldom travel with, any peach-size cup or glass will do); and *Peaches in*

Marsala made by chilling peeled peach halves in cream Marsala. The latter is such a favorite of ours that we travel with a small bottle of Marsala just for this recipe—which can also be used with canned peaches: just replace the can juice with cream Marsala and put the can in the refrigerator for a few hours. A very nice finishing touch for Peaches in Marsala is a dusting of nutmeg.

Pears

The most popular variety of pear is the Bartlett, mainly produced in California, Washington, and Oregon, available from early August through November. Several popular fall and winter varieties of pear are grown in the same area—Anjou, Bosc, Winter Nellis, and Comice. There are *many* other varieties of pears which are also delicious.

Look for firm pears of all varieties. The best color depends on variety. For Bartletts, look for a pale yellow to rich yellow color; Anjou or Comiel—light green to yellowish green; Bosc—greenish yellow to brownish yellow; Winter Nellis—medium to light green. Pears will ripen at room temperature, and they will be slightly soft when ready to eat.

Though there are many delightful uses for raw pears (team some of the less common varieties with cheese for a continental dessert). They are also good baked like apples or poached in wine or cream—until tender.

Persimmons

Persimmons grown in California are sweet, plumlike Asian fruits that look somewhat like heart-shaped tomatoes. Two varieties are available, the Hachiya and the Fuyu. Cultivated persimmons are good eaten raw if they are ripe. They are available on the market in late fall and early winter. A different kind of persimmon grows wild in the eastern states; it is good in preserves and puddings but is not eaten as a dessert fruit.

Look for market persimmons that are plump and smooth with the stem attached. Persimmons will ripen at room temperature. Persimmons *must* be ripe to taste good: Hichiyas will be a deep orange-red and will feel soft when squeezed; Fuyus will be the same rich glossy color but will be slightly firm when ripe. Once they are ripe, eat the persimmons immediately.

Persimmons are eaten whole, including the skin; they are almost jelly-like. For a fun, decorative presentation make *Persimmon Stars*: Score the skin from the tip almost to the base at several equal intervals; place the persimmon base-down on the plate and peel down each section of skin into points around the persimmon. You can get fancier by sprinkling it with a tablespoon of fruit-flavored brandy.

Pineapples

Pineapples are available all year but are most abundant March through June. Hawaii, Puerto Rico, and Mexico are principal suppliers. There are several varieties from the very small sugar pineapple (4 to 6 inches long) to the conical Brazilian pineapple (12 to 14 inches long).

A mature green pineapple will turn to golden yellow, orange yellow, or reddish brown, depending on the variety, within a few days at room temperature. Many are already fully colored when you find them in the market; delivery to market is timed so that they are near their peak of sweetness.

Look for bright color, fragrant pineapple odor, and pineapples that are firm, plump, and heavy for their size—the larger the fruit, the greater the proportion of edible flesh. The pineapple will be a little soft at the bottom when it is ripe.

Plums

There are more than a dozen varieties of plums marketed in the summer. Some common varieties are the Santa Rosa, a good-eating red plum with yellow flesh; the greengage, a green-yellow plum with yellow flesh good for baking; the Kelsey, a large yellow plum with yellow flesh, juicy but bland; and the small blue-black Italian prune plum, which comes in late summer and is good for baking (this is the kind commonly dried to make prunes). Damson plums are small, purple cooking plums that may grow wild. Beach plums are a wild native plum that grow in the East from Virginia on up the coast and around the Great Lakes; they are not good raw but make a tasty jam or jelly which is sold in the region.

Since plums, like the other fruits in their family, are fairly fragile, often locally grown varieties are best. Look for ripe fruit with good color—ripe plums yield to gentle pressure. (The Kelsey will ripen if bought green.)

To prepare any of the plums that are eaten as dessert fruit, just wash and serve—the skin is good. To add plums to fruit salads or to use them in baking, halve the plums and pit.

If you happen to come by some beach plums and want to do *something* with them, make *Beach Jam*: Combine 1 part washed pitted beach plums, 1 part sugar, 1 part water in a large saucepan; simmer over medium heat, stirring frequently, until very thick and syrupy (15 minutes or more). Test with a spoon: when it drops a drop at a time, it's done. Cool and use like ordinary jam or as ice cream topping (keep refrigerated).

Pomegranates

Pomegranates are an ancient tropical fruit. They are the principal flavor of grenadine. Pomegranates from California are available in markets in the fall. Look for deep-red large pomegranates with smooth unbroken skin.

The edible parts of the pomegranate are the seeds and their surrounding jelly-like red pulp. To get at the seeds, cut away the skin or quarter the fruit; scoop the seed clusters out of the membrane. Pomegranate seeds make beautiful jewel-like additions to various salads and desserts or can be eaten with a spoon.

Prickly Pears

This unusual fruit that grows on a cactus is fun to try. Prickly pears or cactus pears are grown in desert areas of the Southwest and are occasionally available in markets from midsummer to midwinter. Depending on the variety, their flesh may be either yellow or magenta.

Look for firm pears with a yellow to reddish color. They may have very sharp, fine spines, which are usually removed before marketing—but beware.

To eat a prickly pear either peel and slice or peel back the skin and eat with a spoon as you would a small melon—its flavor is often compared to watermelon (and you have to deal with the seeds similarly).

Tangelos

Tangelos are a cross between a tangerine and grapefruit, resembling a tangerine but juicier and slightly more difficult to peel. They are available in the same season as tangerines, and they are selected and used the same way.

Tangerines

Tangerines belong to a family of small Chinese oranges with loose, easy-to-peel skins—the mandarins. Other members of the family are the satsumas, the type of mandarin orange found in cans.

Florida is the chief American source of tangerines. Considerable quantities of tangerines and similar types of oranges are produced in California and Arizona, some in Texas, and a few are imported. Tangerines are available throughout the winter.

Look for deep yellow or orange color and a bright luster as your best sign of fresh, mature, good-flavored tangerines. Juicy fruits are heavy for their size.

Ugli Fruit

This fruit that lives up to its name looks like a lumpy grapefruit, one of its parents (the other parent is a tangerine). Ugli fruits are sweeter than grapefruits and easier to peel and section. They are available in late fall and early winter.

Look for fruits that aren't obviously blemished (mottling is natural) and that are heavy for their size. Use ugli fruit like grapefruit (but serve it in segments).

Artichokes to Zucchini

VEGETABLE STAND NEXT STOP

We can almost hear you now: "Trying the strange beautiful fruits of America may be an adventure, experimenting with fresh seafoods may be an adventure, but no one is going to tell me a parsnip is an adventure." Maybe not, but how about eating a delicious thistle, an ancient Aztec favorite, or a cactus pad if you never have? (Try artichokes, jicama, and nopales.)

Still, most of us don't look forward to eating our peas with quite the enthusiasm we reserve for strawberries and steaks—unless, perhaps, they are the tender first peas of spring just hours from the garden.

And nothing expresses quite as well the way Americans are eating today as the salad bar—for RVers, every day is a salad day, and every roadside stand is a salad bar.

And what a deal! You can sample everything on the stand, throw half away when you're full or if it doesn't suit you, and still come out ahead of a stop at a fastfood restaurant. Maybe there's more adventure to vegetables than you thought?

Artichokes

The globe artichoke is the large, unopened flower bud of a plant belonging to the thistle family. Produced only in California, artichokes are shipped in limited amounts most of the year, but the peak of the crop comes in April and May.

Look for plump, globular artichokes that are heavy in relation to size and compact with thick, green, fresh-looking scales (the leaf-like parts). Size is not important in relation to quality. See the recipe for *Monterey Bay Artichokes*.

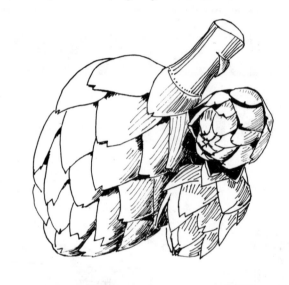

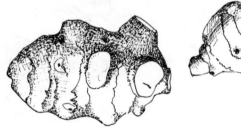

Note: The misnamed Jerusalem artichoke is the tuber of the American sunflower plant, unrelated to the artichoke but resembling it in flavor. Jerusalem artichokes can be served raw in salads—wash, peel, and slice. Or cook the slices in a small amount of boiling salted water in a covered saucepan until tender (about 10 to 15 minutes); serve with lemon-butter or cheese sauce. (Jerusalem artichokes discolor rapidly after peeling; to prevent that, dip the slices in cold water mixed with a little vinegar.) Sunchoke is a new marketing name for Jerusalem artichoke.

Asparagus

Considered by many a harbinger of spring and a tonic, fresh asparagus is the kind of roadstand treat you won't want to pass up. California, New Jersey, Washington, and Michigan are the chief sources of asparagus, available from mid-February through June, with peak supply from April to June. Very little is available after the end of June.

Look for closed, compact tips, smooth round spears, and a fresh appearance. A rich green color should cover most of the spear. Stalks should be tender almost as far down as the green extends.

To prepare, wash very thoroughly—sand often gets lodged in the scales. Snap the bottom off each spear wherever it breaks naturally, and discard. Cook asparagus spears in a covered saucepan or skillet until tender (10 to 13 minutes, less if you are using as a salad). Serve hot with lemon-butter or hollandaise sauce or cold, marinated in a vinaigrette or Italian dressing.

Beans

Snap beans, produced commercially in many states, are available throughout the year. Most beans found in the market will be the common green podded varieties, but large green pole beans and yellow wax beans are occasionally available.

Look for a fresh, bright appearance with good color for the variety. Get young, tender beans with pods in a firm, crisp condition.

To prepare, wash the beans, cut off the ends, and pull off the strings. Use beans whole, in short pieces, or sliced in long diagonal strips (French-style). Cook the beans in a small amount of salted boiling water in a covered saucepan until tender (13 to 15 minutes for 1-inch pieces; 20 to 25 minutes for whole).

For a pot of green snap beans with an Italian accent, replace the salted water with a jar of spaghetti sauce and proceed as above, adding water if needed. If you add some well-browned Italian sausage, it is a main dish.

Snap beans are good with basil, dill, marjoram, mint, oregano, savory, tarragon, or thyme.

Note: There are a large number of other bean varieties popular in America. Most are sold dried and require considerable preparation time, making them impractical for the RV cook. Fortunately, the favorite varieties are available precooked in cans or bottles—ideal for RV dining. Some beans eaten shelled—for example, lima beans—are sold fresh. Fresh shelled beans can be cooked like snap beans in salted boiling water until tender.

Bean Sprouts

The delicate shoots of various seeds and legumes—mung beans, alfalfa, wheat—have become a familiar addition to American salads and sandwiches. They are available all year since they can be grown anywhere (even in an RV!)

Look for sprouts that are crisp and fresh-looking, especially the tips. Alfalfa and wheat sprouts should be bright green; bean sprouts should be plump and white. Keep sprouts refrigerated.

To serve, rinse and pat dry with paper towels just before using them. The finer sprouts are especially good in tossed salads and layered with tomato and avocado in club sandwiches. Bean sprouts are also good raw, or cook them briefly with other vegetables in Oriental main dishes like stir-fried beef or sukiyaki.

Beets

Beets, available year round, are grown in most parts of the nation. Many beets are sold in bunches with the tops still attached (the tops can be used as greens).

Look for beets that are firm, smooth, round, a rich deep-red color, and with a slender tap root (the large main root).

To prepare, cut off the roots and most of the stems; wash well. If you are cooking the beets whole, don't bother to peel first. If you are cooking them sliced, cubed, or shredded, peel first. Cook the beets in salted boiling water until tender. Whole beets should be cooked in boiling water to cover for about 40 minutes then cooled and peeled. For sliced or cubed beets, use less water and cook for about 15 to 20 minutes. For shredded beets, cook about 10 minutes.

A variety of spices and herbs enhance beets: allspice, bay leaves, caraway seed, cloves, dill weed, ginger, savory, or thyme. They are also good just plain with butter. Or chill and toss with Italian dressing.

Note: Canned and bottled beets compare favorably in flavor with fresh cooked beets and under ordinary circumstances are a better idea than fresh for the RV cook.

Broccoli

A member of the cabbage family, and a close relative of cauliflower, broccoli is available throughout the year but—because broccoli grows better in cool weather—is least abundant in July and August. California is the heaviest producer, but Texas, New Jersey, Oregon, Florida, Pennsylvania, and other states produce large amounts of broccoli.

Look for a firm, compact cluster of small flower buds, with none opened enough to show the bright yellow flower. Bud clusters should be dark green or sage green—or even green with a decidedly purplish cast. Stems should not be too thick or tough.

To prepare, soak broccoli in cold salt water, trim off outer leaves, and slice into spears or just use the florets.

Broccoli florets can be used raw in tossed salads or with dips. Or cook these little "trees" in a small amount of salted boiling water in a covered saucepan until tender (about 5 to 8 minutes for florets; about 9 to 12 minutes for broccoli with split stalks). Serve with cheese sauce, hollandaise, or lemon-butter. A pinch of caraway seed, dill weed, or tarragon will enhance broccoli.

Brussels Sprouts

Another close relative of the cabbage, Brussels sprouts develop as enlarged buds on a tall stem, one sprout appearing where each main leaf is attached. Most Brussels sprouts are produced in California, New York, and Oregon, and some are imported. Although they are available about 10 months of the year, peak season is October through December.

Look for unblemished sprouts with a fresh, bright-green color, tight fitting outer leaves, and a firm body. Small sprouts are usually the best.

To prepare, trim off any wilted leaves and stems; soak in cold salted water briefly. If the sprouts are small and tender, you can include them raw in a tray of vegetable dippers.

Cook Brussels sprouts in a small amount of salted boiling water in a covered saucepan *just* until tender (about 15 minutes); try not to overcook. Small tender Brussels sprouts can also be cooked in a skillet with a little butter or oil. Brussels sprouts are good with crumbled bacon and various cheese sauces. Herbs that enhance Brussels sprouts are basil, caraway seeds, dill weed, sage, or thyme.

Cabbage

Three major groups of cabbage varieties are available: smooth-leaved green cabbage, crinkly-leaved green Savoy cabbage, and red cabbage. All types are suitable for any use, although the Savoy and red varieties are more in demand for use in slaws and salads.

Cabbage may be sold fresh (called "new" cabbage) or from storage (called "old" cabbage). New cabbage is available throughout the year, since it is grown in many states. In winter, California, Florida, and Texas market most new cabbage. Many northern states grow cabbage for late summer and fall shipment or to be held in storage for winter sale.

Look for firm or hard heads of cabbage that are heavy for their size. Outer leaves should be a good green or red color (depending on type), reasonably fresh, and free from serious blemishes. The outer leaves (called "wrapper" leaves) fit loosely on the head and are usually discarded, but too many loose wrapper leaves on a head cause extra waste.

Some early-crop cabbage may be soft or only fairly firm but is suitable for immediate use if the leaves are fresh and crisp. Cabbage out of storage is usually trimmed of all outer leaves and lacks green color but is satisfactory if not wilted or discolored.

Cooked cabbage dishes tend to be overwhelming in the RV and are not recommended. However, fresh cabbage salads and slaws are popular. Wash the head, quarter and core, and cut into shreds with a knife. Toss with your favorite slaw dressing. An old-time favorite is a simple dressing of cream with sugar and vinegar (½ cup whipping cream, 2 tablespoons each sugar and vinegar).

Caraway seed, celery seed, dill seed, savory, and tarragon are seasonings often added to cabbage slaws.

Carrots

Freshly harvested carrots are available the year round. California and Texas market most of them, but many other states produce large quantities. Young tender carrots are best for raw carrot sticks. Larger carrots are used primarily for cooking or shredding. In either case, don't eat any green "sunburned" areas.

Cook carrots, sliced or diced, in 1-inch salted boiling water in a covered saucepan until tender (about 10 to 20 minutes).

Carrots are good with allspice, bay leaves, caraway seed, dill seed, dill weed, mace, fennel, ginger, marjoram, mint, nutmeg, or thyme.

Glazed Carrots are a treat, especially with tiny whole "baby" carrots: Cook 1 pound of whole small carrots as above (they don't take too long because they are tender). In a skillet melt ¼ cup (½ stick) butter over medium-high heat; stir in 2 tablespoons of your choice of sugar, honey, frozen orange juice concentrate, *or* orange marmalade. Add the drained carrots, and cook, turning the carrots frequently, until shiny (about 5 minutes). Salt and pepper to taste.

Cauliflower

Though most abundant from September through January, cauliflower is available during every month of the year. California, New York, Oregon, Texas, and Michigan are major sources. The white, edible portion is called the curd.

Look for white to creamy-white, compact, solid, and clean unblemished curds. A slightly granular or "ricey" texture of the curd will not hurt the eating quality if the surface is compact.

To prepare, wash cauliflower and remove all the leaves and the stem. Cut or break cauliflower head into florets if desired. Cauliflower florets can be used raw in tossed salads or with dips. Or cook the cauliflower in a small amount of salted boiling water in a covered saucepan until *just* tender (about 8 to 12 minutes for florets; 20 to 24 minutes for whole).

Cauliflower is enhanced by cheese sauces and various seasonings—caraway seed, celery salt, dill seed, dill weed, mace, or tarragon.

Celery

Celery, a popular vegetable for a variety of uses, is available throughout the year. Production is concentrated in California, Florida, Michigan, and New York. Most celery is of the so-called "Pascal" type which includes thick-branched green varieties.

To prepare, wash and trim stalks. You can freshen celery somewhat by soaking the butt end in water for a few minutes. Serve fresh raw celery stalks plain, with salt, or with dips. Fill stalks with plain or flavored cheese spreads or have your children make *Ants on a Log* (peanut butter filled celery with raisins scattered along the top).

Chinese Cabbage

Primarily a salad vegetable, Chinese cabbage plants are elongated, with some varieties developing a firm head and others an open, leafy form. Look for fresh, crisp green plants that are free from blemishes or decay.

To prepare, wash and cut off the tough bottom part of the head. Slice or shred and add to slaws or mixed salads.

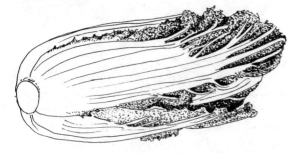

Cooked Chinese cabbage doesn't have the strong odor of ordinary cabbage. If you are stir-frying vegetables and have some on board, add a few leaves sliced into strips.

Note: Bok choy, another vegetable popular in Chinese recipes, is sometimes also called Chinese cabbage and is used in much the same way. Bok choy has long white stems and large dark green shiny leaves. Sometimes bok choy is called Chinese chard, and the leaves can be used like ordinary Swiss chard greens.

Corn

Sweet corn is available practically every month of the year, but is most plentiful from early May until mid-September. A large number of states produce sweet corn during the spring and summer; midwinter supplies generally come from south Florida. Most supplies are yellow-kernel corn, but some white corn is sold.

Corn should be refrigerated immediately after being picked and kept moist until used. Look for fresh husks with good green color, silk ends that are free from decay or worm injury, and stem ends that are not too discolored or dried. See *Perfect Corn on the Cob* and *Heartland Corn Roast*.

Cucumbers

Although cucumbers are produced at various times in many states—and imported during the colder months—the supply is most plentiful in the summer months when these cool-tasting vegetables are most welcome. Small cucumbers are usually made into pickles. There are a few special varieties of cucumbers you may find in the market in addition to the ordinary old-fashioned cucumbers—the English or Chinese cucumber, long, thin, rather elegant vegetables (the skin is so delicate is doesn't need to be peeled); and the apple or lemon cucumber, a small, pale-yellow, round cucumber.

Cucumbers are most usually used raw—peeled and cut into sticks or slices—in salads or with dips. Dill weed and cucumber is a classic combination. Add a pinch of dill weed to vinegar and oil or to yogurt or sour cream and toss with cucumber slices for a delightful cool summer salad. If you don't have dill weed, try crumbled mint or another salad herb.

Eggplant

Eggplant or aubergine is actually a very large berry that is a distant relative of potatoes, tomatoes, and peppers. Eggplant is most plentiful during the late summer, but is available all year to some extent. Look for firm, heavy, smooth, and uniformly dark purple eggplants (there is a light variety but it is seldom seen on the market).

Eggplant is often used in complex Meditarranean and Near Eastern recipes. One of the simplest recipes is *Egged Eggplant*: Peel eggplant, cut off the cap, and cut crosswise into ¼-inch slices. Generously salt and pepper slices. Dip slices into a beaten egg, and then into either crushed crackers or flour (you can add a few tablespoons of grated Parmesan cheese to the crumbs or flour). Cook eggplant slices in a skillet in a little hot oil until lightly browned and tender (about 2 minutes on each side).

For *Easy Eggplant Parmigiana*: Layer Egged Eggplant, cooked as above, in a baking pan with ½ cup grated Parmesan cheese, a 15½-ounce jar of spaghetti sauce, and 8 ounces of sliced or shredded mozzarella cheese. Bake at 400° until heated through and the cheese is melted and bubbly (about 20 minutes).

Greens

A large number of widely differing species of plants are grown for use as cooked "greens." The better known kinds are spinach, kale, collards, turnip greens, beet greens, chard or Swiss chard, mustard greens, broccoli leaves, chicory, endive, escarole, dandelion, watercress, and sorrel. Many others, some wild, are used as greens to a limited extent. Look for leaves that are fresh, young, tender, and free from blemishes and tiny insects.

How to cook greens is a matter of considerable debate, with time recommended for cooking ranging from a few minutes to a few hours—partly related to the maturity and variety of greens. If you are not already a fan of cooked greens, a vacation trip is probably not the time to try them. If you are, then you know how you and yours like them cooked.

Chicory, Endive, Escarole

These vegetables, used mainly in salads, are available practically all year round—but most abundantly in the winter and spring. Chicory or endive has narrow, notched edges and crinkly leaves resembling the dandelion leaf. Chicory plants often have "blanched" yellowish leaves in the center, these are preferred by many people. Escarole leaves are much broader and less crinkly then those of chicory.

Witloof or Belgian endive is a compact, cigar-shaped plant which is creamy white. The small shoots are kept from becoming green by being grown in complete darkness. Belgian (or French) endive is imported.

Look for freshness, crispness, tenderness, and a good green color of the outer leaves except in Belgian endive.

To prepare, remove any withered leaves, wash and dry leaves, and split lengthwise or tear into pieces. Add to mixed green salads or serve alone with a vinaigrette dressing. If you are using Belgian endive, cut out the bitter, conical core at the base.

Lettuce

Among the nation's leading vegetables, lettuce owes its prominence to the growing popularity of salads in our diets. It's available throughout the year, at various seasons, from California, Arizona, New York, New Jersey, Texas, Colorado, New Mexico, Wisconsin, and other states. Four types of lettuce are generally sold: iceberg, butter-head, romaine, and leaf.

Iceberg lettuce is the major group. Heads are large, round, and solid, with medium-green outer leaves and lighter green or pale-green inner leaves.

Butter-head lettuce, including the Big Boston and Bibb varieties, has a smaller head than iceberg. This type will be slightly flat on top and have soft, succulent, light-green leaves in a rosette pattern in the center.

Romaine lettuce plants are tall and cylindrical, with crisp, dark-green leaves in a loosely folded head.

Leaf lettuce includes many varieties—none with a compact head. Leaves are broad, tender, succulent, fairly smooth, and vary in color according to variety. It is grown mainly in greenhouses or on truck farms.

Spinach

Popeye's favorite has become a very popular salad green in mixed salads or starring on its own. Spinach can, of course, be cooked. But most Americans, at home and on the road, prefer to let someone else do the preparation of cooked spinach—frozen spinach is one of the most popular frozen vegetables.

Fresh spinach is available all year with peak season in April and May. Look for leaves that are large, crisp, fresh, and dark green. Keep refrigerated in a sealable plastic bag.

To prepare, trim off tough stems and immerse in a bowl of tepid water; lift out leaves and discard sandy water. Repeat until there's no sand in the bowl. Tear leaves into bite-size pieces and serve in a salad. See *Coronado Spinach Salad* for an especially good one.

A tasty way of cooking spinach is *Roman Spinach*: In a covered skillet, cook about a pound of trimmed and well-washed spinach leaves (in the water that is left on the leaves after washing) over medium heat until the leaves are tender and wilted. (Or substitute a 10-inch package of frozen spinach, cooked according to package directions). Drain off any liquid and pour ¼ cup of bottled Italian dressing over the spinach; fry briefly over high heat. Break in 3 eggs and scramble well with spinach. Cook until eggs are set (you may want to reduce heat if eggs seem to be cooking too fast). Salt and pepper to taste and sprinkle generously with grated Parmesan cheese.

Watercress

Watercress is a small, round-leaved plant that grows naturally (or may be cultivated) along the banks of freshwater streams and ponds. It is prized as an ingredient in mixed green salads and as a garnish because of its spicy flavor.

Look for watercress that is fresh, crisp, and rich green. To keep watercress fresh, put it in a sealable plastic bag with a little water and stand the bag up in the refrigerator so its "feet" stay wet.

Jicama

Jicama is a very old vegetable of the Americas that is new again. It is a brown tuber that looks somewhat like a turnip and tastes much like water chestnut. In Mexico it is used like a potato or eaten raw. Look for small jicama that are relatively free of blemishes. Choose and store like potatoes.

Raw peeled and sliced jicama is very good. We were introduced to jicama several summers ago in two dramatically different settings: served like sliced cucumbers with French dressing at a Mexican family picnic on the beach in Mazatlan, and included in a dazzling array of crudités with an appetizer dip at a garden party at the J. Paul Getty Museum. Both ways are well worth trying.

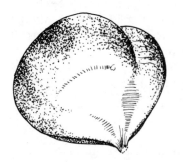

Kohlrabies

Kohlrabi (sometimes called cabbage turnip) looks like a root vegetable but develops above the ground. Kohlrabi leaves can be used as cooked greens. Kohlrabi is available throughout the summer and fall with peak supply in June and July. Look for fresh, crisp globes.

Kohlrabi is good raw in slaw, salads, or as a relish—peel off tough outer skin and slice. Thin slices can be added to sukiyaki or tempura or cooked in a small amount of boiling salted water in a covered pan until tender (about 25 minutes). Serve cooked kohlrabi tossed with sour cream or mashed.

Mushrooms

Grown in houses, abandoned mines, cellars, or caves, mushrooms are available the year round in varying amounts. Most come from Pennsylvania, but many are produced in California, New York, Ohio, and Illinois, as well as other states.

We usually describe mushrooms as having caps, the wide portion on top; gills, the numerous rows of paper-thin tissue seen underneath the cap when it opens; and a stem.

Look for young mushrooms that are small to medium in size for using raw; large mushrooms are good for cooking and stuffing. Caps should be either closed around the stem or moderately open with pink or light-tan gills. The surface of the cap should be white or creamy—or light brown if from some producing areas. See the index for various mushroom recipes.

Nopales

If you ever wonder what a cactus tastes like, try nopales—leaf-like cactus pads that can be eaten as a vegetable (they taste like firm green beans).

To prepare, carefully cut out the "eyes" with the thorns (use the tip of your potato peeler). Slice in thin strips or dice. Cook in boiling salted water to cover in a covered saucepan until tender but firm (about 10 minutes).

For *Nopales Mexicali*: Mix cooked drained nopales with an equal amount of mild picante sauce and heat through.

Okra

Okra is the immature seed pod of the okra plant, grown and marketed locally in southern states.

Look for small tender pods (the tips will bend with very slight pressure). They should be unblemished and have a bright green color.

Okra is used in various Southern specialties, especially gumbos and stews. A simple old-fashioned way of preparing okra by itself is known in Oklahoma as *Okie Okra*: Wash okra pods, cut off stems, and slice crosswise in ½-inch slices. Shake slices in salted flour or cornmeal or a combination of both. Meanwhile, fry a couple of slices of bacon in a skillet, remove the bacon. Cook the okra in the bacon fat over low heat until lightly browned (about 30 minutes), covering the skillet for the first half of the cooking.

Onions

George Washington's favorite vegetable, onions add flavor to many of America's favorite dishes, but tend to be overwhelming when cooked in an RV's close quarters. Consequently, we have tended to use them with limitations throughout this book—covering pans when onions are called for, substituting instant minced onion when possible (it doesn't require preparation). When you do want regular onions, there are a large variety to choose from.

Dried Onions, Shallots, and Garlic

Most onions, including bulbous yellow Spanish onions, yellow and white boiling onions, and large white Bermuda onions are dried or cured after harvesting, as are their pungent relatives garlic and shallots. Dried onions are available year round, with some seasonal variations.

Several onions are known as sweet onions—for example, Spanish onions, red Italian onions, Bermuda onions, Maui sweets, and Walla-Walla sweets—these are all good raw in salads or sandwiches.

Some of the sweet onions are special enough to deal with on their own: Washington's Walla-Walla onions are so sweet, local RVers claim to eat them like apples. Two local recipes worth trying are *Baked Walla-Walla Sweets*: Peel onions, cut in half, dot with butter and brown sugar, and bake in a baking pan in a 350° oven until soft (about 20 minutes).

For *Walla-Walla Onion and Cucumber Salad*: Slice onions and peeled cucumbers very thin; toss with sour cream.

Shallots are a prized member of the onion family with a flavor halfway between onion and garlic. They grow in cloves like garlic, are somewhat larger, and have a papery brown skin.

Garlic is the most potent member of the onion family with lots of legendary side effects. You're not likely to have vampires around—or anyone else—if you do much cooking with whole garlic cloves in the RV. Incidentally, the whole group of cloves is a head, the individual bulblets are the cloves.

Scallions and Leeks

Fresh onions include the small slender scallions, also called green onions (and sometimes mistakenly called shallots), and leeks, their large mild-flavored relatives. They are available year round, with a peak season in the summer.

Scallions, most usually eaten raw as a relish or chopped or sliced into salads, need only washing and trimming—slice off the root and most of the tops.

Leeks, much larger fresh onions, can be eaten raw but are more usually added to soups and stews. Wash thoroughly and trim as you would scallions but leave only an inch or so of the tops.

Peas

Perenially popular, peas are best when they are very fresh and young. General George Washington was nearly lured to his death by a plate of the first fresh peas of spring. Pea season begins in April and varies by region; they are grown extensively in Washington, Wisconsin, Minnesota, Oregon, Idaho, Delaware, and, as usual, California. Look for pods that are fresh, crisp, and bright green. Test a pod to see that the peas are small, bright, and tender.

Shell and wash fresh peas just before cooking. Cook in boiling salted water in a covered saucepan just until tender (about 10 minutes; less for young delicate peas, more for mature peas). Fresh black-eyed peas can be prepared the same way. Peas are enhanced by mint, thyme, chervil, basil, dill weed, savory, rosemary, marjoram, and chives.

Note: Fresh snow peas or Chinese pea pods are a delicacy, eaten pod and all. Look for flat crisp pods with the peas undeveloped. To prepare, wash and trim the ends. Serve raw as a vegetable dipper or in salads. Or stir-fry or steam *very* briefly, to retain crispness (1 or 2 minutes).

Peppers

There are several pepper varieties used in American cooking—green or red bell peppers; yellow or green banana; red, green or yellow chilies; cayenne and jalapeño peppers. Most of the peppers you'll find in the market, and the ones most commonly used, are the sweet green bell peppers. They are available in varying amounts throughout the year but are most plentiful during late summer. (Fully matured peppers of the same type have a bright-red color.)

In sweet green bell peppers, look for medium-

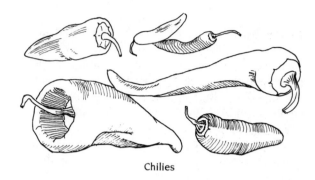

Chilies

to dark-green color, glossy sheen, and relatively heavy weight. Most of the hot peppers require special preparation and are not recommended for the RV cook.

Raw green bell pepper is good chopped in salads, cut in strips for vegetable dippers, or halved and stuffed. A nutritious Midwestern campers' snack is pepper wedges filled with plain or herbed cottage cheese.

Potatoes

For practical purposes, potatoes can be put into three groups, although the distinctions between them are not clear-cut, and there is much overlapping.

"New" potatoes is a term most frequently used to describe those freshly harvested and marketed during the late winter or early spring. The name is also widely used in later crop producing areas to designate freshly dug potatoes which are not quite fully matured. Best use of new potatoes is boiling or creaming. They vary widely in size and shape, depending upon variety, and are likely to display "skinning" or "feathering" of the outer layer of skin. This skinning usually affects only their appearance.

General purpose potatoes include the great majority offered for sale in the markets, both round and long types like the California Long White, also called the White Rose. They are amply available throughout the year. As the term implies, they are used for boiling, frying, and baking, although many of the common varieties are not considered to be best for baking.

Baking potatoes include the Russet Burbank, known as the Idaho potato whether or not it's grown in Idaho, a long variety with fine, scaly netting on the skin and the most widely grown and best known among this group.

Look for well-shaped, firm potatoes that are free from blemishes. Potatoes with large skinned and discolored areas are undesirable. Avoid sprouted potatoes and those with green color. The green portions, which contain the alkaloid solanin, may penetrate the flesh and make the potato bitter.

Note: Asparagus potatoes, also called Danish potatoes, are small, long, delicate potatoes that are cooked like new potatoes.

Radishes

Radishes, available the year round, are most plentiful from May through July. California and Florida produce most of our winter and spring supplies, while several northern states provide radishes the rest of the year. Radishes can be red or white.

Look for medium-size radishes (about an inch) that are plump, round, firm, and a good color for the variety.

Radish Flowers are an easy and attractive garnish: Wash the radish, trim off the top and the small tap root, and make four vertical cuts from the root end almost to the leaf end. Or after trimming, make several cuts in both directions from the root end almost to the leaf end. Place radishes in cold water in the refrigerator and leave for a few hours or overnight.

Note: Daikon (Japanese radish) is a large white radish, slightly hotter than ordinary radishes. It is often used in Oriental salads and soups or as a relish, for example, accompanying sashimi. Lo bok (Chinese turnip) resembles ordinary radishes in flavor and is used like daikon.

Rhubarb

There are fruits used like vegetables—tomatoes, eggplant—but rhubarb, sometimes called pie plant, is a vegetable used like a fruit in sweetened sauces and pies. Very limited supplies of rhubarb are available during most of the year, with most supplies available from January to June, when it is often used as an old-time spring tonic.

Look for fresh, firm rhubarb stems with a bright, glossy appearance. Stems should have quite a bit of pink or red on them.

To use rhubarb, cut off the leafy portions and discard—*they are poisonous*. Peel the stalks. For an old-fashioned spring treat, dip the tart stalks in sugar and eat raw. Or you can cook peeled and cut-up rhubarb along with other fruits such as strawberries.

Root Vegetables: Turnips, Rutabagas, Parsnips, Celeriac

Besides carrots, radishes, and beets, various less popular vegetables are cultivated for their roots, among them, turnips, rutabagas, parsnips, and celeriac or celery roots. They are all available mostly in the fall and winter. Root vegetables are sometimes called for in historic and ethnic American recipes but are not widely popular. There were various points in our history when they were lifesavers: 1894-1895 on the Cherokee Strip has been immortalized as the Year of the Turnip—"On turnips sure we nearly choked/Without those turnips we'd have croaked."

The most popular turnip has white flesh and a purple top. Rutabagas are somewhat larger than turnips and have yellow flesh. Parsnips look like large pale carrots. Celeriac are knobby brownish roots.

Look for turnips and celeriac that are relatively small and parsnips that are fairly thin. In general, look for roots that are firm and free from serious blemishes.

To prepare any of these roots as a vegetable by itself, wash, peel or cut off the skin, slice or cube, and cook in boiling salted water to cover in a covered saucepan until tender (about 10 to 20 minutes for turnips, 20 to 30 minutes for rutabagas, 15 to 20 minutes for parsnips, and 10 to 15 minutes for celeriac). Any of these vegetables can be served mashed like potatoes or mashed with potatoes. Celeriac is sometimes cut into thin sticks and eaten raw with a spicy salad dressing.

Squash

All squashes are edible gourds, but there their similarities end. In one small town in Washington we encountered a score of squash varieties wildly different from each other—tiny, huge; pale-yellow, black-green; smooth, hairy; delicate skinned, tough shelled; some that can be eaten raw, some that take long slow cooking. Squashes were favorite foods in this country long before Europeans came, and they still are—only now there are more choices.

Summer Squash

Summer squash includes those varieties which are harvested while still immature and when the entire squash is tender and edible, including the skin. They include the yellow crookneck, the large yellow straightneck, the greenish-white pattypan or scalloped squash, and the slender green or yellow zucchini. Some of these squash are available at all times of the year. You can identify a tender summer squash by its skin: it will be glossy and neither hard nor tough.

See *Zucchini Frittata* for one popular way of cooking summer squash. Another is a Pacific Coast way of preparing a memorable summer treat, a *Pan of Pattypan*: Wash and thinly slice pattypan squash. In a skillet cook the squash in a few tablespoons of butter over medium heat until just lightly golden and almost transparent. That's it—these little squashes are so sweet, they taste like they've been candied.

Raw summer squash can be washed and sliced or cut into sticks for use as vegetable dippers or in salads.

Winter Squash

Winter squashes are those varieties which are marketed only when fully mature. Some of the most important varieties are the small corrugated acorn or Danish squash (available all year round), butternut, buttercup, green and blue Hubbard, green and gold delicious, turban, and banana. Winter squash is most plentiful from early fall until late winter.

Look for full maturity, indicated by a hard, tough rind. Also look for squash that is heavy for its size (meaning a thick wall, and more edible flesh). Slight variations in skin color do not affect flavor. See index for squash recipes.

Other Squash

There are a few other squash that do not neatly fit into the summer/winter squash categories: pumpkin, the star of Halloween, Thanksgiving, and picturesque harvest tables; spaghetti squash, a large bright-yellow squash with flesh that turns into spaghetti-like strands when cooked; and chayote (also called vegetable pear and mirliton in the South), a tender-skinned, tropical squash with a large, single seed and a taste somewhat like melon.

Pumpkins are available extensively in the fall; spaghetti squash are available from August through February; chayote from October through April.

Look for handsome pumpkins (odds are you aren't going to cook it anyway); select spaghetti squash like a winter squash; and choose and use chayote more or less like summer squash—its looks vary so much it is hard to describe how it should look, but, in general, the harder the chayote the better.

Spaghetti squash is one of the few fresh vegetables that usually comes with a label telling you what to do with it. In case yours doesn't: Cut squash in half lengthwise and clean out seeds. Place squash, cut side down, in a pot with 2 inches of water. (Obviously you need a big pot if you are doing both halves.) Cover and boil until tender (about 20 to 30 minutes). Scrape out the strands with a fork and toss with hot spaghetti sauce or butter and sprinkle with grated Parmesan cheese.

Note: We sometimes wonder whether we are passing along too much advice on familiar foods, then we remember a dear friend, who is otherwise a good cook, who spent most of one day baking pumpkin pie "from scratch" for the first time—using the stringy stuff around the seeds.

Sweet Potatoes and Yams

Two types of sweet potatoes are available in varying amounts the year round.

Moist sweet potatoes, called yams in America, are the most common type. They have orange-colored flesh and are very sweet. (The true yam is the root of a tropical vine which is not grown commercially in the U.S.) Dry sweet potatoes have a pale-colored flesh, low in moisture.

Most sweet potatoes are grown in the southern tier and some eastern states. California is also a heavy producer.

Look for well-shaped, firm sweet potatoes with smooth, bright, uniformly colored skins, free from signs of decay. Because they are more perishable than white potatoes, extra care should be used in selecting sweet potatoes. Sweet potatoes should not be stored in the refrigerator.

Though their natural sweetness is often enhanced by candying or glazing, yams can be cooked and served like white potatoes. A simple and popular Southern recipe for *Breakfast Yams* is ideal for the RV at any meal: Peel 4 to 6 medium yams and cut into thin slices (as you would for scalloped potatoes). Cook in ¼ cup (½ stick) melted butter in a covered skillet over low heat until tender, about 5 minutes on each side. Remove the cover, turn the heat up, and cook for a few minutes more. Season to taste with salt and pepper.

Taro

A group of plants with starchy tuberous roots are called taro or dasheen and are widely cultivated and used in the Pacific. Taro root is a staple in Hawaii. Depending on the variety, both leaves and root can be toxic if improperly cooked. We do not recommend experimenting with taro without some local expert advice.

Tomatoes

One of our most popular crops, tomatoes are available throughout the year, although seasonally the price and flavor rise and fall in inverse ratio. Florida, California, Texas, and a number of other states are major producers, and imports supplement domestic supplies from late winter to early spring. There are several varieties of tomatoes: most are bright red, a few yellow.

The best flavored tomatoes are "home grown" on local farms which have allowed them to ripen completely before being picked. If the tomatoes need further ripening, keep them in a dark place, not in sunlight. Unless they are fully ripened, don't store tomatoes in the refrigerator—the cold temperature can keep them from ripening even after they are removed from the refrigerator. However, once tomatoes are ripe, you may keep them refrigerated for some time.

One of the best and simplest ways of serving garden-fresh ripe tomatoes, especially if you have the good fortune to have fresh basil too, is *Italian Tomato Salad*: Sprinkle sliced tomatoes (any variety) with Italian dressing or vinegar-and-oil dressing and fresh or dried chopped basil. If you have garlic, you can add a crushed clove to the bowl. For a continental version of the recipe, add cubes of mozzarella cheese and sliced black olives.

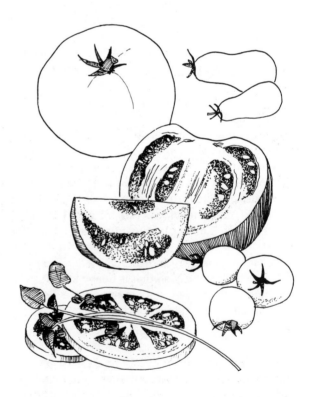

Meats and Seafood

TODAY'S SPECIAL

Using local specials for your meal mainstays is both adventurous and advantageous: prices differ wildly by availability; rarities in some parts of the country are commonplace in others; fresh seafood is abundant near most of the country's campgrounds. But making the most of these opportunities is not always simple, so we put together some information that may help you with unfamiliar mainstays and even your favorites—they may be marketed differently or sold under a different name down the road.

Beef and Veal

Beef is the meat that Americans eat in greatest quantity, more than a 100 pounds each a year. Veal usually comes from cattle less than 3 months old. Beef comes from more mature animals—usually 15 to 30 months old. Baby beef comes from animals only 7 to 10 months old.

Fresh meat usually reaches the consumer within 6 to 10 days. Some high-quality beef, however, is "aged" under controlled circumstances to develop additional tenderness and flavor.

Cured meat is treated with curing ingredients—primarily salt and sugar. After curing, the meat may be smoked with a nonresinous wood such as hickory for added flavor. Cuts of beef frequently cured are the brisket (called corned beef when cured), the tongue, and some sausages and luncheon meats. Dried beef, another cured product, is usually made from the round.

Tenderized beef may have been treated with liquid or powdered tenderizers (though the latter are usually put on by the cook) or by mechanical treatment (these are the scored steaks such as "minute" steak or cubed steak).

USDA Choice is the beef grade most commonly found in retail markets. USDA Prime, the highest grade, may be found in some retail markets, but, alas, most of it goes to hotels and restaurants.

Look for beef with lean that is a uniform, bright, light to deep red; veal that is grayish pink. Fine-textured, firm lean is preferable to coarse-textured, soft lean. The color of fat is not an indication of quality.

Veal should be cooked fairly well done to make it tender. Beef is considered rare when it has an internal temperature of 140°, medium at 160°, and well done at 170°. Veal is considered well done at 170°, too.

Besides hamburger, RVers probably buy more steaks than anything else, which can be confusing because there are regional and local variations in the names of various cuts. Here's a thumbnail guide that may help.

The most tender meat is from the upper-middle sections (rib and loin):

Tenderloin, the most tender of all steaks, has no bone and very little fat. The center cut is sometimes called chateaubriand; the lower steaks, tournedos or filet mignon.

Porterhouse, often considered the best steak, has a generous section of tenderloin and is a big steak.

T-bone, very similar to the porterhouse steak, has a smaller amount of tenderloin.

Top Loin (club steak), like the porterhouse and the T-bone, is cut from the short loin but has no tenderloin. It's a nice individual-serving steak.

Top loin (strip steak) is the same as the large muscle in both the porterhouse and the T-bone with the tenderloin removed. This flavorful steak is often sold as a New York Strip steak or a Kansas City steak.

Rib, cut from the rib section and including the rib bone, is a tender, flavorful steak. It is also called a club steak.

Ribeye, cut from the eye of beef rib, is a very tender, flavorful steak that is boneless and has little fat. The ribeye is often called a Delmonico steak (a name used for a cut of chuck steak too).

Less tender steaks include:

Sirloin, a large steak that can be fairly tender if it is one with a long, flat bone. If the sirloin is cut into two boneless steaks, top sirloin and bottom sirloin, the top sirloin is better.

Sirloin tip, a boneless steak, is less tender than the regular sirloin but still a candidate for broiling and pan-broiling.

Round, an economical steak with little waste, has three muscles which vary in tenderness: top round, the most tender, can be broiled; bottom round, not as tender as top; eye-of-round, also a less tender cut than top but can be pan-broiled when sliced thin.

Flank, a boneless steak with very little fat, is a less tender cut than most steaks but flavorful and adaptable to several cooking methods that make the most of it. Also known as London Broil.

Chuck steaks have many regional names—California, Western, Cheyenne, petite butter, finger, breakfast, his 'n hers, etc. The two main cuts are blade chuck, a flavorful, economical steak, but varying in tenderness; and arm chuck, a flavorful but fairly tough cut often used for Swiss steak. (Ground chuck is a popular hamburger meat.)

Fish

Odds are you are leveled up near a lake, river, stream, or an ocean—Fish Country. And odds are you are more likely to be dealing with fresh fish on the road than at home whether you bag it, beg it, or buy it. And odds are you are a bit confused about fish varieties.

Well, that's not surprising. There are so many kinds of fish available in the United States and Canada that it took a 145-page publication of the American Fisheries Society just to list the names.

Generally, fish are divided into saltwater fish and freshwater fish, though there are some families that have species in both and some species that spend part of their life in both.

Another way of categorizing fish is by lean and fat so you have a clue to how they are best cooked. Lean fish—like sea bass, red snapper, and ocean perch—are good poached, steamed, and fried; or, if they are well basted, can be baked, broiled, or barbecued. Fat fish—like mackerel, sablefish, and shad—are best for broiling, baking, and grilling. The fish that are midway—like salmon, kingfish, and pompano—can be cooked either like lean or fat fish. But then there's trout, which is fairly fat, and is perhaps the all-time American favorite fried

fish. So these categories are only general guidelines at best.

However it's categorized, the fish you're interested in is probably sitting in your sink right now. We wish we could have scouted all the fish you might be eating, but there are more than 200 edible species of American fish. With luck, maybe yours is among the fish that are described in this thumbnail guide to some of the most popular.

Butterfish (also called silver dollar and Pacific pompano) are small, mild, delicate, moderately fat, saltwater fish from the East and West Coast. They can be cooked like pan-size trout.

Catfish (including blue catfish, channel catfish, bullheads, flathead catfish) are mild, firm, lean, freshwater fish found throughout the Mississippi Valley from the Great Lakes to Mexico and in other inland lakes and rivers. Catfish should be skinned before cooking: be careful of their barbs. See *Mississippi Valley Catfish Fry* or cook filleted catfish like other mild fillets.

Cod (Atlantic or Pacific), famous historic fish used extensively in New England and other parts of the world, are mild, flaky, large, lean, saltwater fish. Fresh cod is used in a great many ways. Try *Cape Cod Chowder* or cook fillets like ocean perch. Skip the salted cod which requires extensive fussing with changes of water before it can be cooked. Young small cod is often marketed as scrod.

Grunnion (California) are tiny, delicate, saltwater fish that come up on shore in late spring to spawn and are gathered by hand on West Coast beaches. If you're there during the "grunnion run," you'll get lots of local advice. Or cook them like smelt, which they resemble. See *Great Lakes Smelt Fry*.

Haddock, closely related to cod but usually smaller, are mild, flaky, lean saltwater fish from the Northeast coast. Young haddock is often marketed as scrod. Smoked haddock is known as finnan haddie. Cook fresh haddock fillets like other mild fish fillets.

Halibut (Pacific) are mild, tender, lean, very large, saltwater fish of the West Coast sold in steaks or fillets. Chicken halibut are small fish (6 to 10 pounds) sold whole. See *Seawife's Halibut* and *Teriyaki Sea Steaks*.

Kingfish, largest of the mackerel family, are distinctively flavored, moderately fat, saltwater fish

from the waters off Florida and the Gulf. Kingfish are sold mostly as steaks or fillets that can be cooked like salmon.

Lingcod (blue cod, buffalo cod) are not true cod but greenling, and are large, fine flavored, lean, saltwater fish of the West Coast available whole or in steaks or fillets. Don't be put off by lingcod with greenish flesh; it is a normal characteristic of the species. This delicately flavored fish should not be overwhelmed with spicy sauces. Try the fillets cooked like *Poached Pacific Perch* or *Snappy Oven-fried Snapper*.

Mackerel (including Spanish mackerel, Atlantic mackerel or Boston mackerel, Pacific mackerel) are distinctively flavored, fat, saltwater fish of the East and West coast, that are sold whole (1 to 4 pounds) or filleted. They are usually broiled or baked, though some people like pan-fried mackerel in spite of its high fat content. Try whole mackerel prepared like *Champion Fish in Foil* or *Hudson River Shad Bake*.

Mullet (there are *many* varieties), favored fish of the ancient world and now especially popular in the South, are mild, moderately fat, saltwater fish mostly from the southeastern coast and Gulf. They are usually sold whole (pan-size to 3 pounds) and can be cooked like trout.

Ocean perch, among the most extensively used fish in America, are various mild, lean, saltwater rockfish commonly sold as fillets. The most widely marketed are the tender Atlantic ocean perch, also called redfish. Those marketed as Pacific ocean perch are somewhat firmer and larger fish. Use like other mild fillets or see *Poached Pacific Perch*.

Perch (including walleye or walleyed pike, yellow perch, sauger or sand pike) are small, prized, fine flavored, lean, freshwater fish of northern lakes and rivers. Cook whole freshwater perch like trout or use fillets like other mild fillets.

Pike (including northern pike, muskellunge) are large, firm, mild, lean, freshwater fish of northern lakes and rivers. Closely related to perch, pike can be cooked the same way or like trout. See *Champion Fish in Foil*..

Pompano (Florida pompano), prized fish of the Gulf, are distinctively flavored, firm, moderately fat, saltwater fish. The whole fish (pan-size to 3 pounds) are frequently broiled or barbecued, amply basted with butter or oil. Fillets are used in various southern specialties—see *Mardi Gras Pompano*.

Porgy (scup) are small, mild, flaky, lean, saltwater fish mostly of the East Coast, usually sold whole. Any of the several varieties of porgy can be prepared like other pan-size fish and are especially popular pan-fried—see *Brookside Trout*.

Red snapper, prized fish of the Gulf and southern coasts, are distinctively flavored, lean, saltwater fish. Snapper is excellent prepared almost any way. See *Lone Star Red Snapper*. Pacific red snapper is an unrelated rockfish.

Rockfish are medium-size, mild, firm, lean, saltwater fish of the East and West coasts. There are many varieties; some are sold under more specific names such as ocean perch and Pacific red snapper. See *Poached Pacific Perch* and *Snappy Oven-Fried Snapper* or use like other mild fillets.

Sablefish (Black cod, Alaska cod) are buttery, very fat, saltwater fish of the West Coast about the size of salmon. Sablefish is often smoked (can be eaten as is or broiled). Fresh sablefish is sold whole in in fillets or steaks and is good broiled, baked, or barbecued. See *Teriyaki Sea Steaks*.

Salmon (including chinook or king, coho or silver, sockeye or red, Atlantic salmon, pink salmon) are rich, distinctively flavored, moderately fat fish that are caught along the Pacific Coast, the Atlantic Coast, and in inland waters including the Great Lakes. Most of these much-sought-after fish spend part of their life cycle at sea, returning to freshwater streams and rivers to spawn or meet their fate at the hands of fisherfolk. See index for various salmon recipes.

Sea bass are mild, lean, saltwater fish of both the Atlantic and Pacific, ranging from pan-size to 600 pounds depending on variety—common sea bass or black sea bass, striped sea bass, giant sea bass, etc. To confuse matters, there are the fresh water bass (sunfish) plus several other fish called bass that are in different families. Bass as a general rule can be cooked like other mild fish.

Shad are mild, bony, fat, saltwater fish of the East and West coasts. See *Hudson River Shad Bake*. The shad roe is also a delicacy and is sold with the eggs intact in the set of pouches. To prepare, wash the set carefully (do not break the membrane or separate the set); melt ½ cup (1 stick) butter in a skillet; turn the roe carefully in the warm butter until well coated; and simmer gently, covered, for about 15 minutes, turning once. Salt and pepper to taste. Shad roe is usually served with lemon wedges, toast, and bacon.

Smelt are tiny, tasty fish of the Northeast and West Coast as well as inland waters. Ocean smelt include the oily eulachon or Columbia River smelt and the surf smelt or whitebait. Rainbow smelt are lean abundant fish of the Great Lakes. See *Great Lakes Smelt Fry*.

Sole and **Flounder** (including Dover sole, petrale sole, fluke or lemon sole, winter flounder, summer flounder, sand dab) are mild, distinctively flavored, flaky, lean, saltwater flatfish of the West and East coasts. Sole is so popular that many related fish are sold as sole—most of the East Coast sole is actually flounder. Sole and flounder are usually sold as fillets. See *Sole Veronique*. Greenland turbot is a similar, related flatfish that is imported.

Striped bass (sometimes called rockfish), prized fish caught on the East and Wests coasts, are large, mild, lean, saltwater fish. Large whole fish are often stuffed and baked or poached like salmon. Small striped bass, fillets, and steaks, are used like other mild fish.

Sunfish are firm, lean, freshwater fish found throughout the country, usually pan-size. Included in this large family of American fisherman's favorites are bluegill, largemouthed bass, smallmouthed bass, spotted bass, the crappies, and the sunfishes; many of these have charming local names—pumpkin seed, bachelor perch, copper belly, calico fish. Sunfish are most usually pan-fried or cooked over the coals. See *Lickety-Split Small Fry*.

Swordfish are huge (200 to 600 pounds), distinctively flavored, coarse textured, moderately fat, saltwater fish of the East and West Coast. Barbecued swordfish steaks are popular.

Trout (including rainbow trout, brook trout, cutthroat trout, lake trout, Dolly Varden, brown trout) are prized, firm, fat, freshwater fish from throughout the country. A few varieties also go to sea—steelhead, a kind of rainbow, and sea-run cutthroat (which has the delightful scientific name *Salmo clarki clarki*). Trout are usually cooked whole. See the index for various trout recipes.

Whitefish (including lake whitefish, chub, lake herring) are firm, fat, freshwater fish of the Great Lakes and other inland waters. Lake whitefish is the mildest and largest. Whitefish is often smoked. Fresh whitefish can be cooked almost any way; try the trout recipes. See *Champion Fish in Foil*.

If fisherman's luck hasn't made your choice for you, the following information may be helpful in the fish market.

Fresh and frozen fish are marketed in various forms or cuts (you can, of course, duplicate these cuts with freshly caught fish):

Whole fish, in market terminology, are fish as they come from the water. Before cooking, the fish must be eviscerated and, depending on the species, scaled. In this cookbook, the term "whole fish" refers to a dressed fish.

Dressed fish have scales and entrails removed; sometimes the head, tail, and/or fins are also removed. The midsection or whole body of a large dressed fish is sometimes called a fish roast.

Fillets are the sides of the fish cut lengthwise away from the backbone. The fillets may or may not be skinless. For butterfly fillets, the two sides of the fish are cut lengthwise away from the backbone and held together by the uncut fish and skin of the belly; they are cooked like one fillet.

Steaks are cross section slices from large dressed fish, usually cut ⅝ to 1 inch thick. A cross section of the backbone is the only bone in a steak.

Chunks are cross sections of large dressed fish. A cross section of the backbone is the only bone in a chunk.

Fish are also extensively sold in various prepared forms: frozen (for example, fish sticks and fish cakes), smoked, and canned. Incidentally, in some fishing areas you can have your own catch canned or smoked.

When you are buying fresh, whole or dressed fish, look for firm flesh; a mild odor; bright, clear, full eyes; and shiny, unfaded skin. Fresh cut fish should have a mild odor and fresh appearance with no signs of drying. Frozen fish should have little or no odor and should preferably be solidly frozen when bought (for best results defrost in the refrigerator just before cooking).

When your fish came from the water directly to you, you are sure of its freshness, but then you probably have to do the scaling, cleaning, and/or filleting yourself.

To scale a fish, first wash it, then place it on a cutting board with one hand holding it firmly by the head. Holding a knife almost vertically, scrape off the scales, starting at the tail and scraping toward the head. Be sure to remove all the scales around the fins and head.

To clean a fish, with a sharp knife cut the entire length of the belly from the vent to the head. Remove the intestines. Both cleaning and scaling are best done outside.

To fillet a fish, with a sharp knife cut along the back of the fish from the tail to the head. Then cut down to the backbone just back of the collarbone. Turn the knife flat and cut the flesh away from the backbone and rib bones. Lift off the whole side of the fish or fillet in one piece. Turn the fish over and cut the fillet from the other side.

If you wish, you may skin the fillets. Place the fillet, skin side down, on a cutting board. Hold the tail end tightly with your fingers and with a sharp knife cut down through the flesh to the skin about ½ inch from the end of the fillet. Flatten the knife against the skin and cut fhe flesh away from the skin by sliding the knife forward while holding the tail end of the skin firmly between your fingers.

Now you're ready to cook the fish—and your choices are vast. Check the index for a couple dozen recipes for fresh fish to get you started.

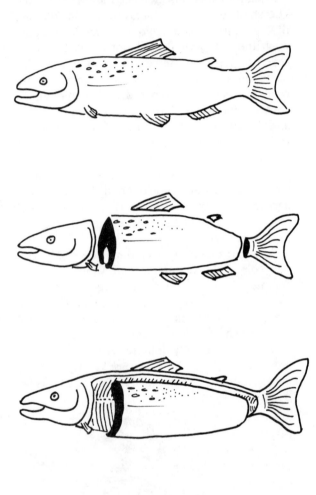

Game

Although RVers probably eat more game than Americans as a whole, they don't necessarily eat it in their RVs since most game is aged. More to the point, most hunters know how to deal with the basics of field cooking better than we do (we do our hunting of wildlife with fieldglasses and camera), and for the more adventurous there are already excellent books on game and wildlife cooking. Consequently, we defer on this specialized subject to those more experienced. In a pinch, you can almost always get local advice. If you've legally come by some critter you or your fellow campers don't know how to deal with, try the local historical society or museum (there are 5,500 musuems in America—one's bound to be close by): a great number of them sell regional/historic cookbooks with recipes for everything from moose nose to beaver tail.

Lamb

Americans eat less lamb than any of the other commercially marketed meats, less than 2 pounds each a year. Lamb is meat from young sheep usually less than a year old. Almost all the sheep annually sold for meat are marketed as lamb. Most of the federally graded lamb on the retail market is USDA Prime or USDA Choice, but not all lamb is federally graded.

Meat from high-quality, young lambs has pink, firm, fine-textured lean. The lean meat from older, high-quality lambs is light red. The color of the fat is not an indication of quality.

Generally, lamb should be cooked at low to moderate temperatures for the most tender, juicy, and flavorful results. Lamb is usually preferred medium or even well done (though many good cooks say overcooking lamb ruins it). Lamb is considered medium when it has a grayish-tan interior with a tinge of pink and an internal temperature of 170°

Pork

Americans eat more than 60 pounds of pork each a year, much of it in ham, bacon, sausage, and luncheon meats. Pork is meat from hogs, usually under one year of age. It is sold fresh, cured, or cured and smoked.

Many pork cuts are cured to add distinctive flavor and variety. Before adequate refrigeration became common, pork was treated with a heavy salt brine to preserve it. Nowadays less salt is used because meats are cured primarily for flavor, not for preservation. "Country style" hams, available in some areas, are heavily salted and may require soaking before cooking, making them rather impractical for the RV.

After treatment with the curing ingredients, the meat may be smoked with a nonresinous wood for added flavor. Hickory is one of the most popular.

Almost all cured and smoked hams are labeled either "fully cooked" or "cook before eating." Obviously, in most cases the fully cooked hams would be a better bet for the RV cook.

Other forms of cured pork available include picnic shoulder, shoulder butt, Canadian bacon (made from boneless pork loin), bacon, and smoked loin chops.

Sausages and luncheon meats include fresh and smoked sausages to be cooked before eating and ready-to-serve sausages and luncheon meats.

Fresh pork sausage is made from ground pork mixed with seasonings. It is sold in bulk or stuffed into casings. Link sausages may be fresh or smoked in casings or skinless; both must be cooked before eating.

Ready-to-serve sausages, such as hot dogs and luncheon meats, are fully cooked and can be served cold or heated.

Look for meat, either fresh or cured, that has a high proportion of lean to fat and bone. The flesh should be firm and fine textured. Color of the lean in fresh pork may range from grayish pink to red. Lean cured pork has a typical deep-pink color. Unlike other meats, pork is not usually federally graded.

Cured meats can be kept in the refrigerator slightly longer than fresh pork, but even ham, bacon, and hot dogs should be used within a week. Frozen cured meat loses quality rapidly and should be used as soon as possible.

Caution: Fresh pork must *always* be thoroughly cooked. A very small percentage of pork is infected with trichinae, microscopic organisms that can live in pork and be transmitted to humans. Severe illnesses can result unless the organism is destroyed by cooking or other procedure. Raw pork and pork products, including bacon and fresh sausage, should never be tasted before cooking.

Cook pork at low to moderate temperatures for the most flavorful, tender, and juicy results and to avoid shrinkage. Fresh pork should be cooked to an internal temperature of 170°. Cured hams labeled "cook for eating" should be heated to an internal temperature of 160°.

Poultry

Americans need little introduction to poultry. Judging from the tons of chicken bought year-round and coast-to-coast, there must be at least a chicken in every pot. And turkey, the homely bird that Benjamin Franklin thought should be our national symbol, is not only the star of American holiday feasts but, more and more, a versatile year-round meat.

Classes of chilled and frozen chicken usually found in retail stores indicate whether the chicken is young or mature. Young chickens include broiler-fryers, Rock Cornish game hens (a small special-breed chicken, usually weighing about a pound), roasters, and capons; while mature birds include hens, baking chickens, and stewing chickens.

Canned chicken comes boned or whole. There are numerous other frozen and canned chicken products on the market ranging from frozen precooked fried chicken to chicken hot dogs.

Turkeys marketed as whole birds are usually frozen, though chilled turkeys are sometimes available, especially during the holiday season. It's unlikely that a whole turkey will fit in an RV oven, but, when the occasion warrants it, you might try a boneless raw turkey roast (available in all white meat, all dark meat, or a combination of both), whole turkey breast, or a halved or quartered turkey. (Be sure to take your tape measure or ruler with you to the market.) Turkey parts, cuts, and products are good on their own or as stand-ins for other meats—turkey ham, turkey hot dogs, ground turkey, turkey scallops (used like veal scallops).

Considerably less used poultry are ducks and geese. Ducks are usually marketed young, weigh about 3 to 7 pounds, and are mostly frozen, ready-to-cook whole birds. Geese are marketed young, weigh about 6 to 12 pounds, and are chilled or frozen, ready-to-cook whole birds.

Buy only poultry bearing the U.S. wholesome-ness stamp and the official USDA grade shield. We recommend buying U.S. Grade A poultry, the finest available. Grade A birds are fully fleshed and meaty, well-finished, attractive, and practically free from defects.

Don't keep chilled, raw poultry for over a few days. Defrost frozen poultry most safely and conveniently in the refrigerator and use promptly after thawing.

Poultry is usually cooked thoroughly, but there the guidelines end—there are literally hundreds of ways of cooking poultry that are popular in America.

Turkey roasts are done when the interior temperature reaches 170° to 175°. Whole birds are done when a leg moves easily in the socket, parts when they are tender when pierced with a fork (clear juices are another sign). Then there are those who tell by pinching (don't ask us how they tell) and other means of divination. We have sometimes eaten half the chicken trying to determine if it is "done" yet.

Shellfish

The mollusks and crustaceans of coastal North America have been brightening dinnertime as long as there have been people here. In addition to the ancient favorites, there are a few introduced through marine culture, and a few, like Alaskan king crab, added thanks to modern fishery. Unfortunately, some American shellfish have become rarities due to pollution and mismanagement of resources. But shellfish are still many Americans' idea of a feast, and there is still, happily, plenty to feast on.

Abalone are large mild univalves (one-shell mollusks). Most American abalone are from California and do not leave the state. (Some frozen abalone is imported from Mexico and Japan.)

Removing and cleaning the edible stemlike muscle from this sea snail is a formidable task for the uninitiated and one you'd probably just as well forego unless you are in some peculiar circumstance where you have access to considerable fresh abalone—in which case you'll find guidance on how to do it. But if you want to try this highly prized delicacy while in California in the spring or fall, check the markets for prepared abalone steaks—thin slices that have been pounded to make them tender (a necessity). The steaks should be cream to beige and smell fresh. Cook within a day. If the abalone is purchased frozen, defrost only in the refrigerator and cook immediately after thawing.

Abalone needs only the briefest cooking or it will turn leathery. The simplest and most usual preparation is to coat the steaks with seasoned flour (or leave the steaks plain) and cook in melted butter in a skillet over medium-high heat for just 1 minute, turning once. Serve with lemon wedges.

Note: In parts of America, other sea snails are popular, including the large, beautiful conch of Florida and the tiny periwinkles of the Atlantic. (Conch preparation is even trickier than abalone. Live periwinkles are poached briefly, but on special request from our young sons—who have pet snails—we are not including more specific instruction.)

Clams, ever popular seashore meal-makers, come in many varieties and sizes and are abundant on both coasts. You can buy clams, but they are more fun to dig if you have the opportunity—clamdigging is one of America's favorite family sports, especially popular with RVers.

Some of the principal clams that you might come across are:

Soft-shelled clams (also called long-necked clams, steamer clams, Eastern clams) are tender clams abundant on both coasts. They are 2 to 4 inches across and are mostly used for steaming.

Hard-shelled clams (also called little-necked clams, quahog, round clams) is a general name used on the East Coast for a tender clam of various sizes—the largest are called chowder clams,

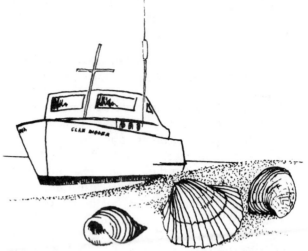

medium to small ones are called cherrystones, and sometimes the small ones are called littlenecks. On the West Coast another small, tender variety of clam with a shell somewhat like a cockle is called the Pacific littleneck. Partly depending on their size these tender clams are eaten raw, steamed, or in chowders or other dishes.

Butter clams (resemble quahog and are sometimes called that) are hard-shelled clams of the Pacific Coast, usually about 2 to 3 inches across. They are steamed and used in chowders like the other hard-shelled clams.

Razor clams, especially popular in the Northwest, are large, long, meaty clams distinguished by a thin, oval shell with a lacquerlike coating. They are usually about 5 inches long and require special preparation before frying and using in chowders or fritters.

Gaper clams (also called blue clams, horse clams, Empires, bluenecks) are very large clams (more than a pound), prepared like razor clams. Little gaper clams look like soft-shelled clams.

There are several other clams used for cooking, ranging from the pretty cockle clam with its scalloped rayed shell to the oddity of the Pacific Coast, the intimidating huge geoduck clam, which weighs up to 7 pounds.

Often there are free or inexpensive pamphlets available in coastal parks that will give you all the specifics about preparing (and digging) the local varieties.

Clams are sold live in their shells or shucked (and occasionally frozen). Live clams usually keep their shells tightly closed; tap any open ones—if they don't close up, reject them. Shucked clams should be fresh smelling and evenly colored; use immediately. Clams are also available canned; use the minced ones like fresh, the smoked ones as appetizers.

To dig your own clams, you don't really need any special equipment, though your RV refrigerator would be a dream-come-true for generations of clam-diggers who struggled with the problem of keeping their clams fresh and alive until cooking time. Contact the local fish and game department or park rangers for information on quarantines, digging methods, tides, regulations, limits, seasons, etc. *Cautions:* In some seasons black portions of clams can contain a lethal poison; some clamming areas have become polluted.

To clean freshly dug clams (market clams have usually been cleaned), first sort through and discard any that are broken or open—varieties with protruding necks should retract a little when poked; scrub well under cold water (treat softshell clams gently to avoid breaking their shells); put the clams in a bowl of cold salted water in the refrigerator for an hour or more so they clean themselves of sand (if you can't fit them in the refrigerator, do it in the sink). Rinse the clams thoroughly again. They are now ready for steaming, opening, or storing in the refrigerator for a few days.

Some varieties of large clams require further cleaning, trimming, and preparation before cooking—for example, large softshells, razor clams, gaper clams, and geoduck clams.

See the index for various clam recipes.

Crabs are such a fearsome-looking lot you have to admire—and be grateful to—the first person with enough courage to eat one. If you were the first to come to eyeball to eyeball with an enormous Alaska king crab (some can be 9 feet from claw tip to claw tip), you might well have wondered who was going to be dinner.

There are several very different crabs that come from the coastal areas of the country but all have that distinctive, sweet, delicate meat that Americans like so much. The most common market varieties are:

Alaska king crab are very long-legged, deep-water crabs from Alaskan waters. Only the legs and claws are eaten. They are only available frozen, usually in the shell. See *Kodiak King Crab Legs on the Half Shell.*

Blue crab (often called by a state name—Florida crab, Maryland crab) are small crabs with meaty bodies and claws found from the mid-Atlantic Coast to the Gulf. They are sold whole—live, cooked, or frozen; and as cooked crabmeat—fresh or frozen (lump meat is considered choice). See *Charleston She-Crab Soup* and *Eastern Shore Crab Appetizer.*

During the summer, blue crabs that have molted (a natural stage of development) are sold as softshell crabs. These small crabs are sold live or killed and cleaned (if only live are available, have the fish market kill and clean them). Softshell crabs are fried whole and eaten entirely, shell and all.

Dungeness crab are greatly appreciated large crabs of the Pacific Coast—they are our idea of what a crab ought to be, a lot of delicious meat in both body and claws. They are available whole—live and cooked, and as cooked crabmeat—fresh or frozen. See index for recipes.

Snow crab (spider crab) are long-legged crabs from the Pacific. Although smaller than king crab, they are marketed similarly—leg and claw meat, usually frozen. See *Snow Crab Ball.*

Stone crab (Florida stone crab, Atlantic stone crab) are small crabs with very large, heavy claws from the southern Atlantic. Only the claws are eaten, and they are "harvested": a single claw is removed and the live crabs are returned to the sea to regenerate the missing claw. See *Florida Stone Crab Claws.*

Although crabs are available live, unless you are having a crab boil (or caught them yourself), we recommend that you have them cooked at the market, which is usually an option. Since crabs are ordinarily just boiled or steamed in salted water for most purposes, you'll save yourself a lot of trouble. (To cook a live crab you can follow the directions for cooking a live lobster—see *Maine Boiled Lobster.*) If you are buying live crabs, they should be very lively. When using frozen crab, defrost completely in the refrigerator. Use all crabmeat quickly.

Crabmeat from all types of crab can be used in any recipe calling for crabmeat. See the index for recipes.

For a *Southern Crab Boil:* In a very large pot, add crab boil seasoning according to the package instructions and sliced lemon to enough boiling water to cover several small crabs per person (about ¼ cup seasoning and 1 lemon for each 6 to 8 quarts of water). Bring water and seasonings to a rolling boil before plunging crabs in head first. Boil for about 20 minutes, stirring once halfway through. Serve with melted butter, icy beer, and a plate of dill pickles, celery, and olives. For a traditional touch, set your camp table with layers of old newspaper and have a mountain of paper napkins on hand.

Lobster, the big red shellfish with the equally big pricetag, is one of the most popular premium meal mainstays in America. There are two principal kinds of lobster: the American lobster has huge claws and comes from the northeast coast, notably Maine; and the spiny lobster (rock lobster), which has insignificant claws and comes from the southern and Gulf coasts and California (many are imported from other parts of the world).

American lobsters are sold live, or occasionally, cooked and shelled. When buying a live lobster, look for a lively one. (Incidentally, if you've never dealt with a live lobster, you may be surprised to discover that they aren't red, but a mottled black.) American lobsters are often sold by weight names, for example, chickens (1 pound); quarters (1¼ pounds); deuces (2 pounds); and jumbos (over 2½ pounds up to about 4 pounds).

Spiny lobsters are mostly sold as frozen lobster tails (their only meaty part); the frozen tails are usually uncooked. Occasionally live spiny lobsters

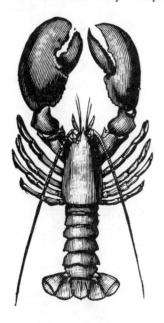

are for sale. Completely defrost frozen lobster only in the refrigerator before cooking.

See the index for how to cook a whole live lobster and for other recipes.

To cook frozen lobster tail, thaw completely and boil in salted water lilke a whole lobster until opaque (follow package instructions for timing, or estimate about 1 or 2 minutes cooking time for each ounce of the largest tail).

Note: Langostinas are shrimp-size imported lobsters sold frozen and ready-to-eat when defrosted. They can be used in recipes calling for cooked lobster.

Mussels are an abundant, easily gathered, distinctively flavored, tender, bivalve mollusk found on both coasts. They have handsome, readily identified, dark-blue, elongated shells, usually about 2 to 4 inches long, and richly colored flesh.

If you buy mussels in the market make sure they are alive—the shells will be tightly closed. The smallest mussels are considered the choicest. Use immediately.

Gathering mussels is almost as easy as getting them in the market. They attach themselves in clusters to rocks and pilings and are sometimes washed up in such numbers the beach seems paved with them. All you have to do is pull or cut them off the rocks and head back to your RV. Caution: Mussels are subject to "red tide": check for local quarantine especially on the Pacific Coast. (Don't worry about the mussels you find in the market, they have been checked.) Check also for any local regulations or limits.

To clean mussel shells for cooking, scrape off any barnacles and encrustations, and scrub them vigorously (use a wire brush or steel wool if you have them) under running water. Some people like to soak them in cold water in the refrigerator for an hour or two like clams. Just before cooking, check again that they are all alive, rinse again, and pull off the beards (called byssus) if you like (sometimes they are cooked with their "whiskers" which act like a handle for dipping the steamed mussels).

Serve mussels raw or steamed like clams, or see *Beachcomber's Mussels*.

Oysters, an all-American favorite since antiquity, comes from both coasts and are available all year but are best from September through April. The principal species of these popular mollusks are the familiar Eastern oysters (cove oysters) from the Atlantic Coast; Olympia oysters (Western oysters), small prized native oysters of the Pacific Coast, now quite scarce; and Pacific oysters (Japanese oysters), which come in various sizes from very small to large—the smallest are most choice. Since oysters reflect local conditions, many are marketed under local names—Blue Point, Chincoteague, Quilcene.

Oysters are sold live in their shells or shucked. Live oysters should have their shells tightly closed (or close up when you prod them). Shucked oysters should be fresh smelling and evenly colored; use immediately (unless they are labelled as specially packed for longer refrigeration). Smoked canned oysters are served as appetizers.

To clean live oysters, scrub the shells thoroughly under cold running water and drain. Keep refrigerated until time to serve or cook.

See index for various oyster recipes.

Scallops are delicately flavored, tender mollusks of all the coastal areas, though most in the markets are from the East Coast or imported. There are two main types, the small, delicate bay scallops (cape scallops) from estuaries and bays, and the larger sea scallops from ocean waters.

Scallops are sold shucked and trimmed—in this country only the round hinge muscle is used. Look for scallops that are even colored and fresh smelling. Use scallops immediately.

Either bay or sea scallops can be used in any recipe calling for scallops. See index.

Shrimp, by some estimates the most popular seafood in America, are found on all of the country's coasts and in hundreds of species. In addition, much shrimp is imported. Fortunately, since all of the market varieties are tender and sweet, the only significant difference in shrimp is their size.

Shrimp of all sizes are sold raw and cooked, shelled and unshelled, fresh and frozen. The tiny shrimp—Pacific, Alaskan, Maine—are usually sold cooked, peeled, and cleaned (life is too short to spend your RV time peeling 150 to 180 shrimp to get a pound for a salad: don't be tempted by a "bargain" on unshelled tiny shrimp). Medium shrimp and large shrimp mostly come from Florida and the Gulf. They are usually sold headless, but may have shells or not. In their raw state, shrimp may have slightly pinkish or grayish shells depending on the variety. If you have your choice of raw or cooked shrimp and are feeling the least bit ambitious, buy raw shrimp and cook them yourself rather than having them steamed at the market: shrimp readily absorb flavoring during cooking. Fresh shrimp should be firm and smell sweet (an ammonia smell is a signal of deterioration).

To clean shrimp, shell before or after cooking and devein. (Most people don't bother to devein small shrimp). To shell, pull back the legs and the shell will come with them; the tail end can stay or be pulled off. To devein, slit shrimp along the back with a small sharp knife and lift out the intestinal vein. See index for shrimp recipes.

Notes: Crayfish (crawfish, crawdad, ecrevisse) and prawns are similar freshwater crustaceans with edible tails that can be cooked in some of the same ways as shrimp—for example, crayfish are often boiled like shrimp, and prawns are often substituted in elegant shrimp dishes. Crayfish, native shellfish very popular in some locales, are found throughout the country and cultivated as well. Prawns, especially the Malaysian prawn, are cultivated in Hawaii and the Southeast.

The enormous imported tiger shrimp is almost as big as a small lobster tail and can be used accordingly.

OVER
THE COALS

THE BASICS OF BARBECUING

The American enthusiasm for cooking out has been going strong since at least the seventeenth century. In the nineteenth century the tradition was kept alive and well by gargantuan gastronomic outdoor occasions—political barbecues and burgoos, oyster roasts and clambakes—and by those people on the move who did not have much of a choice about cooking out. The on-the-road accomplishment of the cowboy cook of the late nineteenth century is still celebrated in legend and in restaurants and recipes dubbed "chuckwagon." Then in the twentieth century, the family barbecue spread like starter on coals across the patios, porches, and RV parks of America, and the coals show no sign of cooling.

Although RVs may have just about any cooking appliance from the instantaneous convenience of a simple burner through thermostatically monitored ovens to computer-controlled microwave ranges, a whole lot of grilling paraphernalia goes on the road along with other amenities of the good life. With all the technology available, why do so many RVers cook out? To begin with, there are lots of foods that taste better when cooked in the smoke over the coals. Then there are foods which leave aromas that you'd just as soon not live with after dinner. And there are times when the prospect of heating up your rig with the broiler

or the oven at 400° for an hour can dim your appetite for even the most delectable dish. Plus, with part of the meal preparation outside and part inside, the cooking is usually shared and everyone has more time to enjoy the sunset. Besides, it's fun.

Wherever you're camped, there's a pretty good chance that your campsite has at least a firepit and, maybe, a built-in outdoor barbeque grill—constant reminders and temptations to enjoy what has been termed the "American Barbecue Mania."

We have included the basics of barbecuing in this section for those of you who, for the first time, have caught or cadged a fish too big for the pan—too big even to fit into the RV oven; and for you who suspect you might be passing up a culinary delight every time you light the fire just for fun; and for you nonbarbecuers from the North who discover why the South had summer kitchens outside the house; and for you adventurers who want to do something new on vacation.

If you are already accomplished in the great American backyard pastime or do campfire cooking as vacation recreation, pass up the basic how-to information and skip to the recipes for some of the easiest and best of America's over-the-coal favorites. We hope all of you will find among them eating adventures that are new for you.

Equipment

Firebox barbecue equipment that RVers may use ranges from a terra cotta flowerpot with several briquets for cooking shish kebabs to a huge gas-fired grill with a motorized spit that will take a large turkey. Considering the premium most of us put on space in our RVs, finding the minimum of equipment that will get the job done makes sense.

In general there are two basic types of portable metal fireboxes: a simple brazier suited for relatively quick cooking of flat foods (under 2 inches thick) such as hamburgers, hot dogs, small fish, and steak; and grills with a lid or cover which reflects the heat back on the food from all sides, holds the flavor-imparting smoke around the food, and virtually eliminates flare-ups which can char the food. The flavor of some foods is substantially improved by being covered, and if you have an open brazier or use those in campsites, sometimes a cover should be improvised from aluminum foil.

Accessories for grilling are legion: there are manual and electrically driven spits; griddles; shish kebab sets; wok pans; drip pans; barbecue brushes; wire brushes; long-handled forks, spatulas, tongs, and skewers; hinged wire barbecue baskets or broilers; thermometers; fish baskets; insulated mits; and, indispensable, aluminum foil. Fortunately, you can get along fine with just a few essentials and your regular RV utensils.

If you are on the road without *any* outdoor cooking equipment, with a little ingenuity and aluminum foil you can cook just about anything on a campsite or park grill. However, life will be a lot easier with a couple of other simple accessories: tongs, important both for moving hot charcoal briquets or coals and for lifting and turning hot food (you probably have a pair to fish hot dogs and corn on the cob out of boiling water); a long-handled wire broiler, also called a barbecue basket grill, to hold delicate fish, burgers, and hot

Since your fire isn't going to be all that big, your regular cooking utensils and hot pads or mit will do nicely.

A nice addition for something fun to do with your campfire or for impromptu snacks over the RV stove burner is a long-handled pie cooker: put in a slice of bread; add jam, pie filling, cheese, canned stew, or spaghetti sauce and mozzarella; top with another slice of bread and close the halves, trimming off the crusts hanging out; and toast over the heat for an almost instant snack treat.

The Fire

Thinking ahead, you can make cleaning easier by lining your metal grill with aluminum foil to catch the drippings—be sure not to cover air circulation holes in the firebox.

No matter what fuel you use, the important thing is to have hot coals, not a blazing fire—leaping flames are for gathering around to tell fish or ghost stories. If you are at a campground and deciding to try barbecuing for the first time, wood may be the only fuel at hand. If you have a choice, hardwoods, the deciduous trees more available in the East, burn slower and more evenly; the soft pine woods common in the West burn faster and are harder to maintain at a steady temperature. In either case, start your fire well ahead of when you expect to start cooking, allow at least an hour to build up a bed of coals, and be ready to put dinner on as soon as the coals are ready so you have full advantage of the short happy life of the glowing embers.

By far the heat source most frequently and easily used is charcoal briquets, hard little pillows of compressed charcoal, available in almost any grocery store.

You can start briquets with a chimney made from a good-sized can (a 2-pound coffee can) with the bottom as well as the top removed. Punch holes around the bottom edge with an old-fashioned beer can punch opener, and/or set it up on a tripod of three briquets to allow plenty of air to flow up through the can. Crumple a couple of sheets of newspaper as starter at the bottom end of the can and put the briquets on top. Light the bottom and, in about half an hour, remove the chimney and spread out the now hot coals.

dogs safely, make turning easy, and keep your food off the dirty grill at the campground; a stiff wire brush to clean your grill (handy, but a piece of crumpled aluminum foil will also work); a 1-inch brush to apply bastes and sauces; a meat thermometer to take some of the guesswork out of determining when dinner is done; and, if you are using an open grill, a plastic spray bottle for water to put down flare-ups (recycle a clean, empty window cleaner bottle). If you like shish kebabs, you can use either metal skewers or inexpensive disposable bamboo skewers available at grocery stores.

Commercial liquid starter is what most outdoor cooks use to get briquets started: Liquid starter makes a one-match fire easy. *Never use gasoline or alcohol and never put liquid starter on hot coals. All fires are potentially dangerous and should be treated with respect.*

If you have a covered grill with vents, face the vents into the wind and remove the cover. Make a pyramid of about 20 or 30 briquets or, if you want to be precise, spread briquets one layer deep over an area slightly larger than the size of what you intend to cook, then pile them into a pyramid. Soak the pile with liquid starter and allow a couple of minutes for the starter to soak in. (When in doubt, read the directions.) Light the briquets around the bottom. It will take about 30 minutes for the charcoal to be ready for cooking—glowing at night, covered with a light coating of gray ash in the light. When they are ready, spread the coals out one layer deep for most cooking.

Use indirect heat and a drip pan for cooking roasts and whole birds. Fashion a drip pan from aluminum foil and bank the coals around or beside it. Catching the dripping fat will prevent flare-ups—or excessive smoke in a covered grill—and will help to keep the grill clean. If you wish to use this slower cooking method on an open grill, you will need to fashion an aluminum foil tent/lid to trap and reflect back some of the heat.

Fireside Tips

• Always grill in the open air: fires produce carbon monoxide that can accumulate dangerously in an enclosed area. And start up away from overhanging branches and other inflammables to avoid a bigger fire than you want.

• Clean your grill before beginning with a stiff wire brush or crumpled aluminum foil.

• Rub the grill well with fat cut from your meat for additional cleaning and, more important, to keep the food from searing itself to the grill. Use cooking oil, margarine, butter, or nonstick vegetable coating on the grill for fish or when you otherwise don't have any fat. *Caution:* Don't spray vegetable coating into the fire or coals.

• Before using a campfire pie cooker or other metal pans, coat the outside with nonstick vegetable coating or ordinary soap to make cleanup a lot easier. If you must use a pan, line the pan with aluminum foil; or, if possible, shape a pan from aluminum foil and throw it away after cooking.

• It is very important to allow enough time for the fire to develop before beginning to cook.

• If you are burning wood and trying to get more air onto the fire, a foot pump (if you have one along for tires or sports equipment) makes a dandy bellows—much easier than getting giddy from blowing.

• If you don't have a wire grill basket to keep fish or other fragile foods from falling apart or into the fire when turned, make one from heavy aluminum foil or a double thickness of regular foil. Tear off a piece of foil as long as your fish or other grilling candidate and twice as wide. Punch pencil-size holes in the sheet and oil or butter it. Put in on the grill, oiled side up, and place the fish on half of it. When the first side is cooked, fold the extra half over the fish, turn the entire aluminum foil-and-fish sandwich over, and unfold the top (formerly the bottom) aluminum. Cook the other side.

• If your grill doesn't have a lid, improvise one from aluminum foil. (Remember, it isn't cooking with wood or charcoal that gives that special flavor, it is the smoke.) Tear off two pieces of foil 24 or more inches long. Fold and seal the two sheets together along the long edge. Pleat it down the middle the other way for strength and form it into a tent/lid. Don't cover the fire completely and punch a few vent holes near the top to keep from smothering the fire.

• A fine way to cook over a fire is a sealed aluminum foil pouch—although the flavor comes from what is inside the pouch not from the fire. To make a foil pouch tear off a piece of foil several inches longer than the food to be cooked and a few inches more than twice as wide. Center the food in the foil and bring the top and bottom edges of the foil together. Roll the edges together, folding them to make a snug seal across the center of the food. Then roll each end in to make a custom-fit package for the food. The center fold of the package can be opened to check if the food is finished cooking without spilling the contents, and all but the most liquid contents can be turned on the grill without leakage.

• If you have a covered grill, wipe the grease from inside the lid with paper towels while the lid is still warm.

• If you have a covered grill, close the vents after cooking to smother the fire and you can relight the remaining charcoal for the next cookout.

More Fireside Chat

The unpredictable nature of outdoor cooking calls for a spirit of adventure and a relaxed attitude. Cooking times are always approximate, particularly in RV outdoor cooking—you can be in different circumstances every time you start a fire. It would tax a computer to adjust cooking times to accommodate all the variables that make a difference: heat of the fire, the distance of the food from the heat, the size and beginning temperature of the food being prepared, the altitude of your campsite, the air temperature, the wind, the equipment you are using, the humidity ... and, for all we know, the phases of the moon and the position of the planets.

How hot is hot: To determine the temperature of the coals, use this rule of thumb: if you can't hold your hand near the grill for more than 2 seconds, it is a hot fire (about 400°); if 3 or 4 seconds is the limit, it is a medium fire (350°); and if you pull away at about 5 seconds it is a low heat fire (about 300°). You can make a hotter fire by arranging the charcoal closer together and cool the fire down by separating the coals. More charcoal burning will, of course, make a hotter fire; and moving the food from above the hottest part of the grill (not necessarily the center) will reduce the cooking heat. If your grill rack is adjustable, move it closer or further from the coals to adjust the temperature.

Flavor bonuses: Sprinkle on seasonings from high enough to allow some to fall into the coals to flavor the smoke. For certain foods putting garlic, onions, and sprigs of herbs directly on the coals will add a tantalizing extra. And you can give the flavor of the smoke distinction by adding a cup of damp hickory, mesquite, or alder chips to the hot coals. Chips and chunks of aromatic woods should be soaked in water for at least 30 minutes before tossing on the hot coals. You can often buy aromatic wood chips where you purchase charcoal briquets.

Fat's on the fire: Maybe that old saying has something to do with the undesirability of too much fat dripping onto the coals and causing charring flare-ups. Trim all excess fat from your meats and there will still be plenty to flavor both the smoke and the meat. If you do leave fat around the edges of steak, slash it every inch or so to keep the meat from curling.

Keep it juicy: To retain juices in your steaks, hamburgers, and other meats, sear the meat on each side before beginning the serious cooking. If you are using a covered grill, you do this by leaving the top off for the first few minutes on each side of the piece of meat. On an open grill you try for the same effect by putting the meat over the hottest part of the grill at the beginning of the cooking. Larger pieces to be cooked by the indirect method can be seared over the hot coals at the edge of the grill before placing the meat above the drip pan. Use tongs when you turn meat or fish to prevent the loss of juices.

A word about fish: It may surprise you to learn that the first recorded barbeques in America's long tradition of barbecuing were of fish: for example, sturgeon roasted in Virginia in the seventeenth century. But it should be no surprise to any fish lover that many full-flavored fish are enhanced by barbecuing. Compared to meat, fish are lean and do not exude self-basting oils during cooking. Consequently, even the fattier fish need some special handling if cooked directly on a grill rather than in an aluminum foil package. Liberally oil the grill or barbecue basket grill or a homemade aluminum foil support to keep fish from searing onto the metal. The fish should be basted frequently as it is grilling. Fish contain very little connective tissue and can break up during handling—use a basket grill or the foil support to turn them. Don't overcook fish in or out of a foil package. Allow a total cooking time of 10 minutes per inch of thickness, including stuffing, measured at the thickest point. For example, a stuffed fish measuring 2 inches at the thickest point should only be cooked about 20 minutes, 10 minutes on each side if turned. At least that is the accepted rule of thumb.

Telling when it's done: As the old chuckwagon cook said, "You can tell when the food is done, when it's cooked." Other hints like fish flaking readily with a fork or juices running clear when the chicken is done are handy visual clues we've included in the recipes. A more reliable method is to check internal temperature of the meat or fish with a meat thermometer.

A word about barbecue sauces: One would have to devote a book to the subject of barbecue sauces to even give a fair sampling of all the kinds that are popular in the country. Two types are widely available commercially—the spicy tomato-based sauces marketed as "barbecue sauce" and teriyaki sauces. Generally, barbecue sauces have in common something sour, something sweet, something with a little heat. The sour can be lemon, wine, vinegar; the sweet can be syrup, brown sugar, molasses, honey; the heat can be hot sauce, ginger, mustard, chili powder. Plus, of course, any-

thing else that is flavorful.

For example, to 1 cup of spaghetti sauce or ketchup, add 3 tablespoons vinegar, 3 tablespoons brown sugar, and 1 teaspoon prepared mustard or several dashes of hot sauce. Heat for a few minutes.

Or for something a little different, try one of these less typical barbecue sauces.

Mississippi Lemon Barbecue Sauce

1 6-ounce can frozen lemonade
 concentrate
1 cup ketchup
¼ cup prepared mustard
¼ cup Worcestershire sauce
Pepper to taste

Thoroughly mix together all ingredients and cook over low heat until thick (about 20 minutes or longer if you have the time). Use sauce to baste chicken or pork.

Alabama Onion Barbecue Sauce

½ cup (1 stick) butter
1 medium onion, chopped
1 tablespoon soy sauce
1 tablespoon Worcestershire
 sauce
1 tablespoon lemon juice
 (½ lemon)
1 cup vinegar

Melt butter in a small saucepan, stir in onion and cook, covered, for a few minutes over medium heat. Stir in the remaining ingredients and heat through. Use sauce to baste chicken, turkey, pork chops, beef or pork ribs, etc.

Sea Steaks to Sunset Stew

A SAMPLER OF GREAT AMERICAN OUTDOOR RECIPES

PACIFIC CORNUCOPIA

All recipes serve four unless otherwise stated.

Longhouse Salmon

Salmon has been called the staff of life for the early Indians of the Northwest Coast and they cooked, preserved, and served it in as many ways as other cultures have done with their own mainstays. But one method—barbecuing split salmon over alder wood—has had such enduring and widespread popularity that it is what is meant all along the coast when you hear someone is having Indian-style salmon. Many regional restaurants and special events feature alder-smoked or alder-barbecued salmon, and if you want to experience a culinary time-trip with all the setting, you can park your RV and take a 45-minute boat ride from Seattle to Blake Island State Park. However, we found that cooking salmon "Indian-style" was much too delicious to leave to such occasions. With a little ingenuity and fudging on the time-honored method of flattening the fish between two upright poles with splints of wood bracing it open, it is easy, too—just use your barbecue basket grill. Incidentally, the pre-European contact Indians used a strong-flavored eulachon or seal oil to baste the fish. Our recipe comes from a more modern tradition.

Whole salmon,* cleaned with head, tail and backfin removed
½ cup (1 stick) butter, melted
2 tablespoons brown sugar
2 tablespoons lemon juice
Alder wood or alder wood chips

Thoroughly oil a hinged barbecue basket grill. Butterfly salmon from the stomach side and remove backbone. Leave the skin intact, but trim any white membrane from the inside of the fish. Wipe the fish with a damp paper towel inside and outside. Place opened salmon in the barbecue basket grill. Grill salmon, skin side down, 10 to 12 inches from hot alder coals or charcoal to which a cup of damp alder wood chips have been added. After about 10 minutes brush the salmon with mixture of butter, brown sugar, and lemon; turn the salmon and brush the skin side with the butter mixture; and continue grilling the salmon until it flakes easily (about 10 minutes more).

Variation: If alder is unavailable, you will still enjoy salmon prepared this way over an ordinary charcoal fire or try substituting hickory chips for the alder wood chips.

*The length is what is critical—the body of the fish should fit the longest dimension of your barbecue basket grill; you can probably do a 3- to 5-pound salmon.

Pacific Stuffed Salmon

Stuffing salmon with everything from soup to nuts seems to be a Northwest Coast exercise in creativity. It is not unusual in this region, accustomed as it is to an abundance of these silvery beauties, for cooks to barbecue-bake the fish smothered in vibrant combinations of onions, garlic, peppers, tomatoes, and herbs or stuffed with highly flavored mixtures of seaweed, crumbs, and spices. But if having a whole fresh salmon is a rare and special delicacy for you, you may be happier with the subtler enhancement favored by our northern neighbors. We came by both this delightful traditional recipe and the handsome coho salmon which sold us on it through the generosity of a fisherman we met in a Vancouver Island forest campground.

Whole salmon or salmon roast, cleaned
1 apple, sliced thin
1 8-ounce package herb-seasoned stuffing
½ cup raisins
½ + cup walnuts, broken or chopped
Butter

Rinse fish in cool water and pat dry with paper towels. Lay fish on large piece of buttered heavy-duty foil. Line cavity of fish with layer of overlapping apple slices. Prepare packaged stuffing as directed on package, stirring in raisins and walnuts. Stuff cavity of fish with 1 to 2 cups of the prepared stuffing depending on the size of the fish. Dot outside of fish with bits of butter (a few tablespoons for a 6- to 8-pound fish). Measure stuffed fish at thickest point. Enclose fish in foil. Lay pouch on grill and bake over hot coals for about 10 minutes per inch of thickness. Check to see if the fish is done—cut a slit in thick part near backbone and see if flesh is opaque. If not, continue baking as long as needed.

Tip: Wrap the leftover stuffing and any leftover apple slices in aluminum foil and bake alongside the fish.

Teriyaki Steak Strips

Teriyaki, the "shining broiled" beef steak of Japan, may be more popular in America than in its home country. You can make it in a few minutes if you use lean tender beef like sirloin or tenderloin sliced in ¼-inch slices and dipped in bottled teriyaki sauce—simply grill the strips for a minute on each side. Less expensive and only slightly more trouble is teriyaki flank steak.

1½- to 2-pound flank steak
½ cup bottled teriyaki sauce

Remove the membrane and trim the steak if it needs it. Cut meat into 1-inch-wide diagonal strips. Put steak and teriyaki sauce in a sealable plastic bag and allow to marinate for at least an hour, preferably 4 hours to overnight, turning the bag from time to time. (Refrigerate if you are marinating for more than an hour or two.) Remove steak from marinade, allowing the excess marinade to drain back into the bag. (Pour the leftover marinade into a small container.) Broil the steak strips over hot coals for about 2 minutes on each side, brushing with the leftover marinade as they are grilling. Serve with rice and a simple stir-fried vegetable to complete your Japanese steakhouse dinner.

Note: Teriyaki glaze (see *Teriyaki Sea Steaks*) is a traditional finishing touch, nice but not necessary.

Teriyaki Sea Steaks

Pacific salmon or halibut steaks rival beef steak in some parts of the Northwest. Sea steaks are a breeze to grill and can be subtly and easily enhanced by various simple bastes—lemon or lime juice and melted butter, bottled Italian dressing, or herbs in melted butter or lemon juice. Or try this delicious contribution of the Japanese to Pacific Coast cuisine: sea steaks marinated and glazed with teriyaki sauce.

4 halibut or salmon steaks,
each about ¾ inch thick
½ cup bottled teriyaki sauce*
1 tablespoon oil
¼ cup bottled teriyaki glaze*
(optional)

Rinse sea steaks and pat dry with paper towels. Place steaks in a sealable plastic bag and pour teriyaki sauce and oil over the steaks. Marinate the steaks for 30 to 45 minutes, turning the bag from time to time. Remove the steaks allowing the excess marinade to drain back into the bag. (Pour the leftover marinade into a small container like a paper or plastic cup.) Broil the steaks over hot coals on an oiled grill or in an oiled barbecue basket. Grill for 3 minutes on each side or until fish flakes easily with a fork, brushing the steaks as they are grilling with the leftover marinade.

Teriyaki steaks are excellent if you stop here. But they are even better with the glaze. You can use heated bottled glaze or make your own *Teriyaki Glaze*: In a small saucepan heat ¼ cup of teriyaki sauce and 1 tablespoon sugar to simmer. Immediately reduce heat; stir in 2 teaspoons of cornstarch mixed with 1 tablespoon water and cook, stirring constantly, until it is a clear syrup. (The whole process takes only a minute or two.) Pour hot glaze over sea steaks when you serve them.

*We suggest you use bottled *Kikkoman* teriyaki sauce and teriyaki glaze. The packaged teriyaki sauces are convenient to carry but inconvenient to deal with if the whole contents are not used. Leftover bottled teriyaki sauces are good sprinkled on rice, vegetables, meats, and in other recipes.

Kodiak King Crab Legs on the Half Shell

King crab legs can be charcoal-broiled much like you would do lobster tail and are just as special a treat. Unless you are in rare circumstances, even in Alaska the crab legs are likely to be precooked and frozen. Defrost carefully in the refrigerator to preserve flavor.

4 Alaska king crab legs
½ cup (1 stick) butter, melted
⅛ teaspoon garlic powder
(optional)
1 tablespoon lemon juice
Pepper to taste

Cut a strip of shell 1 inch wide down the length of each leg. (Easier said than done, but with a small sharp knife or kitchen scissors you can do it.) Mix butter, garlic powder, and lemon juice and brush the crabmeat generously with the mixture. Broil the crab legs, shell side down, over hot coals, basting from time to time with the flavored butter, until the crabmeat is heated through. Sprinkle liberally with pepper and serve the legs in their half shells with more melted butter.

Hibachi Tidbits

Charcoal-broiling tasty tidbits to order is another popular Japanese contribution to American entertaining. Hibachi smoke wafts from Hawaiian lanaiis, California patios, and Washington decks as guests custom-cook such regional favorites as Angelenos, Shrimp Pupus, and Rumaki. You can have the same fun anywhere you have a fire. Add a pitcher of Sangria or Luau Punch and you have a party.

Angelenos

You may know these out-of-this-world morsels as Angels on Horseback or Devils on Horseback.

12 medium oysters, shucked
6 thin lean bacon slices,
  cut in halves
Pepper, preferably freshly
  ground

Sprinkle oysters with pepper and wrap a slice of bacon around each, securing by running a toothpick completely through the oyster. Grill over hot coals just until bacon is crisp, a few minutes on each side (turn with tongs).

Shrimp Pupus

The Hawaiian *pupu* is to the islands what *antipasto* is to Italy and *hors d'oeuvres* are to France, a meal before the meal made up of an array of mouth-watering appetizers.

12 uncooked large shrimps,
  shelled and deveined
6 thin lean bacon slices,
  cut in halves
6 scallions (green onions)

Ginger-Soy Marinade:
¼ cup soy sauce,
1 tablespoon sugar,
⅛ teaspoon ground ginger

Mix soy sauce, sugar and ginger. Marinate shrimp in the ginger-soy mixture while preparing the scallions. Cut the roots of the scallions and trim most of the tops, leaving about a 2-inch piece of scallion. Split scallions in half lengthwise. Lay scallion half on each shrimp and wrap a piece of bacon around, securing bacon with a toothpick run through the bundle. Grill over hot coals until bacon is crisp and shrimp is pink, 4 or 5 minutes on each side (turn with tongs).

Rumaki

6 chicken livers, halved
6 water chestnuts, halved
6 thin lean bacon slices,
  cut in halves
¼ cup Ginger-Soy Marinade
  (see *Shrimp Pupus*)

Marinate chicken livers and water chestnuts in the ginger-soy mixture while the coals are getting hot (or longer). Wrap liver half and chestnut half in piece of bacon, securing bacon with a toothpick run through the bundle. Grill over hot coals until bacon is crisp, 4 or 5 minutes on each side (turn with tongs).

Luau Ribs

5 pounds lean beef short ribs
  for barbecuing
1 cup bottled teriyaki sauce
1 cup red wine
2 tablespoons salad oil,
  preferably sesame oil
1 tablespoon sesame seeds
2 tablespoons brown sugar (or
  substitute white sugar)
1 teaspoon ground ginger *or*
  1 small piece of fresh ginger,
  crushed (optional)
4 scallions (green onions)
  including stems, chopped
Pepper to taste

On both sides of each bone, make cuts at about ¾-inch intervals almost to the bone. Mix remaining ingredients. Pour over ribs in sealable plastic bag or bags and marinate for at least an hour (in a pinch, you can skip this step). Turn the bag from time to time. Refrigerate the ribs if marinating more than an hour. (You can marinate them overnight or longer.) To cook the ribs, drain excess marinade and grill over medium-hot coals, turning and basting often with the leftover marinade, until the ribs are well browned and crisp, about 30 minutes.

Variation: Frequently Hawaiian cooks include crushed or minced garlic in the rib marinade—some use as many as 6 cloves of garlic for this amount of marinade.

Birds of Paradise

We won fourth prize in the Taylor California Cellars Great American Wine Cookout Contest with these elegant little "birds." Turkey scallops, thin slices of breast meat, play the role of veal scallops in this recipe inspired by *saltimbocca*, the Italian and American favorite so good its name means "jump in your mouth."

6 turkey scallops (about 1 pound)
6 slices Danish-style or boiled
  ham about 4 inches square
  (about 6 ounces)
6 slices Swiss cheese about 4
  inches square
½ pound fresh mushrooms,
  cleaned and sliced
½ cup butter
2 tablespoons dried chervil or
  parsley
½ cup Marsala or sherry

Between two pieces of wax paper, plastic wrap, or foil, roll out each scallop gently until it is as rectangular as possible and roughly 4 inches square. Saute sliced mushrooms in a skillet over medium-high heat in about half the butter. Stir in half the Marsala and half of the chervil. On each scallop lay one slice of ham and one slice of cheese. Mound a few tablespoons of mushroom toward end of scallop-ham-cheese stack and roll up like a jelly roll. Secure with toothpick. Melt remaining butter and stir in remaining Marsala and chervil to make a basting sauce. Broil "birds" over hot coals for 5 minutes on each side, basting frequently with sauce. Use an oiled hinged barbecue basket grill if you have one for easy turning or broil on oiled regular grill, turning carefully with tongs. Use a lid on the grill if you have one for the last few minutes on each side to enhance the barbecue flavor. Serve "birds" with rice or buttered noodles. "Birds" are more attractive—and easier to divide into four servings—if you slice them into halves or thirds.

Tips: The Swiss cheese will roll more easily if it is at room temperature. And if the cheese or ham slices are rectangular, trim them to squares for easier handling and cooking—save the trimmings for sandwiches.

Gold Coast Rock Cornish Game Hens

"A hot bird and a cold bottle"—quail and champagne—is what big spenders and their ladies used to order for an intimate supper in the Gay Nineties. It's still a combination designed to make you feel like romantic millionaires on the town, but the bird today is more likely to be a tender little game hen, and you rather than the hotel's French chef will have to do just a bit of preparation—a minor inconvenience greatly outweighed by having your pick of wonderful settings for your private dining room. To serve two for a moonlight supper:

2 1-pound Rock Cornish game hens, defrosted if frozen
¼ cup (½ stick) butter, melted
½ cup sherry
Salt and pepper

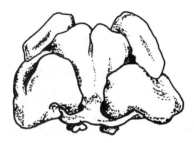

Remove giblets and discard or save for some other use. Wash birds inside and out and pat dry with paper towels. Flatten the birds for easy grilling by removing the backbone and crushing the breastbone: Hold each bird on its neck with backbone facing you and with a sharp knife or kitchen scissors cut down one side of its backbone from tail to neck; lay the bird on its side and cut the backbone off and discard the backbone; lay the bird breast side up and tuck the tips of the wings behind the back; with your hand press down hard on the bird flattening its breast; and, finally, with a small knife make 1-inch slits in skin between the thighs and the breast and push the end of each leg through its slit. This is much easier to do than it sounds. You now have a tidy little parcel that to the French fancy looks a bit like a toad (*crapaud*), which is why they call this method of preparing hens *crapaudine*.

Mix sherry and melted butter and brush the birds liberally with the mixture on both sides. Salt and pepper the birds generously. Brown the birds, skin side down, on an oiled grill over medium-hot coals for 5 minutes. Turn the birds over and continue cooking for 10 to 20 minutes until the game hens are cooked through—the juices will run clear when the thigh is pierced with a fork. Baste the birds a couple of times with the sherry-butter while it is grilling. Serve with chilled California champagne and a loaf of sourdough bread.

Variation: It takes longer, but small birds are also easy to barbecue whole and uncut, with or without stuffing. Remove giblets and wash birds as directed above. Salt and pepper insides liberally; brush butter-sherry mixture over and in each bird. Place birds breast up on cooking grill, and cover and cook using the indirect method of barbecuing for about one hour, brushing the birds with butter-sherry and rearranging them from time to time to ensure even cooking.

MOUNTAIN AND DESERT

Old West Barbecued Beef

Beef is the hands-down favorite of outdoor cooks all over the country, and more steaks and burgers are grilled in RV campsites than probably everything else put together. Nowhere is this truer than in the Mountain West which has been cattle country for more than a century and where people take their beef seriously. There are many who argue that a good piece of meat (and in these parts they won't deal in anything else) needs no more embellishment than the smoke of a charcoal or wood fire to raise it to perfection—and we are inclined to agree. For best results, choose steaks at least an inch thick and try not to overcook the meat since too long a stint on the grill can turn even a great steak into a "dry-as-prairie-dust" piece of leather.

Blue-Ribbon Steaks

1 3- to 4-pound porterhouse or
T-bone steak, cut 2 inches
thick, *or* 4 serving-size filet, rib,
club, sirloin, or T-bone steaks
cut at least 1 inch thick
Salt and pepper

Trim excess fat from outer edge of steak (save a piece of the fat and rub the grill with it). Slit remaining fat every 2 or 3 inches (just the fat not the meat). Broil steaks on greased grill over hot coals to desired doneness, turning once with tongs. If you are using a covered grill, a 2-inch steak will take at least 8 minutes on each side for rare, 10 minutes on each side for medium, and 12 minutes on each side for well done. A 1-inch steak will take about 4 minutes on each side for rare, 5 minutes on each side for medium, and 6 minutes on each side for well done. If you are using an open grill, you may have to add several minutes to the times, especially if it is cool and breezy or you are at a high altitude. When the steak is almost cooked, salt and pepper to taste. (This is the point when you can dash on seasoned salt or steak seasoning from a few feet above the grill to give it a little aromatic dazzle.) To serve the large thick steak, carve it in thin slanting slices.

Open Range Steak Barbecue

Of course, if you have a hankering for some gussied-up beef, Western cooks have been perfecting that since the days of the longhorn. The ultimate outdoor feast of the Southwest is the Barbecue with a capital B, an occasion on the grand scale of the open range and with a lineage misted in lore.

No one quite agrees on the origin of the word *barbecue*, let alone who should get credit for *the* Barbecue—a genuine American institution that ranks with the New England clambake. Some think that the word *barbecue*—like lariats, chaps, and spurs—came from south of the border, named after a wooden grill called a *barbacoa*. Others credit the French, who have a phrase for roasting on a spit: "from whiskers to tail," *barbe a' queue*. Whatever its source, say "Barbecue" and you can almost smell the tangy aroma of roasting basted beef carried on the clear air of an unspoiled Western grassland and hear the lowing of a herd off in the distance.

To experience an authentic full-scale Western Barbecue, you'll have to get yourself invited to some 1000-acre spread on a special occasion or luck into a community celebration on something like Founders' Day. The main event is likely to be whole side of beef or more—although even on Texas ranches they barbecue a variety of meats like pork, lamb, kid, and chicken. The trimmings might include coleslaw, potato salad, and beans; relishes—anything from dill pickle chips to jalapeño peppers; corn on the cob; cornbread, biscuits, or Texas toast (thick slices of French bread spread with garlic butter and grilled); and, depending on where it is, any number of Mexican specialties.

About 4 pounds steak, at least 1 inch thick (see the steaks in Blue-Ribbon Steaks for suggestions)

½ cup barbecue sauce*

Trim excess fat from outer edge of steak and slit remaining fat every 2 or 3 inches. While the coals are getting hot, put steak or steaks into a sealable plastic bag and pour barbecue sauce over meat. Seal bag and turn the bag from time to time to distribute the sauce. When the coals are hot, remove the steak from the bag allowing the excess barbecue sauce to run back into the bag. Broil steak on greased grill to desired doneness, turning once with tongs and basting with leftover barbecue sauce from time to time. See Blue-Ribbon Steaks for approximate broiling times.

*There are as many barbecue sauces as there are outdoor cooks in the West—maybe more. Although those who make a business or an art of the Barbecue often mix up their secret formulas by the bucket, they swear that a fraction of this or that can make a difference—and maybe it does. In any case, barbecue sauce recipes tend to be complicated and seem like a lot of trouble if you only want a dab, especially when there are so many good ones commercially available. If you have a chance, we heartily recommend trying one of the regional bottled barbeque sauces, for example, *Bill Johnson's Famous Barbeque Sauce* out of Phoenix, or *Ol' Hired Hand's BBQ Sauce*, originally from San Angelo, Texas. Try to avoid sauces that add "smoke flavor": your Open Range Barbecue will supply the real thing. If for some reason, you'd still like to make your own sauce, see A *word about barbecue sauces* earlier in this chapter.

Chuck Wagon Chuck

Tough cuts get to be fit fare for tenderfoots and hard-to-please rangehands with this Southwestern barbecue secret. Choose a round, flank, or chuck steak or roast at least 1 inch thick, preferably more—up to 2½ inches thick. If you have time you can marinate the steak overnight or for several hours and skip the tenderizer.

**3- to 4-pound chuck steak,
cut about 1½ inches thick
Unseasoned meat tenderizer
1 tablespoon chili can carne
seasoning
½ cup bottled Italian dressing**

Apply tenderizer to meat according to package directions but going a little easy on the tenderizer. Trim excess fat from edges of meat. In a small container (a paper cup will do) mix Italian dressing and chili con carne seasoning. Put steak in a sealable plastic freezer bag and pour dressing-chili mixture in bag over meat. Seal bag and leave at room temperature (or in refrigerator) for ½ to 2 hours or more, turning bag to distribute marinade from time to time. When coals are ready, remove steak from bag, allowing excess marinade to drain back into bag, and grill for about 30 to 40 minutes (15 to 20 minutes on each side) or until steak is well browned outside and done to your taste inside. For covered grills, reduce cooking time by 10 minutes and be sure to leave the lid off for a few minutes on each side to sear the meat. A chuck roast 2½ inches thick will take about 55 minutes and should be basted with the leftover marinade from time to time. A flank steak will usually only take 5 to 7 minutes on each side.

Chuck Wagon Baked Beans

Campfire beans, the ever popular side dish of many a cookout, come to the table straight from the can or gussied-up with a dash of this and that according to the cook's whim. This spicy Colorado recipe takes a bit of the fire with it to the table.

**1 28-ounce can baked beans
(the originator of this recipe
insists on Bush's)
½ cup hot pepper rings or sliced
pepperocini
¼ cup maple pancake syrup**

Combine ingredients in a small ovenproof pan (a cake pan or a saucepan or skillet with heatproof handle.) Bake uncovered on an open or covered grill for 45 minutes. Actually, the beans are fully cooked when you start, so all you really *need* to do is heat the beans through.

Hamburger with a Surprise

Multimillion-dollar ad campaigns have been waged on the premise that charcoal-broiled burgers are better, and, according to generations of campers, nothing beats the burgers *you* broil in the great outdoors. Everyone has a hot tip for making the perfect burger—a couple of tablespoons of steak sauce or soy sauce mixed into the hamburger or a bit of ice water or ice in the center to keep the middle rare. The basic technique is simple and the results foolproof: use lean hamburger, don't overhandle the meat, make your patties at least ¾ inch thick (no more than 4 to a pound), sear the meat by leaving the lid off for 1 or 2 minutes on each side if you are using a covered grill, use a hinged barbecue basket grill for easy turning or use a pancake turner, and broil for about 3 minutes on each side for rare or 5 minutes on each side for well done. What you do in addition to make your burgers special is limited only by your imagination.

1½ pounds lean ground beef
Choice of fillings: 2 slices of Swiss,
Monterey Jack, or Cheddar
cheese; thin onion slices and
2 slices of American process
cheese; 2 ounces of Roquefort
or blue cheese formed into 4
small flattened balls; pickle
relish, mustard, and small
cubes of American cheese;
4-ounce can of mushrooms
broiled in butter; or 4-ounce
can of chopped green chilies
(more than enough)

Divide the meat into eight equal portions (about a ⅓ cup for each). Shape each portion into a large (about 4 inches) patty. (If you measure the meat with a measuring cup and use wax paper or plastic wrap on top and bottom when you flatten the patties, you'll have virtually no cleanup and clean hands.)

Using half of the patties as bottoms arrange your choice of filling in the center of each patty—use half a slice of cheese (break off the corners) or a couple of tablespoons of chopped filling for each, leaving at least a ½-inch border. You can also add a pinch or sprinkle of seasoning to the filling at this point. Top with remaining 4 patties, sealing edges well. Broil as usual increasing time slightly.

Fiesta Burgers

The flavor is in and on this upper Rio Grande specialty.

1½ pounds lean ground beef
¾ cup green chile salsa*
1 tomato, sliced
Guacamole (see index)

Mix green chile salsa into ground beef. Shape meat into 4 patties about ¾ inch thick. Broil as usual to desired doneness. Top each burger with 1 or 2 slices of tomato and a dollop of guacamole and serve on grilled hamburger buns brushed with butter. Nacho or corn tortilla chips are a nice complement and handy for the remaining guacamole.

Territorial House Gourmet Green Salsa from Corrales, New Mexico, is excellent and authentic. If green chile salsa isn't available, substitute a picante sauce.

Mile High Cracked Pepper Steak

High living is nothing new to the High Country. You would have been as likely to dine in the grand style on such epicurean specialties as Steak au Poivre—accompanied by a vintage bordeaux—in the sandstone castles of the 1880s as in the high-rises of the 1980s. It may even taste better in your open-air dining room.

4 small New York steaks or club steaks, cut 1 inch thick
1 tablespoon black peppercorns, crushed, *or* 2 teaspoons coarsely ground black pepper
¼ cup brandy *

Spread pepper over both sides of steaks and push the pepper hard into the surface of the meat with the back of a spoon. Let steaks rest at room temperature while coals are getting hot—about 30 minutes. Broil steaks on lightly greased grill over hot coals to desired doneness, turning once with tongs. Rare will take about 5 minutes on each side, medium about 6 minutes on each side, and well done about 7 minutes on each side. Transfer steaks to a heatproof pan or plate. In your smallest pan, warm the brandy (you can do this right on the grill) and then ignite the brandy and pour or spoon over steaks. *Caution*: Turn off your over-the-range fan if you do this on the stovetop.

Tips: Since you are unlikely to have a mortar and pestle with you, a simple neat alternate way to crack peppercorns is to put them in a sealed plastic sandwich bag, lay it on your cutting board, and, holding a metal tablespoon loosely by the end of the handle, tap the peppercorns with the back of the spoon.

Note: The flames can blaze up quite high when you light the brandy, so be careful that your hand is not above the pan: use a fireplace match or light a little of the warm brandy in a spoon, stand back and pour the flaming brandy into the brandy in the pan.

*Miniature brandy bottles are usually 1/10 pint or 50 milliliters, just a little less than a ¼ cup and fine for this recipe.

HEARTLAND

Illinois Brat Broil

The popular Heartland brat broil is a gourmet version of the American wiener roast with a strong German accent. Grilled bratwurst of veal and/or pork and other German sausages are served on brat buns (like the individual loaves of French bread used for submarine sandwiches) with mustard and, sometimes, sauerkraut. Beer is an essential ingredient of a traditional brat broil, both to drink icy cold and to cook the brats. And, as at most other summer picnics in this part of the country, corn on the cob and potato salad are usually on the menu.

8 bratwurst
1 12-ounce can or bottle of beer (flat beer is OK)
8 brat buns or French rolls

On your RV stovetop simmer the bratwurst and beer in a covered pan until cooked through (grey in the middle), about 20 minutes. Drain bratwurst and broil on charcoal grill over hot coals until nicely browned on all sides (about 10 minutes). Serve hot from the grill on a split roll with mustard on hand for each person to add to taste.

Heartland Corn Roast

Although corn on the cob plays a feature role in many of America's summer cookouts, in the Heartland it is often the star of the menu. You can take your pick of ways to roast corn on the cob—all of them good but each a little different—in or out of the husk, on the coals or on the grill. And the variations and additions within those variables are legion. Times on roasting corn are wildly approximate, based not only on the usual barbecue variables but also on your preference, the tenderness of the corn, and how long it's been since it was standing in the field. Corn roasted in its husk comes out suntanned. Corn in foil is more like boiled corn.

8 to 12 ears of fresh corn in husks

Peel back the corn husk on each ear and remove the silk. Lay the husk back in place and tie with string or a strip of husk. Soak corn ears in cold water from 5 minutes to an hour. Shake off excess water. Roast the corn directly on coals for 8 to 15 minutes *or* on the grill over medium-hot to hot coals for 15 to 30 minutes, turning the corn from time to time as it is roasting. Strip off husks and serve hot corn immediately with butter, salt, and pepper.

Corn in Foil

8 to 12 ears of fresh corn
Butter

Strip husks and silk from corn ears and rinse the corn ears in water. Butter ears of corn with soft butter. Wrap each ear separately in a piece of heavy-duty foil. Place directly on the coals for 10 to 15 minutes *or* on the grill over medium-hot to hot coals for 15 to 20 minutes, turning the corn from time to time as it is roasting. Serve with additional butter, salt, and pepper.

Tip: A Corn Country tip for easy buttering of hot corn is to fill a large clean coffee can ⅔ full of water, add 2 sticks (1 cup) of butter, and heat the water and butter until the butter is melted. The butter floats on top and, as each hot ear of corn is dipped into the can, the ears come out evenly coated with melted butter.

Champion Fish in Foil

From the thousands and thousands of lakes and the streams and rivers of the Heartland comes a bounty that has fed the dreams of fishermen and the bellies of the lucky since the dawn of history. In the late 1600s, Baron La Horton, a French traveler to Michigan, wrote of "trout as big as one's thigh." If you should happen to come by one of them—or a more petite specimen—or of any of the many other good-eating varieties that abound in the region, light the fire and prepare to enjoy one of America's most legendary meals.

This is a succulent solution to cooking the big ones that don't get away—trout, pike, salmon, whitefish.

Whole fish, cleaned
1 lemon, sliced thin
1 sweet onion, sliced thin
White wine or vermouth
Salt and pepper
Butter

Rinse fish in cool water and pat dry with paper towels. Generously salt and pepper fish inside and out. Lay fish on large piece of buttered heavy-duty foil. Line cavity of fish with layer of overlapping lemon slices alternating with onion slices. Measure stuffed fish at thickest point. Sprinkle several tablespoons of wine over fish (about 4 to 6 for a 5-pound fish.) Enclose fish in foil. Lay pouch on grill and bake over hot coals for about 10 minutes per inch of thickness. Check to see if the fish is done—cut a slit in thick part near backbone and see if flesh is opaque. If not, continue baking as long as needed; the fish is unlikely to get dry using this method even if it takes considerably longer to cook than the 10-minute-per-inch rule of thumb. If it does seem to be getting dry when you check it, dribble in a tablespoon or two of melted butter or oil.

Tip: This is a delicious way of cooking smaller fish like 1-pound trout as well as the big ones. Follow the same directions, wrapping each fish separately. We know fisherfolk who like this recipe so well that they travel with a bottle of vermouth just for this purpose. Of course, since you have the vermouth and the lemon peel, you might want to make a Martini while the fish is cooking.

Lickety-Split Small Fry

When your catch from lake, stream, or supermarket comes up several pounds shy of the record, skip the frying pan and broil the fish directly over the coals. With this fuss-free recipe, no one will remember that they were small, they'll only remember how good they tasted.

4 to 8 ½- to 1-pound fish (trout, walleye, salmon, sunfish, rockfish, sea bass, baby blues, etc.), cleaned
1 cup bottled Italian dressing

Thoroughly oil a hinged barbecue basket grill. Rinse cleaned whole fish in cool water and pat dry inside and out. Pour dressing into and over outside of each fish and leave to marinate for up to an hour if you have the time. (Try using a plastic bag for this step to save cleanup.) Place fish in basket grill with a little space between fish. Grill over hot coals for about 7 to 10 minutes per side (less if they are very small fish) or until flesh appears opaque and fish flakes easily when tested with a fork. While the fish are cooking, baste with leftover marinade from time to time. When fish are cooked, lift side of grill carefully, loosening any skin stuck to the grill with a tip of a knife.

Cornbelt Fish

Fish and corn are popular flavor-mates across the country. In mid-America, where a supply of both may be located within walking distance from camp, an old favorite of the region's fishermen is preparing fish *in* corn—husks that is.

8 ½-pound fish, cleaned
1 cup (2 sticks) butter
Lemon juice (a 2½-ounce plastic lemon will be more than enough)
Salt and pepper
8 cornhusks, whole but with silk removed

Rinse cleaned fish in cool water and pat dry inside and out. Fish may be deheaded if you prefer. Soak cornhusks in water about 5 minutes. In the cavity of each fish place a 2-tablespoon chunk of butter and squirt about a teaspoon of lemon juice. Sprinkle each fish generously with salt and pepper inside and out. Lay each fish in a whole cornhusk with the head end at the stem end of the husk. Tie cornhusk at tail end with a string or strip of cornhusk. Place husk-wrapped fish directly on bed of hot coals and cook about 15 minutes or until fish flakes easily when tested with a fork.

Tip: To get the cornhusks off the ears of corn as a whole intact husk, peel the leaves of the husk back and down a few at a time until the entire ear of corn is uncovered. Break the ear from the stem and wipe out the corn silk clinging to the husk. Fold the leaves of the husk back to their original position.

Fresh Lemon Trout

Another delicious alternative to pan-frying your catch is this fresh lemon treatment. It enhances various small (¾ to 1 pound) fish from the bluefish of the Atlantic to the rockfish of the Pacific, but it is custom-made for the several kinds of trout in the inland waters.

4 1-pound trout, cleaned but left whole
Salad oil
4 lemons
Salt and pepper

Thoroughly oil a hinged barbecue basket grill. Rinse cleaned whole fish in cool water and pat dry inside and out. Generously salt and pepper cavity of fish. Slice two of the lemons and fill the cavity of each fish with a layer of lemon slices (a half lemon to each fish). Cut remaining lemons into wedges and use a couple to rub the outside of each fish. Save the rest of the lemon wedges to serve with the fish. Generously rub each fish with oil and sprinkle generously with salt and pepper. Place fish in basket grill with a little space between fish. Grill over hot coals for about 7 to 10 minutes per side or until flesh appears opaque and fish flakes easily when tested with a fork. When fish is cooked, lift side of grill carefully, loosening any skin stuck to the grill with the tip of a knife.

Variation: One of the best destinies for fresh mint other than a julep glass is the inside of a trout. Add a handful of washed and bruised mint along with the lemon slices, for *Fresh Mint Trout.*

CRADLE OF LIBERTY

All recipes serve four unless otherwise stated.

Orangerie Lamb

Much of the lamb raised in America ends up on tables in the Northeast served in traditional American, Middle Eastern, or Mediterranean specialties. Among the many exotic and complex recipes, none is more time-honored and prized than lamb prepared over the coals. With no more than a generous sprinkle of salt and pepper, skewered 2-inch chunks of lamb chops and steaks are enhanced by simply barbecuing. You can easily add traditional flavor accents by throwing a cut garlic clove in the fire while grilling or brushing the lamb before and during grilling with bottled mint sauce or bottled Italian or garlic dressing. Almost as easy is this fragrant orange-honey baste.

4 lamb steaks or lamb chops
¼ cup (½ stick) butter, melted
Grated peel of a large orange (about 1 tablespoon)
1 tablespoon honey
1 teaspoon dried chervil or parsley
Salt and pepper

Mix butter, orange peel, honey, and chervil. Brush lamb on both sides with mixture. Cook chops directly on grill or in a barbecue basket grill over hot coals for about 5 minutes on each side, brushing with butter mixture from time to time, until cooked to desired doneness. Season to taste with salt and pepper.

Variation: For a more traditional sauce, substitute 1 tablespoon chopped fresh mint or 1 teaspoon dried mint for the chervil and omit the orange peel.

Roquefort Lamb

Two flavorful additions give grilled lamb the gourmet treatment.

4 lamb steaks or lamb chops
4 ounces Roquefort or blue
cheese
1 garlic clove, crushed

Mash the cheese to a paste with the garlic in a small container (preferably disposable). Lightly spread both sides of lamb with cheese mixture. Cook lamb directly on grill or in a barbecue basket grill over hot coals for about 5 minutes on one side. Turn and spread top side with remaining cheese and cook for another 5 minutes or so until the bottom is browned and lamb is cooked to desired doneness. (If you are used to cooking lamb very well done, try cooking it more like you like your steaks.)

Variation: Substitute a herb-and-garlic triple-cream cheese such as Boursin for the Roquefort and garlic.

New England Beach Bake

The most famous and longest-running favorite of America's cookout feasts, the New England clambake is an experience no visitor to the region should miss if the opportunity presents itself. An authentic, traditional clambake is an elaborate production that takes several hours: digging the firepit and lining it with selected stones, laying the fire, removing the coals and layering the pit with seaweed and food, closing the bake, the actual cooking, and, finally, the moment everyone has been waiting for—the opening of the bake.

Besides clams, the bake may include other shellfish such as oysters, hard-shell crabs, and lobsters, as well as fish chunks or fillets, meat, chicken, white and sweet potatoes, onions, and, almost as necessary as the clams, corn, usually baked in the husk. Whether the clambake is to feed 6 or 600, a good deal of effort is involved and at least some special equipment. You can, of course, make a foil-pouch dinner with some of the elements of a clambake—rockweed, clams, precooked chicken, corn, and precooked lobster. But you can't foilwrap the main ingredient of a clambake—its centuries-old link with the past as a communal event. The gathering and the occasion are at least as important as the food. It seems to us, you can no more have an individual clambake than a one-man parade. It would be better to enjoy the incredibly easy, maybe even tastier, perhaps as popular, and at least as ancient method of baking clams on the beach: simply heating them over the coals until they pop open.

80 clams, cleaned and well-
scrubbed (see index)
1 cup (2 sticks) butter, melted

Choose either Eastern hard-shell or soft-shell clams, allowing more or less than 20 a serving depending on their size and your appetites. (Several West Coast varieties of clams can be prepared this way also). Arrange clams directly on grill and cook over low heat coals until clams begin to open (about 3 to 5 minutes); turn clams over and continue to cook until they pop wide open. Meanwhile, melt butter in a small saucepan and set it on or near the grill. Protecting your hand from the hot shell, pick up a clam and drain juices into the pan with the butter. Serve clams straight from the grill with the clam-flavored butter and bread.

Charcoal-Broiled Maine Lobster

An all-American favorite, broiled lobster is at its best when done over the coals. Though some recipes call for splitting the live lobster, we think this technique is less traumatic (for cook and lobster) and gives better results.

4 1- to 2-pound live lobsters
½ cup (1 stick) butter, melted
Vegetable oil

Plunge the live lobsters into vigorously boiling water. Boil for 5 minutes. Remove the lobsters and allow to cool for easier handling. (In the likelihood that you don't have a kettle large enough for four lobsters, do them one or two at a time.) Split each lobster in half lengthwise through the middle and rinse out its entrails. Brush the cut side of the lobster with butter. Place the lobster halves flesh side down on a well-oiled grill and broil over medium-hot coals for about 6 minutes. Turn over the lobster halves and brush with butter generously. Continue brushing the lobster halves with butter from time to time and broiling until the flesh is opaque—check at about 10 minutes. Serve with a cup of melted butter and lemon wedges.

Skewered Sea Scallops

Either sea scallops or large bay scallops can be used in this barbecue favorite. The recipe makes a generous main course for four scallop fanciers. If the market price is steep, you may want to make half as much and serve it as an appetizer or part of a mixed grill: a surf-and-turf plate of skewered scallops and a small steak, for example.

2 pounds scallops
12 strips lean bacon
¼ cup lemon juice
Salt and pepper
½ cup (1 stick) butter, melted

If you are using frozen scallops, defrost completely in refrigerator. If scallops are very large (more than 2 inches across), cut scallops in half. Rinse the scallops in cool water and pat dry with paper towels. Cut bacon into 2-inch pieces and fry for a few minutes until partially cooked. Drain on paper towels. Mix lemon juice, about a teaspoon of salt, and a generous dash of pepper in a small container (a paper or plastic cup will work well). Drop in scallops one at a time and coat well. Alternately thread bacon and scallops snugly on 8 metal or wooden skewers and brush with melted butter. Broil the scallops over hot coals, turning from time to time and basting with the melted butter frequently, until bacon is crisp and scallops are opaque throughout (about 10 minutes or longer).

Variations: For those who can't bear to tamper with the distinctive flavor of scallops, skip the bacon in the above recipe. For those who like to gild lillies, add a finely grated onion and/or a chopped garlic clove to the lemon coating. More subtle additions are a teaspoon of chopped fresh dill or dried chervil or parsley stirred into the melted butter.

Hudson River Shad Bake

Early explorers of America's Atlantic coastal rivers found such "an abundance of fish, lying so thicke with their heads above the water" that Captain John Smith reported that they "attempted to catch them with a frying pan." One of the most populous and popular of the fish of the Hudson, Connecticut, and Delaware rivers was the spring migrant scientifically known as "most delicious shad." George Washington, Thomas Jefferson, and countless other Americans have looked forward to shad season and the incomparable flavor of barbecued shad. In some Hudson River towns the shad bake is as popular as the clambake is in New England. Planked shad, boned whole shad nailed to a board through bacon strips and cooked as the Indians did with the board propped almost upright beside a long firepit, is the most famous shad recipe and the way to do it if you are having a few hundred people for dinner. For a more intimate gathering try this adaptation.

2 ½ to 3 pounds shad, filleted but with skin left on*
½ cup (1 stick) butter
3 tablespoons sherry
Salt and pepper

Rinse fillet in cool water and pat dry with paper towels. Leave skin on fillet and line skin side of fillet with aluminum foil bringing the foil up around the fish like a shallow pan. Melt the butter in a small saucepan and stir in sherry. Dribble the butter-sherry sauce over and under the fillet so that it is well-coated on both sides. Bake shad in a covered grill over medium-hot coals for about 20 minutes, lifting lid to baste with sauce occasionally. Do not turn the shad over. The shad is done when its flesh is opaque and flakes easily when tested with a fork. Salt and pepper the shad to taste before serving.

Variations: Omit the sherry and about half the butter and bake the shad with two or three strips of bacon laid across the top of the fillet. Or add a sprinkle of thyme or paprika before baking.

*Shad is such a bony fish that you may have to pay dearly to buy it boned—worth it in our opinion. Otherwise, follow the general directions for filleting fish. Good luck.

DIXIE

Mahogany Chicken

There seem to be at least as many recipes for Southern barbecued chicken as there are for fried chicken, although the outdoor cooks seem less bound by tradition and may use almost anything on the pantry shelf from peanut butter to puffed rice to give distinction to their creation. Two bottle sauces you're likely to have on hand give Mahogany Chicken its color and character. We can see why a version of this recipe is purported to be a favorite of former President Jimmy Carter.

4 whole chicken breasts
3 tablespoons butter, melted
2 tablespoons Worcestershire
  sauce
1 tablespoon soy sauce

Wash chicken breasts and pat dry with paper towels. Mix butter, Worcestershire sauce, and soy sauce. Brush breasts generously with butter mixture. Place chicken, skin side up, on a lightly oiled grill over low-heat coals. Cook, turning and basting with butter mixture occasionally, for 30 to 40 minutes or until chicken is cooked through. If you are using other chicken parts or chicken halves increase the cooking time.

Orange Blossom Pork with Yams

A good old-fashioned dinner that would be an ideal choice for some leisurely Sunday afternoon dining Southern-style. The cooking time is longer than most of our recipes—a good reason for roasting the loin outside your RV. And, of course, the barbecue smoke is a flavor bonus. For an extra touch try adding a couple of handfuls of damp hickory chips on the coals midway through the cooking.

2½ to 3½ pounds lean rolled
  pork loin (no thicker than 3
  inches)
Salt and pepper
½ cup orange marmalade
4 yams (choose serving-size yams
  that are on the long side rather
  than chubby for easier baking)
Butter

Rinse loin with cool water and pat dry with paper towels. Generously salt and pepper loin on all sides. To cook the loin use a covered grill and the indirect method of barbecuing with a drip pan. Place the loin over the drip pan on oiled grill and roast for about 1½ hours or until pork is thoroughly cooked. Meanwhile, scrub yams, pat dry, rub with butter, pierce skin, and wrap each yam in foil. After the pork has been cooking about a half hour, add a half dozen coals to the fire and arrange the yams alongside the loin. In another half hour, turn the yams, check to see if the meat is cooking evenly—if not, rearrange the loin—and begin basting with marmalade. Continue to brush the loin frequently with the marmalade until the pork is done (170°).

Bourbon London Broil

There are some bourbon fanciers who think a splashful of America's finest does wonders for almost anything from canapes to cakes. And, if this recipe is any indication, they may be right.

1½- to 2-pound flank steak
¼ cup bourbon
¼ cup honey
¼ cup soy sauce
2 tablespoons lemon juice

Mix bourbon, honey, soy sauce, and lemon with ¾ cup water. Score flank steak with light diagonal cuts on both sides. Put steak and marinade in a sealable plastic bag and allow to marinate in the refrigerator for at least an hour, preferably 4 hours to overnight. Remove steak from marinade and grill 5 minutes on each side so it is browned on the outside but still rare in the center. Let rest for a few minutes before slicing in thin slices across the grain.

Variation: Substitute ¼ cup red or white wine and ¼ cup soy sauce for the bourbon marinade; turn the bag occasionally while marinating.

Buccaneer's Shrimp

From the southern coast of America—Florida and the Gulf—comes some of the world's finest and largest shrimp, prime candidates for grilling and baking in various luscious ways. Peppery shrimp swimming in butter baked over the coals of a driftwood fire on a moonlit beach is the stuff dreams are made of, but you'll enjoy Buccaneer's Shrimp almost as much in a landlocked campground.

2 pounds unshelled raw shrimp, deheaded
1½ cups (3 sticks) butter
2 or 3 tablespoons coarse black pepper

Make a large baking pan of aluminum foil. Combine shrimp, chunks of butter, and pepper in pan. Bake in a covered grill over hot coals until pink (about 15 to 30 minutes). Serve with lime or lemon wedges and the best bread you can find.

Imperial Shrimp Toby

A famed specialty of Morgan City, Louisiana, Imperial Shrimp Toby can be prepared in the same way as Buccaneer's Shrimp.

2 pounds unshelled raw shrimp, deheaded
½ cup (1 stick) butter
¼ cup sherry
2 tablespoons Worcestershire sauce
Hot pepper sauce*
Salt and pepper

Make a large baking pan of aluminum foil. Spread the shrimp in the pan; sprinkle with salt, pepper, sherry, Worcestershire, and hot pepper sauce (to taste, go lightly if you are tender-mouths). Dot with butter. Bake in a covered grill over hot coals until pink (about 15 to 30 minutes).

*Louisiana is famous for its hot pepper sauces such as *Tabasco* and *RedHot! Sauce.*

Carolina Oyster Roast

Almost as rich in lore and time-honored as the New England clambake, the Southern oyster roast is a delightful and traditional way to enjoy this popular shellfish. As experienced by generations of Southerners from Maryland to Georgia, the oysters, steamed by the bushelful over an open fire, are but the prelude to a full-scale picnic. The other foods served at an oyster roast are not as dictated by tradition as at a clambake, but a familiar follow-up is hot Hopping John and biscuits. In earlier days, when oysters were more plentiful and appetites larger, oyster roasts techniques were evolved to deal with oysters by the wheelbarrowful. Our adaptation is for a more moderate amount.

48 (a dozen for each person) oysters in the shell
Melted butter, lemon wedges, and ketchup or cocktail sauce

Rinse the oysters until they are relatively free of sand—the shells don't have to be scrubbed clean. Arrange as many of the oysters as will fit comfortably on your grill in no more than two layers (about 24 on a 14-inch grill). Drape oysters with several layers of wet paper towels. Roast oysters over medium-hot coals for 20 minutes, sprinkling water over towels as needed to keep them damp (not dripping). The oysters will roast more evenly if midway through you shuffle the oysters around. Serve the hot oysters immediately with bowls of melted butter, lemon wedges, and ketchup or cocktail sauce. The roasting steams the oysters open slightly; have your most deft diner open them the rest of the way for all of you. Meanwhile, put the next batch of oysters on to roast.

SHISH KEBAB, YAKITORI, SHASHLIK, BROCHETTES

As easy as cooking a hot dog—well, almost—and offering infinitely more opportunity for adventurous eating, kebab cooking turns everyone into a creative chef. Kebabs can be cooked on metal or bamboo skewers or even on sharp sticks of green wood over the smallest of makeshift grills or campfires. We think kebab cooking is the most fun when the kebabs grow like a Dagwood Bumstead sandwich out of whatever is on hand. Cut everything into 1- to 2-inch cubes or pieces and make a faint effort to string foods together that take about the same time to cook. If you have a very small fire, make your cubes relatively small. Crowded, tightly packed skewers cook more slowly, so if you like your meat well done give it a little space on the skewer.

Albacore to Zucchini Kebabs

Take your pick from the following possibilities and design your own kebabs. As a rule of thumb, allow 1 to 2 pounds of meat or seafood to serve four. For inspiration think about foods that go together in other dishes like fish with onions, tomatoes, peppers, and mushrooms or liver with onions and bacon. And don't forget that a dab will do—that leftover baked potato or half dozen olives at the back of the refrigerator may be just what you need to balance your creation.

Thread cubes alternately on 4 to 8 skewers putting oily foods next to vegetables or fruits and juicy foods next to dry foods. Brush kebabs with your choice of baste and grill over medium-hot coals on a well-oiled grill. Turn the kebabs now and then as they are cooking and baste frequently. Allow about 15 minutes cooking time for meats (very approximate) and about 10 minutes for fish. Better yet, poke around and taste until it is done to your liking—we've been known to be down to our last kebab before we got it "just right."

Note: If you're still feeling timid, see the two classic combinations that follow to get you started.

Albacore or other firm-fleshed fish fillets
Apples
Apricot halves
Artichoke hearts
Bacon, cut into squares or wrapped around other foods
Brussel sprouts, partially cooked
Bread, cubed and buttered
Cabbage, cut in small wedges or wrapped around other foods
Cantaloupe (use for desserts or tropical main dishes)
Chicken (possibly marinated)*
Chicken livers
Doughnuts (cake-type)
Eggplant, cubed with the skin on
Fishsticks
Frankfurters
Green or red peppers
Grapes
Ham
Idaho potatoes, at least partially cooked
Jalapeños or milder green chiles
King crab legs, defrosted
Lamb (possibly marinated)
Lemon wedges
Lichee nuts
Lime wedges
Liver
Lobster
Maraschino cherries
Marshmallows
Meatballs (make them small and firm)
Mushrooms
New potatoes, partially cooked unless tiny
Olives (pitted or stuffed, black or green)

Onions
Oranges, unpeeled wedges
Oysters (fresh or canned smoked oysters)
Pineapple (fresh or canned)
Pork (possibly marinated and/or precooked)*
Potato products (potato puffs, canned potatoes)
Poundcake, cut in 2-inch cubes and buttered
Quail or other small birds, marinated*
Red snapper
Salmon
Sausages (any variety)
Scallions with part of the tops
Scallops
Shrimp, shelled or unshelled
Spiced crabapples
Sweet pickles
Tomatoes
Turkey, (possibly marinated)*
U.S. Choice Beef in all tender cut (or tenderize tougher cuts)
Veal
Water chestnuts
Yams, precooked or canned
Zucchini or other summer squash

½ to 1 cup of your choice of bastes: melted butter (plain or with a teaspoon of herbs stirred in); salad oil (plain or seasoned); bottled salad dressing (Italian, French, etc.); barbecue sauce; teriyaki sauce; lemon juice and butter or oil.

***These foods should be cut in small (½ inch) cubes.**

Ham and Yam Kebabs

2 pounds cooked ham, cut in
   1-inch cubes
2 pound fresh yams, peeled,
   cooked, and cut in 1-inch
   pieces (or substitute canned
   candied yams and handle very
   gently)
1 medium green pepper, cubed
1 20-ounce can pineapple chunks
   or fresh pineapple, cut in
   chunks
1 10-ounce jar orange marmalade

Thread cubes alternately on 6 to 8 skewers. Brush kebabs with marmalade. Grill over medium-hot coals for 15 to 20 minutes, brushing with marmalade frequently.

Surf and Turf Kebabs

1 pound sirloin steak, cut into
   1¼-inch cubes
16 large shrimp, peeled and
   deveined *or* 16 large scallops
   or 1 12-ounce package frozen
   Alaska king crab legs,
   defrosted, shell and tendons
   removed, and cut into 16 pieces
16 mushroom caps
16 cherry tomatoes
¼ cup (½ stick) butter, melted
¼ cup white or rosé wine

Thread vegetables, steak, and shellfish alternately on 8 skewers, starting and ending with mushroom caps. Mix melted butter and wine and brush kebabs generously. Grill kebabs over medium-hot coals for about 15 minutes, turning occasionally and basting with butter-wine (especially the shellfish) frequently.

SURPRISE PACKAGES

Though most of the time we cook over the coals for the added flavor, foil-wrapped foods can be just the ticket for some circumstances—the fire is already going for something else; a hot meal sounds good but a hot rig doesn't. Well, get out the roll of aluminum foil, put another log on the fire, and treat yourself to some surprisingly easy and tasty fare.

Sunset Stew

1½ pounds lean chuck or sirloin, cut into 1-inch cubes (if you use a tougher cut of beef, use unseasoned tenderizer as directed on package)
4 medium potatoes, peeled and diced
4 carrots, cut into ¼-inch slices
4 teaspoons instant minced onion
1 10½-ounce can condensed beefy mushroom soup
Salt and pepper

Tear off 4 18-inch squares of heavy-duty foil (or use two overlapping layers of regular foil). In the center of each square, place ¼ of the meat, potatoes, carrots, and instant onion (skip for those who don't like onion—this stew is very easy to customize). Pepper generously and salt lightly (skip the salt if you have used tenderizer). Pour ¼ of the condensed soup on each portion (about ¼ cup). Bring up corners of foil and twist at top to make a bundle. Put bundles on grill over hot coals and let bake for an hour while you watch the sunset or take a walk—don't worry about the stew overcooking if you take the long way back, the coals will burn down and keep the stew-bundles nice and warm. Serve in the foil and cut your dishwashing to almost nothing.

Variations: You can make the stew fancier by adding a pinch or dash of your favorite stew seasoning and tossing in another half cup of vegetables in each bundle—sliced celery, sliced or quartered mushrooms, diced turnip, etc. Or you can make a super-streamlined *O'Brien Stew*: Cut the meat cubes a littler smaller; substitute 1 24-ounce package of frozen potatoes O'Brien for the vegetables (about 1½ cups in each bundle); add the soup, salt, and pepper; and cook as above. Lamb can be used instead of beef.

Tips: You can make the bundles earlier in the day and refrigerate. If you get rained out, bake the bundles in the RV oven at 400° for an hour (put the bundles on your baking sheet for easier handling).

La Dolce Vita Chicken

Chicken Cacciatore takes to the sweet life of the RVer with zero mess thanks to foil.

3 pounds of chicken parts
1 15½-ounce jar Italian-style baking sauce *or* chunky garden-style spaghetti sauce
Parmesan cheese, grated

Rinse chicken pieces and pat dry with paper towels. Brown the chicken pieces on grill over medium-hot coals. (If it is more convenient, brown the chicken on the stovetop in ¼ cup cooking oil.) Tear off 2 24-inch pieces of heavy-duty foil. Arrange the chicken pieces on the double layer of foil, spread sauce evenly over chicken, and enclose chicken in foil making a fairly flat neat package. Place chicken package, seam up, on grill and cook over medium-hot coals for 30 minutes or until chicken is cooked through. Serve with grated Parmesan cheese and hot pasta—the traditional accompaniments to one of America's favorite Italian dishes. Or just sprinkle with Parmesan and pass around a fresh loaf of Italian bread to break into chunks for an easy alfresco picnic.

Variations: Change the nationality of La Dolce Vita Chicken by substituting other international baking sauces and omitting the Parmesan cheese.

We doubt if there is much that hasn't been cooked with more or less success in a foil pouch: whole pineapples; biscuits (wrapped loosely in buttered foil so they can rise); various "TV-dinner" combinations (chicken, potato, peas, and carrots; lamb chop, green beans, and potato); every conceivable combination of vegetables cut in small pieces and dotted with herbs and butter; and various local exotica that defied conventional cooking. Experienced mountaineers do it, scouts do it, and you can do it with nothing more than foil and a spirit of adventure. Juicy foods steam in their own juices and don't actually need anything else. Drier foods benefit by a dab of butter or a little liquid. Double wrap foods and seal the openings snugly. Take care not to burn yourself with the escaping steam when you open the packages. And have fun experimenting. Here are a few of the standbys to get you started:

Baked potatoes: Scrub potatoes. Poke thick-skinned potatoes with a fork several times. Rub the whole potato with butter or oil. Wrap in foil. Bake 45 to 60 minutes directly on the coals or on the grill, turn occasionally if convenient.

Potatoes can also be sliced, cubed, halved, or cut in fries or wedges. Drizzle with melted butter or spread with soft butter, season, and wrap in foil—reassemble large pieces to original potato shape or just wrap in package (it's easier if each is an individual serving). Bake as above though they will cook slightly faster if in small pieces.

New potatoes can be cooked in a bunch; scrub a pound of potatoes and pare a band off the middle. Dot with a couple of tablespoons of butter and salt and pepper generously. Enclose in I large foil pouch and bake as above, turning and shifting package occasionally.

Sweet potatoes or yams are cooked the same as baking potatoes.

Baked squash: On a large square of heavy-duty foil, layer sliced summer squashes dotted with butter and sprinkled with salt, pepper, and seasonings of your choice—thin onion rings, a pinch of dried herbs. Seal securely and bake over medium coals until tender (about 15 to 20 minutes).

To bake acorn squash, halve and seed the squash; add a tablespoon of butter and seasonings—salt, pepper, and a teaspoon of brown sugar or maple syrup. Wrap each half securely in heavy-duty foil and bake on coals or grill until tender (about 30 or 40 minutes).

Vegetables: Repackage frozen vegetables combinations in heavy-duty foil to cook them over coals. Then, like the chuckwagon cook said, cook until done. We know that's not a very specific direction, but, after extensive testing, it's the best we can do (check after 15 minutes).

Fresh cut vegetables can be steamed the same way: sprinkle with water, dot with butter, and season before wrapping in foil.

Whole sweet onions can be baked directly on the coals without wrapping in foil. When the outer layers are charred, they are done—just peel off the blackened parts.

Baked apples: Fill cored apples with jam, brown sugar, maple syrup, butter, cinnamon, and/or raisins. Wrap each apple in foil and bake over the coals until tender. Since this is almost always done as a bonus recipe over the dying coals, it is hard to estimate time—just put them on when you take the steaks off and they'll be a nice surprise after dinner.

ROADSIDE RAMBLINGS

Ever since we started working on *The Great American RV Cookbook*, whenever we've leveled up, we've struck up a conversation with our new neighbors about on-the-road cooking. In those exchanges with RVers from all over the continent, we picked up a wealth of roadside wisdom—a treasury of tips to make life easier for the traveling cook.

Altitude

Ups and downs are a challenge to the RV cook—and we don't mean mood changes. Normally a cook who moves from one altitude to another has time to learn to adjust to the new cooking conditions. But the RV cook may be at several radically different altitudes in as many meals. We remember a day when we breakfasted in a seaside ferry dock on Vancouver Island, had lunch a mile high atop Hurricane Ridge, and dinner at a mountain campground of indeterminate altitude. Many cooks may have had a problem adjusting to the high-altitude cooking that day. We found sea level more of a challenge since our home base is a mile high. It all depends on what you are used to. As a simple rule of thumb, the higher you are, the longer it takes to cook. Not only baking, but almost everything will take a little longer—coffee, frozen vegetables, microwave meals. In addition, baking can be tricky at high altitudes, and many recipes (and all packaged baking products) give directions for adjustments if necessary—usually a slightly higher temperature and longer baking time, sometimes a little more flour and liquid. All of the recipes in this book have been tested at least once at high altitude and, unless noted, need no adjustment.

Aluminum Foil

By now it's clear that we think foil is a very useful thing to have in your RV—indispensable for cooking out or baking in. But our enthusiasm isn't due solely to vacation laziness: it is difficult to achieve the level of cleanliness you maintain at home without running out your hot water tank and filling up your holding tank. When you line a pan with foil, it's like starting anew with a pristine pan. Foil (or plastic wrap or wax paper) will also keep your work surface sanitary when you are handling raw meat, poultry, or fish.

If you don't have heavy-duty foil on hand when it's called for, substitute 2 layers of regular foil—although if you're trying to fabricate a pan out of foil, the larger size and greater body of the heavy-duty makes it easier to work with. Incidentally, the shiny and dull sides are otherwise the same: it doesn't make any difference which is where. When you are lining a pan with foil, wet the pan first and the foil will conform more easily.

Cooking in foil pouches isn't only for the oven and over the coals. A Canadian RVer shared this tip for making a steamed foil dinner: wrap fish fillets, covered with a layer of lemon slices, and sliced vegetables in foil, sealing edges well; put the package in a saucepan with a small amount of simmering water; cover and cook until tender and done (about 25 minutes). She also steams meatloaf or plain meatballs, substituting tomato slices for the lemon.

Baking Soda

No RV should be without a box of baking soda. Use it to keep your refrigerator smelling good, to scrub and freshen washable surfaces, and for a battery of bathroom-cabinet purposes. We substitute baking soda for scouring powder in the RV since so many surfaces do double duty and we want to avoid getting cleaning chemicals in our food. It's an ideal polish for stainless steel and an all-purpose deodorizer. Even if your whole water tank needs to be sweetened, baking soda is the answer: drain the tank; add a solution of 1 cup baking soda to 5 gallons of warm water for every 10 gallons of capacity; drive around for 5 miles; drain and flush with fresh water. And, of course, you can use baking soda for baking.

Beer, Wines, and Spirits

It's fun to sample America's local beers, wines, and spirits. In addition, they and their foreign counterparts can put pizzaz in your cooking. The small plastic bottle of sherry we take with us takes up less space than the ketchup and adds considerably more dazzle to our dinners. And there are some recipes where these spirited ingredients add more than flavor, for example, flaming dishes like *Mount Hood Cherries Jubiliee* and *Mile High Cracked Pepper Steak* are fueled by the alcoholic content (which burns off).

You can use cooking wine, which has been heavily salted to make it unpalatable for drinking, but we don't recommend it. On the other hand, even if you use some of the best liquors around, you don't have to invest in large bottles—wine comes in half bottles and serving-size splits; most liquors come in miniature bottles (usually about 1/10 of a pint, a scant 1/4 cup), just right for many recipes and handy to have on hand for guests who don't share your liquor preferences.

If you don't use alcoholic beverages as a matter of principle, you can still enjoy many recipes that call for alcoholic beverages. For recipes where the liquor is mostly for flavor, omit it and go a bit heavier on other seasonings, for example, in a dessert you might substitute a little vanilla or rum extract. Lemon juice can be substituted for small amounts of wine used during the cooking. For recipes calling for a larger amount of wine, try substituting clam juice in fish dishes, fruit juce in fruit dishes. Some cooks use apple juice in place of sherry.

Bread

As far as we're concerned baking bread is something bakeries do. The closest we've come to baking bread in our RV is *Beer Bread* and Pillsbury's Pipin' Hot loaves sold in the refrigerated biscuit section (they're just the thing to have in the back of the refrigerator in case you run out of bread sometime in a remote area). But Bill's oldest daughter assures us that when the bread-baking spirit hits you, making up a loaf or two can be great recreation wherever you are—she has baked bread while floating down the Yukon River in an open boat. So, just in case this uncontrollable urge should strike you sometime, we asked a friend who bakes bread as casually and often as other people make toast to share her recipe: Dissolve 1 package active yeast in 1 cup very warm

water in a large bowl. Add 1 teaspoon salt and 1 tablespoon sugar and go do something until the yeast starts to grow (about 5 minutes). Add 2 tablespoons oil and beat in 1½ cups of flour until smooth. Gradually beat in more flour (exactly how much depends on the weather, the humidity, etc.—anywhere from 1 cup to 1½ cups, occasionally more) until you have a nice soft dough that doesn't muck up your hands too much. Flour surface and knead in just enough flour to keep your hands from sticking while kneading it—use a circular motion to knead: it seems to get the job done more quickly with less effort. Knead until the dough springs back when you poke it (about 10 minutes). Let the dough rise, covered with a cloth or piece of plastic wrap, in a warm place (a good spot is your oven with only the pilot light on) until it has doubled in size (1 or 2 hours). Then punch down, shape into 1 or 2 loaves on a baking sheet, and let the dough rise again at room temperature while you are preheating the oven to 350° (375° for high altitudes). Bake until it makes a hollow sound when thumped (about 25 minutes for the smaller loaves).

We have found delicious breads everywhere from big cities to small towns—some of the best fruit and nut breads we have ever tasted came from Coombs, British Columbia. Look for locally baked ethnic and specialty breads—sourdough, Italian bread, potato bread, pumpernickel, Irish soda bread, pita, various Native American breads, crumpets.

Incidentally, although crumpets are often toasted they are also authentically served pan-warmed: stack crumpets layered with bits of butter in a saucepan, cover, and warm over low heat until heated through.

While we are on the subject, did you ever try pan-toasting ordinary sliced bread? It is an easy way of coming up with a few pieces of buttered toast when you don't have a toaster and without heating your oven: butter a slice of bread on both sides and cook it over medium heat in a skillet, turning once, until it is toasted on both sides.

Cereal

Make the cereals in your pantry do double duty: mash up unsugared varieties to use as crumbs for topping casseroles or vegetable dishes or for coating chicken or fish. Many cereals are good added to trail mix or mixed with nuts for nibbling. Sometime when you're out of popcorn, try heating a pan of toasted cereal (like *Cheerios* or *Rice Krispies*) with a little butter; salt and serve. And when the children feel like making something, there are always cereal cookie bars.

Snap Crackle Snacks

2 tablespoons butter
20 marshmallows *or* 2 cups miniature marshmallows *or* 1 cup marshmallow creme
2½ cups crisp rice cereal
¼ teaspoon vanilla
½ cup of any of the following singly or in combinations: raisins, salted peanuts, sunflower seeds, chopped nuts, coconut, diced dry fruit, or gorp

Butter a 9-inch cake pan (if it's not a non-stick pan, line with foil before buttering). In large saucepan melt butter over low heat. Add marshmallows and stir until melted (it will be an even-colored cream). Stir in vanilla. Cook over low heat, continuing to stir, for another 3 minutes. Turn off heat. Add cereal and any bonus ingredients and stir until well mixed. Press mixture into pan using a buttered piece of waxed paper or foil. When it's cool, cut or break into pieces.

Children

Traveling with tykes in tow makes any trip more eventful and every event more fun. Even if you only occasionally have small travelers along, pack a Rain-or-Shine Kit in a small plastic container and tuck it in an out-of-the-way corner. Here's a list of what we stash in ours:

Birthday candles (for unbirthdays and illuminating sand castles—the effect is magical at dusk; we also pack a couple of little toothpick flags for castles)

Small plastic bottles of food coloring (for play dough and mixing with liquid detergent for easy-to-clean-up finger paints)

Bubble wands (to use with diluted liquid detergent, liquid hand soap, or shampoo—part of the fun is experimenting to find out what works)

Cup of birdseed in a small plastic bag (to keep an interesting bird interested and to make *Pine Cone Bird Feeders*: Spread a pine cone with peanut butter and roll in birdseed; hang from a tree branch with string)

Non-toxic glue stick (for making paper-plate masks, paper-bag puppets, paper hats, and butterfly kites: Cut out a 10-inch wide butterfly shape from stiff paper or a brown-paper grocery bag, glue on decorations and streamers, and tape a 2- or 3-foot piece of string to the underside)

Small skein of string

Package of *Kool-Aid* (also good for snow cones)

Big package of bubble gum (for a family bubble-blowing contest)

Package of Twisteez balloons (we mastered dogs, rabbits, and giraffes from the package directions one morning while waiting in line for a ferry)

Cooky cutter (for cookies and playdough)

If children are regular crew members, you might add straws and a set of popsicle molds with snap-on lids to your kitchen equipment. The kids can make popsicles with the juice or syrup drained off canned fruits or use any mixture of fruit juices for custom-made treats. For a quicker cooler, use

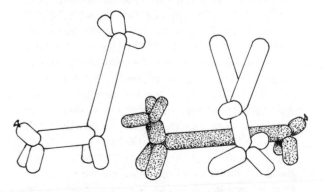

your mouli grater to grind ice cubes into snow for snow cones. To make *Snow Cone Syrup*: Mix 1 package (2-quart size) unsweetened soft drink mix, 1 cup sugar, and ½ cup of water.

If your young travelers have been inspired by the potters at the historic village, let them make small pinch pots and coiled pots from playdough—it's also good for making ornaments and RV-size sculptures (though they don't travel well).

Playdough

2 cups flour
1 cup salt
1 teaspoon oil (optional)
3 drops food coloring (optional)

Mix flour, salt, oil, and about ½ cup of water thoroughly. Add more water until mixture is pliable but not sticky or crumbly. You may have to add more flour to get it just right. Color dough by working in food coloring. Playdough can be stored in a plastic bag in the refrigerator for later use.

Salt can be quite drying, so sculptors should rub a few drops of oil on their hands before they begin.

To make sculptures or pottery permanent let air dry. You can dry the sculptures faster by baking at 325°, but since it takes about ½ hour for every ¼-inch thickness, this method obviously isn't a good idea unless you happen to be baking anyway and it's the dead of winter.

Crackers

Put your snack crackers to work as an ingredient in and on everything from dips to desserts. Savory cracker crumbs are good as crusty coatings and atop vegetables and casseroles. Graham cracker crumbs can go on top of desserts or into a *Graham Cracker Crust*: Mix ¾ cup of fine graham cracker crumbs (mash about 6 ounces of graham crackers in a sealable plastic bag) with 6 tablespoons of melted butter; press evenly into a 9-inch pie pan.

And, the next time the children are roasting marshmallows, don't forget that graham crackers can transform marshmallows into those old campfire favorites, S'mores. For the most popular S'more, you'll also need chocolate candy bars: Sandwich 4 squares of milk chocolate and 1 toasted marshmallow between graham crackers.

Dessert Mixes

Dessert mixes are one of the oldest convenience foods in America (Jell-O was invented in 1845, though it took awhile to catch on). From the turn of the century until today, trading recipes for these jiggly dessert and salad makers has become something of an American pastime. (We once won First Prize in the Great Jell-O/Family Circle Recipe Swap.) You, no doubt, have more than a few in your bag of tricks. One recipe we like because it makes the most of bits and pieces of fresh vegetables is *Harvest Jewel Salad*: Prepare a 3-ounce package of lemon gelatin according to package instructions, adding ½ teaspoon salt with the mix and 1 tablespoon vinegar with the cold water. Chill until thickened. Fold in 1 cup chopped or shredded vegetables (carrots, celery, green pepper, cucumber). Chill until firm (about 3 hours).

Then along came instant puddings to add a new dimension to desserts. "Mom, what's for dessert?" "How about pudding?" "Great!" Five minutes later, a sweet, creamy dessert. What could be better? *Shaker Pudding*, that's what—the practically perfect RV dessert: Put instant pudding ingredients in a jar or shaker with a tight cover and shake *hard* 45 seconds. Pour into serving dishes or leave in container and wait 5 minutes.

You can, of course, add all kinds of goodies to Shaker Pudding: substitute a small can of fruit cocktail for part of the milk or add a small diced banana to the mix and milk before shaking; or add a tablespoon or so of chocolate or butterscotch chips, broken or whole nuts, crumbled cookies, shredded coconut, chopped sweet cherries, or sliced or whole berries to the dessert dishes before pouring in the pudding. For *Mocha Pudding*: Add 1 tablespoon of instant coffee to chocolate pudding ingredients before shaking. For *Rocky Road Pudding*: Add ½ cup miniature marshmallows and ¼ cup chopped walnuts to chocolate pudding ingredients before shaking.

Eggs

Eggs are so endlessly useful to the RV cook there probably should be a reserved spot for them both in the refrigerator and near the top of the shopping list. Not only are eggs an essential ingredient in many recipes, they can turn a side dish into a main dish or stand on their own.

Hard-boiled eggs are especially versatile. Add them to creamed dishes, sandwich fillings, and all kinds of hearty salads—potato, macaroni, rice, tuna; use them to garnish tossed salads, seafood salads, and open-faced sandwiches; and serve them plain or deviled as a snack or appetizer as casual or elegant as you like (*Eggs Romanoff* are simply deviled eggs topped with caviar).

Whole studies have been devoted to cooking the *Perfect Hard-Boiled Egg*. Given the variables of altitude and climate, the personalities of eggs, and with fuel conservation in mind, this is the method we have found most reliable: cover eggs in a saucepan with cold water; heat until water boils; cover pan and turn off the heat. Let the eggs stand for 25 minutes (longer if at a high altitude). Pour off hot water and replace with cool water.

If you are boiling eggs for later use, add a few drops of food coloring after you turn off the heat. You won't have any trouble distinguishing the tinted eggs from your fresh eggs even if they're stored in the same carton.

For soft-boiled eggs, lower the eggs into already boiling water and boil for 3 to 4 minutes. If you cook them for 5 minutes you have *Five-Minute Eggs* or *Eggs Mollet*, which can be used in place of poached eggs.

Speaking of poached eggs, one of the easiest lunches in the world is *Egg Island Soup*: Prepare a can of condensed tomato or tomato bisque soup according to the instructions on the can using a can of milk to dilute it; when the soup is barely simmering, break 4 eggs gently into the soup and poach the eggs in the soup until the whites are set and the yolks are done to your liking (about 3 to 5 minutes).

If omelets aren't in your bag of tricks, now is the time to learn how to make one. With a nonstick pan, there is no trick at all to making perfect omelets. You can serve them as a main dish anytime from daybreak to midnight and fill them with almost anything or nothing. They cost only pennies but are special enough for a champagne supper. For each serving, make one *Perfect Omelet*: Beat 3 eggs seasoned with a sprinkling of salt and pepper (and a pinch of mixed herbs, if you like) in a small bowl until the yolks and whites are well mixed. Heat your skillet over medium heat until

a drop of water dances on it. When the skillet is ready, melt 1 tablespoon of butter until it just begins to bubble. (If the butter browns, your skillet is too hot; wipe out the browned butter and start over with lower heat.) Pour in the eggs and let them cook for a minute or so until the edges are firm. With a spatula or turner lift the edges of the omelet and let the uncooked egg run under the edge. Continue cooking just until the egg is set. Fold the omelet in half or thirds as you tip it onto the plate. Or, add your choice of fillings, such as ½ cup of shredded Cheddar cheese, before folding. If you're serving the omelet without a sauce, "gild" it by running a bit of cold butter over the top.

Equivalents

Knowing how many cups you'll get when you slice a couple of apples or smash a package of crackers into crumbs is handy information. So is knowing how much a cup of shredded cheese weighs when you don't have a scale. By their nature, equivalent measurements are always ballpark figures—Cheddar cheese isn't quite the same density as Swiss; the kind of crackers makes a difference, as does how fine you make the shreds or crumbs. But we still find it useful to have an approximate list of equivalents on hand.

Apples: If you start with 1 pound of apples (about 3), you'll end up with 3 to 3½ cups of apple slices—estimate about 1 cup per medium apple.

Bread Crumbs: When you grate 1 slice of dry bread, you get about ¼ cup of crumbs; fresh bread, at least ½ cup of crumbs.

Butter and Margarine: Each ¼-pound stick is about ½ cup or 8 tablespoons. Use the marks on the wrapper for easy measuring; for most purposes you needn't be exact.

Cheese: Firm cheeses—Cheddar, Monterey Jack, Swiss—make about 1 to 1½ cups of shredded cheese for 4 ounces of weight. We've ordinarily listed cheese ingredients by weight, since it is a more accurate measurement, although a slight variation in the amount of cheese would make no critical difference in any of the recipes in this book.

Crackers and Cookie Crumbs: To make 1 cup of crumbs, you'll need about 15 or 16 graham crackers or 25 saltine crackers or vanilla wafers.

Cream: When you whip 1 cup of heavy whipping cream you get 2 cups of whipped cream.

Lemon: The people who make reconstituted lemon juice think that a lemon makes 2 tablespoons of juice. Most lemons don't know that and make at least 3 tablespoons of juice. If you grate the peel (which is a lot easier to do if you haven't cut the lemon), you'll have 1 to 2 teaspoons of grated lemon rind.

Mushrooms: You will get about 2 to 2½ cups of sliced mushrooms from ½ pound of fresh mushrooms.

Pasta: It takes about 1 cup or ¼ pound of uncooked dry pasta to make 2 cups cooked.

Peas: You have to shell about 1 pound of peas for 1 cup of cooked peas.

Potatoes: If you start with 1 pound of potatoes (about 3), you'll end up with about 2½ cups of potato slices.

Rice: When you cook 1 cup of regular converted rice, you get 3 to 4 cups; when you cook 1 cup of instant rice, you get about 2 cups.

Sugars: Depending on the kind of sugar, a 1-pound box holds 2½ cups (granulated sugar); 3¾ cups (confectioners' sugar); or 2⅓ cups (brown sugar).

Flour

If you are having trouble getting your favorite homemade biscuits to turn out right, it might not be the altitude or the humidity—it could be the flour you are using. Flour is milled from hard and soft varieties of wheat; sometimes flour is blended to suit the baking customs of different regions.

Beyond the unidentified differences in flours, the large companies like *Gold Medal* offer several different types of flour—whole wheat, bleached, all-purpose, instant, self-rising. The last two are especially useful to RVers.

Instant or quick-mixing flour, like *Wondra*, has a slightly granulated quality; it mixes smoothly into sauce, gravies, and batters, and can be used like ordinary all-purpose flour in other recipes. *Wondra* comes in a small pour 'n shake canister, making it especially convenient to use and store.

Self-rising flour is premixed with baking powder and salt, which makes possible various amazingly simple camper's favorites like *Beer Bread* and *Sundae Muffins*.

Flourishes

Somewhere between putting a sprig of parsley on everything and spending hours arranging artistic nouvelle cuisine compositions are the fun flourishes that take only moments to add flair to even the simplest dishes.

With a little practice you can make lemon, lime, and tomato roses to garnish salads, fruit plates, and main dishes. They all use the same technique and take only a sharp paring knife. In the relaxed atmosphere of your RV kitchen, you can master the technique in no time—just try one whenever you aren't using the peel in the recipe.

To make a *Lemon Rose:* Hold the lemon with the stem end up. Cut a thin slice across the top of the lemon but do not cut all the way through. Continue cutting the lemon peel in a continuous spiral from the point where the first slice is attached until all the peel is removed. Gently curl the spiral of peel onto the first slice. When you're making lemon or lime roses, try to cut just the outer peel. (You can make very delicate citrus flowers using a vegetable peeler.)

When you're making tomato roses, you will have to cut more deeply into the flesh with the knife. If you aren't using the roses immediately, refrigerate each in a small plastic bag.

It takes no practice at all to deck cakes or cupcakes with posies of candy-coated, milk-chocolate pieces centered in circles of petals snipped from miniature fruit-flavored marshmallows (cut them in half with scissors). Just as easy are flower garnishes for all kinds of salads. Simply arrange snips or slices of carrot, celery, green pepper, avocado, tomato, oranges, or apples in a wheel, and center with a contrasting round piece or small vegetable. For example, arrange celery slices in pinwheels around carrot slices to top a Harvest Jewel Salad; or arrange cherry tomato halves or wedges around an olive to top a serving of tuna salad.

While you're whipping up a snack, you can perfect cheese rosettes and scrolls piped out of pressurized cans of snack cheese. And, if your family snacks on rolls of fruit leather, you have on hand the makings of a picture-perfect bouquet of elegant *Roll-up Roses* for decorating baked goods: Tear fruit leather into strips (the ragged edge is desirable). Roll into a rosette, pinching the bottom together and flaring out the upper edge of the petal. (These are so easy, we once made roses and camellias for an entire preschool class while we walked through a botanical garden with them—and by the end the preschoolers were making their own.)

For special occasions, flourishes on a grander scale are in order but can be just as easy to make. Since few of us have fancy serving dishes on hand, consider making the presentation in something dramatic but disposable. For example, if you're making a fruit dip for a crowd, serve it in a *Pineapple Bowl*: Slice the top off of a whole ripe pineapple about 1 inch below the bottom of the leaves. Hollow out center of the pineapple with a sharp knife, leaving a firm shell. Cut the removed pineapple into spears. Fill pineapple shell with dip and center in a large tray or platter surrounded with pineapple spears and assorted fruits cut in sections. It will be the hit of the potluck.

Incidentally, a delicious simple *Creamy Fruit Dip* can be made by mixing equal amounts (by weight) of softened cream cheese and marshmallow creme.

Or, perhaps, it's a cheese fondue or dip that's on your open house menu. A *Bread Bowl* is handsome and simple: Cut a horizontal slice off the top of a 1-pound round unsliced loaf of crusty bread (sourdough, rye, pumpernickel). Hollow out the center of the loaf with a sharp knife, leaving a ½-inch shell. Arrange assorted vegetable dippers and large bread cubes cut from the scooped out bread around the bread shell on a large tray or platter. Fill the shell (it will hold about 2 cups) with cheese dip or hot cheese fondue and serve immediately.

You can also serve a hearty, chunky main-dish salad in a bread bowl. For a *Crunchy Bread Bowl*: Spread the inside of the bowl with butter and toast briefly in a 425° oven (you don't have to completely preheat the oven.) Fill the bowl with salad; cut and serve in thick wedges at the table.

Frozen Vegetables

Besides being perhaps the easiest way of putting an interesting vegetable course on the table, frozen vegetables are hard to beat as a basis for speedy but special stovetop meals, especially the seasoned mixed vegetables. With international-style vegetables like those from *Birds Eye*, you can eat your way around the world on a pound of hamburger. Here are a couple of destinations.

Kyoto Beef Bowl
1 pound ground beef
1 10-ounce package frozen Japanese-style vegetables.
1 3-ounce package beef-flavored ramen (Oriental noodle soup)
Teriyaki sauce (optional)

Brown meat in a skillet in large chunks. Drain off excess fat into a heatproof disposable container. Add 2 cups of water and bring to a boil. Add vegetables and bring to a boil again, separating vegetables with a fork. Add noodles and return to simmer. Cover and cook over low heat until noodles and vegetables are tender (about 5 minutes). Stir in contents of the ramen seasoning packet and teriyaki sauce to taste (about ¼ cup).

Munich Beef Spaetzle
1 pound ground beef
2 10-ounce packages frozen Bavarian-style green beans and spaetzle
1 fresh lemon

Grate half the lemon and slice the other half into thin wheels. Brown meat in a skillet in large chunks. Drain off excess fat into a heatproof disposable container. Add vegetables, ½ cup of water, the grated lemon rind, and about a tablespoon of fresh lemon juice. Bring to a full boil, separating vegetables with a fork. Cover and cook over low heat until spaetzle and vegetables are tender (about 5 minutes). Garnish with lemon slices.

Or extend your travels abroad with a package of pasta or rice.

Genoa Pasta Primavera

1 6 to 8-ounce package pasta (seashells, spirals, small bow ties)
1 10-ounce package frozen Italian-style vegetables
¼ cup butter, softened
½ cup grated Parmesan cheese
1 teaspoon dried basil (or, preferably, 2 tablespoons chopped fresh basil)
2 tablespoons finely chopped pine nuts or walnuts (optional)

In separate pans, cook pasta and vegetables according to package instructions. Meanwhile, in a small bowl, mix butter, cheese, basil, and nuts to a paste (this is a *Quick Pesto Sauce*). Drain the pasta and toss immediately with vegetables and pesto until butter is melted and pasta is well coated. Serve with additional butter and Parmesan cheese.

Canton Fried Rice

1 6¼-ounce package fried rice mix with almonds
1 10-ounce package frozen Chinese-style vegetables
2 eggs, slightly beaten

In a skillet cook fried rice mix as directed on package for 10 minutes. Stir in Chinese-style vegetables and quickly return to simmer. Cover and cook for 5 minutes. Stir in beaten eggs and stir-fry until eggs are set. Serve with soy or teriyaki sauce and chopped chives if you have them.

Last but not least, frozen vegetables (broccoli, cauliflower, water chestnuts) are good for salads and you don't even have to cook them—just thaw part or all of a bag of mixed vegetables under cool running water, and add to a mixed green salad or toss with Italian dressing.

Grease

While grease may be necessary to the workings of your RV, it can wreak havoc with your interior.

We remember with sympathy the gracious Southern lady who spent half the day trying to clean her Pace Arrow after "fat popped all over the place" when she fried oysters for her husband. We avoid any deep frying in the RV—it just isn't worth the potential mess.

If you do get grease spatters (even in the kitchen area) clean up immediately: grease can not only cause difficult to remove stains and odors, it is a fire hazard.

And a special note of caution: don't reach for a paper or plastic cup to hold the hot fat drained off during cooking—it can go right through. Use a *heatproof* container, preferably disposable—recycle a dry metal can or use a foil-lined bag made expressly for holding hot grease. If you don't have any old cans or heatproof cups on hand, in desperation, you can pour the hot grease into one of your other pans then wipe it out when it has cooled.

Don't put grease in your drains or holding tanks.

Humidity

If you have transported your kitchen from a dry climate to a humid one, you may be surprised to discover that your potato chips are rubbery, your pasta is pasty, and your cereal isn't talking to you the way it usually does. On the othe hand, if you just drove from the misty coast to the desert—or the high dry plains—you may find that the loaf of bread you left out overnight has turned into a giant crouton. You have the humidity woes.

To complicate matters you can be driving in and out of atmospheres with widely different humidity levels. Fortunately, there is one solution that seems to minimize both problems: keep all your grain products well wrapped or in tightly covered containers to keep air, whatever its moisture content, away from your foods.

If you are coping with a particularly humid area, the covered canisters that some snacks are sold in do a better job of protecting partial contents from getting soggy than a folded down bag; and you can reuse the canisters to keep cookies and crackers crisp.

Leftovers

Perhaps some of the best advice anyone ever gave us is to banish leftovers from your RV kitchen. You can, of course, make exceptions for steak and lobster (since they won't be taking up refrigerator space beyond the next lunchtime) and for chocolate mousse and pecan pie (isn't it nice to have a refrigerator to raid?). We're talking about the dab of noodle casserole and the solitary egg white. You can go back to being the frugal housekeeper when you return to home base.

Measurements and Metrics

Though we've tried to avoid recipes where a tad one way or another makes a difference, if you get too far off the road with your measurements you may end up with paste rather than pie or glue instead of gravy. All measurements are level, which means you fill the cup or spoon and then run a knife blade over the top to cut the excess off; brown sugar is firmly packed into the measuring cup or spoon, but everything else is just spooned in—especially flour and confectioners' sugar.

A great timesaver on the road is to take some time in advance to experiment with some of the common equipment in your kitchen to determine capacities. How close are your teaspoons to a meauring spoon teaspoon? What do the disposable cups you use in the kitchen and/or bath hold? What do they look like with a standard measurement in them, for example, ½ cup? How much does a half egg shell hold? (About 1 tablespoon.)

Using a disposable cup or eggshell for measuring saves clean-ups, especially nice if you're dealing with something messy. So will cutting off the plastic ring, if there is one, that holds your measuring cups or spoons together—you will only have to wash the actual tool you use, instead of the whole set.

You should also know what your pots and pans hold (many are marked). When a recipe on a package calls for a 4-cup baking pan, you can use your 9-inch pie pan; for a 6-cup pan, use your 9-inch cake pan; and for a 15-cup pan, use your 13x9x2-inch baking pan.

Incidentally, the less precise measurements you sometimes run across—a dash, pinch, or sprinkling—are usually meant to be imprecise to encourage you to adjust seasonings to match your taste. Technically, a dash is less than ⅛ teaspoon; a pinch is the amount you can hold between your forefinger and thumb. A jigger is formally 1½ ounces, though in actual practice that is often considered a double shot (2 ¾-ounce "jiggers").

If you're a foreign visitor used to dealing with metric measurements, the following charts will be helpful (and vice-versa for American visitors traveling across the border). We also suggest you buy a set of measuring tools that are marked in both metric and standard American measurements.

Liquid Measure

60 drops = 1 tsp. = ⅓ tbs. = 1/6 oz. = about 5 ml
3 tsp. = 1 tbs. = ½ oz. = about 15 ml
2 tbs. = 1 oz. = about 30 ml
4 tbs. = 2 oz. = about 60 ml = ¼ cup
8 tbs. = 4 oz. = about 120 ml = ½ cup
16 tbs. = 8 oz. = about ¼ l = 1 cup = ½ pint
16 oz. = about ½ l = 2 cups = 1 pint = 1 lb
about 1 l = 4 cups = 2 pints = 2 lbs. = 1 qt.
about 4 l = 4 qts. = 1 gal.

Dry Measure

About 1 liter = 2 pints = 1 quart
8 quarts = 1 peck
4 pecks = 1 bushel

Dry Weights

About 28 grams = 1 ounce
About 225 grams = 8 ounces = ½ pound
About 450 grams = 16 ounces = 1 pound
About 1 kilogram = 2 pounds

Temperature

To reduce degrees Fahrenheit to degrees centigrade, subtract 32° and multiply by 5/9. Some common oven temperatures:

Fahrenheit*	centigrade
250°	121°
300	149
350	176
375	190
400	204
425	218
450	232

To reduce degrees centigrade to degrees Fahrenheit, multiply by 9/5 and add 32°.

  * All degrees given in this book are Fahrenheit.

Linear Measure

1 inch = 2.54 centimeters
12 inches = 1 foot = 0.3048
36 inches = 3 feet = 1 yard = 0.914 meter
5,280 feet = 1,609.3 meters = 1 mile

Odors

One of the chief drawbacks of having your kitchen in your bedroom, and your bathroom within nose distance of your kitchen, is odors. Avoiding stewed cabbage and fried onions will help. So will—according to assorted road wisdom—lighting a match, setting out a bowl of vinegar, boiling a pinch of spice or lemon peel, putting baking soda in your drains and toilet bowl, and various commercial room deodorizers.

For the more common problem of refrigerator odors, use an open box of baking soda or a couple of pieces of charcoal (a fun, tidy way of doing it is with a *Grade* A refrigerator freshener—it looks like an egg). Lemon juice, vinegar, and baking soda are all helpful for deodorizing cooking equipment and hands.

Pasta

A package of spaghetti, a box of macaroni and cheese dinner, a bag of egg noodles—you'll find pasta in practically every RV pantry in one form or another (of course, form makes all the difference in pasta). Easy to store, easy to fix, and the basis of many easy-going American family favorites, pasta needs little introduction. But you may discover some very useful, less familiar pasta if you look beyond the spaghetti and noodle section of the market: frozen ravioli, spaghetti, and noodles make a restaurant-special meal with a pound of browned hamburger or Italian sausage heated with a jar of homestyle spaghetti sauce; small packages of dried tortellini and raviolini, often stocked in the imported foods sections, take just a few inches of cupboard space and can be sauced the same way to make a fun dinner for four; and don't forget the other ethnic pasta stocked with the kosher or Chinese foods.

The only difficulty you might have with pasta is if you are traveling with the basic set of cookware—pasta for four is a tight squeeze in a 2-quart pan. Try this cool, energy-saving way of cooking pastas: bring about half a pan of salted water to a rapid boil, slowly add pasta, return to rapid boiling, stirring to separate (long hard pasta like spaghetti and vermicelli will work if broken into shorter lengths; smaller shapes are a better choice). Boil about 2 minutes, cover, turn off heat, and let sit until pasta is cooked to your preference (about 10 minutes for tiny shells to about 20 minutes for heavier noodles and raviolini).

To keep pasta from sticking together, stir in a little oil while the pasta is boiling.

Plastic Bags

Plastic bags can be, depending on your need, suitcases, salad bowls, or seashore buckets. You can use them to store leftovers, laundry, and letters; or to tote trout, toys or travel brochures.

We have suggested using sealable plastic bags (for example, *Ziploc* bags) for marinading meats and seafood for barbecuing. You can also crisp and toss your salad in a plastic bag—it's easier to find room in the refrigerator for a big bag of greens than a big bowl. And you can use bags to coat foods with seasoned flour or crumbs. While we're on the subject of crumbs, they are easy to make from dry bread, cereal, crackers, or cookies if you put the bread or whatever in a small closed plastic bag and beat, tap, or roll something hard over it. Make chopped nuts or cracked pepper the same way.

Put a scoop of hamburger into a sandwich bag and you can shape your hamburger patties neatly without the meat ever touching your hand or the counter; stack the patties as high as you like to store or carry out to the grill (cut off the edges of the bags to get the hamburgers out).

You can also roll floured pastry dough out in large plastic bags; cut the edges of the bag and peel off the top layer to fit the crust into the pie pan neatly—just like packaged pie crusts.

No matter what your travel recreation is, you'll find uses for bags—storing sea shells or souvenirs; transporting sticky pine cones or wet bathing suits. If you're fisherfolk, fold up a couple for your pocket or pack to use as a disposable creel, sink, or garbage can. And if you catch a surfeit of small fish and have room in your freezer, you can package them with water in a plastic freezer bag and store until you get back to home base or even longer.

And that's just for starters.

Refrigerated Rolls and Biscuits

Having your choice of a variety of freshly baked biscuits, cinnamon buns, or Danish rolls any time you're willing to heat up your oven with absolutely no work and no mess is something of a dream come true for RV cooks. Since a can or two will fit in the most crowded refrigerator, many RVers consider them a staple to have on hand.

Refrigerated crescent rolls are particularly versatile—pat the sections into a pie pan or muffin pan and use as a pie crust substitute or wrap the patched-together sections around fillings for savory or sweet hand pies. Or make *Pigs n' Blankets*: Unroll the dough in a package of refrigerated crescent rolls and separate into 8 triangles; lay a hot dog at shortest side of the triangle and roll the hot dog and dough loosely to the opposite point; place dough-wrapped hot dogs on ungreased foil-lined baking sheet and bake at 375° for 11 to 13 minutes or until golden brown.

Even if you don't have an oven or you don't feel like turning it on, you can still have fresh, hot country biscuits. Try your hand at baking *Skillet Biscuits* on the rangetop: Heat your skillet with the cover on over low heat for a few minutes. Lightly butter the skillet—if the butter browns, the skillet is too hot. Place individual biscuits in skillet slightly separated from each over. Cover and bake 3 minutes. Turn biscuits; cover and bake for about 3 minutes longer or until biscuits are baked through (the biscuits will look like little English muffins).

Sauces and Salad Dressings

Even cooks who are proud of their homemade barbecue sauce, spaghetti sauce, and salad dressings, use commercially prepared sauces. Chances are that the barbecue sauce has a dash or two of *Tabasco*, Worcestershire, or soy sauce, and the spaghetti sauce started with tomato sauce or paste. But even those of us who have been known to make our own mayonnaise at home discover that using a wider variety of prepared sauces on the road can make travel cooking much easier.

Spend some time rating bottled sauces until you find several different kinds that pass your taste test—maybe not quite as good as yours, but good. With a jar of spaghetti sauce, sweet and sour sauce, barbecue sauce, or salsa on hand, your potluck meals can always be interesting.

Here's one for when you get the hungries at an odd hour—*American Woodchuck* (a cousin of Welsh Rarebit and Scotch Woodcock): In a small saucepan mix a 15½-ounce jar of homestyle spaghetti sauce, 1 slightly beaten egg, 1 tablespoon of brown sugar, and about 2 cups of shredded Cheddar cheese. Heat over medium heat, stirring frequently, until cheese is melted and woodchuck is smooth. Serve over crackers or hot buttered toast or English muffins.

Or, when you're rained in, have America's favorite indoor barbecue sandwich, *Sloppy Joes*: Brown 1 pound of hamburger in a skillet and drain off excess fat into a heatproof container. Stir in a 10- to 14-ounce jar of barbecue sauce and ¼ cup chopped onion or a tablespoon of instant minced onion. Cover and simmer for 10 to 15 minutes. Serve on hamburger buns.

Soups

Few things on your pantry shelves are more versatile than soups. Some RVers use dried onion soup to flavor everything from creamy dips to corn on the cob. We feel much the same way about some of the condensed soups—they're good for sauces, savory pies, stovetop meals, and, of course, soups.

Mixing a couple of cans of soup is one of the simplest exercises in creative cooking, and, according to researchers at the Campbell Soup Company, you have pretty good odds of hitting a winner—they have identified 469 successful combinations that can be made with their soups. Or you can add another ingredient or two to make your soup special.

For an old-fashioned *Pacific Corn and Clam Chowder*: Mix a 15-ounce can of condensed New England clam chowder with a 17-ounce can of corn and 1 cup of milk. Heat, stirring occasionally, until chowder is hot but not boiling.

For *Tree Soup*: Mix a 10¾-ounce can of condensed creamy chicken mushroom soup with a 10-ounce package of frozen broccoli florets and 1 can of milk. Bring to a boil over medium-high heat and stir until you get the broccoli florets separated. Lower heat, cover, and simmer until broccoli is tender (about 5 minutes).

If you don't want your vegetables in your soup, try soup on your vegetables. To make a tasty *Two-*

Minute Sauce: In a small saucepan stir well a 10¾-ounce of can condensed cream soup (chicken, chicken and mushroom, mushroom, celery). Stir in ⅓ cup of milk and heat to boiling. Reduce heat and simmer 2 minutes. Serve over vegetables, poultry, fish, or eggs. Or add 1 cup of diced cooked chicken or ham or a can of tuna to make a rich sauce for egg dumplings, noodles, or rice.

Or how about baking a *Simple as Pie*—the makings are probably familiar faces in your pantry. (You can vary the basic recipe by adding a cup of cubed cooked chicken, turkey, or ham, and/or a small drained can of sliced mushrooms or chopped green chilies.

Simple as Pie

1 9-inch pie shell, unbaked
1 cup cubed Monterey Jack cheese (about 4 ounces)
1 10¾-ounce can condensed cream of chicken soup
4 eggs

Preheat oven to 450°. Bake pie shell for about 5 minutes. Arrange cheese cubes on pastry. In a small bowl mix eggs and soup with a fork until well blended. Pour egg-soup mixture over cheese. Reduce oven temperature to 375° and bake pie until golden brown (about 35 to 40 minutes).

Special Diets

Although accomodating special dietary restrictions for medical or religious reasons can be a challenge for the RV cook, the RV is a blessing to travelers in either case since it's far easier to control what goes on in your own kitchen than a restaurant's. Often a simple change in a recipe can make it acceptable—eliminating bacon or not adding salt to the recipe until a salt-free serving has been reserved; substituting margarine for butter, dietetic products for regular brands, nondairy products for dairy.

The cook who wishes to prepare kosher cuisine will find that many of the restricted recipes in this book are adaptable to substitutions. For example, use ½-inch cubes of halibut instead of scallops in *Coquilles St. Jacques*; slices of smoked salmon instead of ham in *Eggs Benedict*.

Cooking for small children is only slightly more inconvenient than it is at home base—while you may enjoy experimenting with new foods, children seem to travel better on their usual fuel. Most of the foods they are used to eating are probably available wherever you are, but one notable difference is water. Small children are sensitive to water changes. If you are in an area where you have some question about the purity of the water supply (for example, the mountains during spring run-off), depend on bottled juices and soft drinks. Anytime you're traveling with a baby, consider taking a special supply of drinking water from home or boiling all water used in preparing the baby's drinks or meals.

Substitutions

Though our first RV meal was only hot dogs, beans, and coffee, it taught us a very important lesson about RV cooking when we got the first burner lit with our last match. The meal—and the day—was saved by a twig from the campsite to carry the fire to the other two burners. Lesson 1: Learn to improvise. The Poor Mother Hubbard's Cupboard List that follows may help you the next time you're out of a critical ingredient.

Butter: Margarine can be used interchangeably with butter for all the recipes in this book, though whipped margarines may not perform the same in some cooking situations. Cooking oil is a satisfactory substitute for ordinary cooking but not where butter flavor is important—better to try a different recipe. In place of butter used for topping (for example, on pancakes or baked potatoes) take a distinctly different flavor approach. For the former, try some sweet alternative—whipping cream, brown sugar, jam. For the latter, you can try one of the many potato-bar toppings or cheese spread (which is good on many vegetables). Mayonnaise can also pinch hit in some situations, for example, the sauce used in *Artichoke Parmesano* is excellent with many vegetables.

Chocolate: Substitute 3 tablespoons cocoa plus 1 tablespoon butter for 1 ounce of unsweetened chocolate; add 4 teaspoons of sugar for a semisweet chocolate.

Cornstarch: Substitute 2 tablespoons of flour, preferably instant flour, for 1 tablespoon of cornstarch for thickening sauces.

Cream: For recipes calling for a cup of heavy whipping cream in cooking, substitute ¾ cup whole milk and ⅓ cup butter; for 1 cup light cream used in cooking, substitute a scant cup of whole milk and 3 tablespoons butter. We have used sour cream (or sour cream substitute) as a substitute for unsweetened whipped cream in several recipes in this book; the usual "sour cream substitutions" (for example, evaporated milk with a tablespoon of lemon juice) would be unsatisfactory for this use.

Flour: You can use instant or granulated flour in place of all-purpose flour for all uses. For stovetop purposes like thickening sauces or coating fish or chicken, you can also use self-rising flour or buttermilk baking mix as a substitute for plain flour. Cornstarch (use half as much) or instant potato flakes are also good as sauce and soup thickeners. Incidentally, you can flour your board, hands, or pan with baking mix.

Herbs and Spices: The fine herbs—dill, chives, parsley—often make pleasing substitutes for one another. Dill and tarragon have many of the same uses. Chervil and parsley are kin. So are basil, oregano, and marjoram. Among the robust herbs, bay and bay laurel or myrtle add much the same flavor (use ¼ to ½ as much of the bay laurel or myrtle). Spices that can often be successfully substituted for each other are cinnamon, nutmeg, and mace, though cinnamon is sweeter and not appropriate for savory dishes. Nutmeg and mace come from the same plant and can be used as mutual substitutes. One teaspoon of dried herbs is the equivalent of 1 tablespoon of chopped fresh herbs.

Vanilla extract and almond extract can be substituted for each other though, obviously, there is a flavor difference.

We have used bottled Italian dressing as an ingredient in many of the recipes in this book because of its pleasant mixture of herbs. Try using it in other recipes that include oil and mixed herbs, for example, *Herbed Green Beans*: Mix ¼ cup of bottled Italian dressing with ½ cup water and bring to a boil; add 1 9-ounce package frozen cut green beans and continue cooking according to package instructions.

Italian dressing: If you're out of bottled Italian dressing, make a classic vinaigrette and add herbs: Mix ¾ cup of oil (preferably olive oil), ¼ cup of vinegar (preferably wine vinegar), 1 teaspoon salt, 1 teaspoon black pepper, and 1 to 2 teaspoons of your choice of dried herbs—chervil, parsley, basil, chives, dill. If you like, you can shake a crushed garlic clove with your dressing—be sure to remove it before using the dressing.

Milk: If you need whole milk for cooking, substitute half evaporated milk and half water or add 1 tablespoon of melted butter to 1 cup of skim milk or milk made from nonfat dry milk. In a pinch, we've substituted hot cocoa mix made according to the package instructions for milk, and discovered that it added an interesting flavor to things like French toast and pancakes.

Mayonnaise: Creamy salad dressing can be used as an alternative for mayonnaise for almost everything. Light salad dressing or dietetic mayonnaise/salad dressing is a satisfactory substitute in most recipes, although when they are used in cooking they may not perform as well.

Mustard: You can substitute 1 tablespoon prepared mustard for 1 teaspoon dry mustard in cooking, sauces, or salad dressings.

Onions: For RV cooking, dried onion is more the standard than a substitute. Use 1 teaspoon instant minced onion for 1 tablespoon fresh; 2 tablespoons, for ½ cup; ¼ cup, for 1 medium onion. The instant dried onion is a less satisfactory substitute for scallions (green onions); try dried chives as a substitute for scallions used in salads. Some people also like onion powder and onion salt.

Syrup: Maple-flavored pancake syrup can be substituted for real maple syrup and, in some recipes, for corn syrup. Honey, molasses, and syrup can often be successfully substituted for each other in recipes. If it's your pancakes that are naked, sprinkle with brown sugar and butter, or heat and stir ½ cup of brown sugar and 1 tablespoon of water in a small saucepan until it comes to a full boil.

Sugars: Substitute 1 cup sugar mixed with ¼ cup liquid for 1 cup corn syrup or honey. In turn, honey can sweeten almost anything that sugar does (in baking, if it is a major substitution, reduce the liquid slightly). When you are out of brown sugar, substitute an equal amount of granulated sugar. In a pinch, granulated sugar can be substituted for confectioners' sugar if it is a minor ingredient. Powdered sugar *is* confectioners' sugar.

Tartar Sauce: Mix 1 cup of mayonnaise with 1 tablespoon finely chopped dill pickle and 1 tablespoon finely chopped onion. Or make a good but less traditional Tartar Sauce with 1 cup of mayonnaise mixed with 2 tablespoons of pickle relish.

Thousand Island Dressing: Mix 1 cup of mayonnaise with 2 tablespoons chili sauce, 1 chopped hard-boiled egg, and salt and pepper to taste. For a southern-styled Thousand Island Dressing: Mix 1 cup mayonnaise with 3 tablespoons of ketchup and 3 tablespoons of pickle relish.

Teriyaki Sauce: While you can substitute bottled teriyaki sauce in most recipes calling for soy sauce, soy sauce is too strong to be substituted directly for teriyaki sauce—dilute with half water or white wine, and add a little sugar.

Vinegar: Though the different vinegars have distinct flavors and traditional uses, you can clean the mineral deposits out of a pan with wine vinegar instead of distilled vinegar and dress your salad with cider vinegar instead of wine vinegar. In a pinch, use vinegars interchangeably. Lemon juice can be substituted for vinegar in cooking and salad dressings.

Water

There's nothing quite so nice about RV travel as having your own water supply, and nothing quite so terrible as when it's lousy. We discovered early in our travels that there can be a world of difference between potable and palatable water. *Always* taste the water before you fill your tank or you risk having to flush the system of unpleasant chemicals. Remember that water is an important ingredient in your cooking—chlorine doesn't do a thing for the flavor of salads, steamed vegetables, soups, spaghetti, or even soda. (The reason your favorite pop tastes different in different parts of the country is the local water supply used by the bottlers—or it could be your ice cubes.) Fortunately, good water is usually available just down the road and almost anyone will be happy to fill a bottle or two for you. In areas where the whole drinking water supply is off-flavored, bottled water is readily available and well worth the minor expense.

INDEX

L

LA DOLCE VITA CHICKEN, 195
LAKE HERRING (whitefish), 155
LAMB, 157
    barbecued lamb, 186
    orangerie lamb, 186
    Roquefort lamb, 187
LANGOSTINAS, 161
LEEKS, 147
    Noah's ark soup, 62
LEFTOVERS, 206
LEMON ROSE, 204
LEMONS, 134
    air freshener, insect repellent, 134
    caviar lemons, 134
    fresh lemonade, 125
    lemon juice, equivalents, 204
    lemon rose, 204
LETTUCE, 144-145
    Monticello salad, 112
LICKETY-SPLIT SMALL FRY, 185
LIMES, 134
    Key lime pie, 123
    lime rose, 204
LINGCOD, 154
LO BOK, 148
LOBSTER, 161
    charcoal broiled Maine lobster, 188
    cooking live lobster, 94, 188
    fettucine Newport, 92
    lobster Newburg, 93
    Maine boiled lobster, 94
    Maine lobster roll, 88
    Maine lobster salad, 88
    varieties and sizes, 161
LONDON BROIL, BOURBON, 191
LONE STAR RED SNAPPER, 50
LONGHOUSE SALMON, 172
LOUISIANA, 110, 113, 117-118, 122,
    124-125, 191
LUAU PUNCH, 36
LUAU RIBS, 176

M

MACKEREL, 154
MAGNOLIA BLOSSOM, 125
MAHOGANY CHICKEN, 190
MAINE, 85, 88, 94, 161-162, 188
MAINE BOILED LOBSTER, 94
MAINE LOBSTER ROLL, 88
MAINE LOBSTER SALAD, 88

MANGOES, 134
    sunbird salad, 112
MANHATTAN CLAM CHOWDER, 85
MANHATTANS TO GO, 106
MAPLE SNOW, 103
MARDI GRAS POMPANO, 118
MARGARITAS, 58
MARINATED MUSHROOMS, 20
MARIONBERRIES
    fresh berry desserts, 32
MARTINIS TO GO, 37
MARYLAND, 119, 160, 192
MARZIPAN CRESCENTS, 61
MASSACHUSETTS, 86, 102, 105-106
MASSACHUSETTS CRANBERRY
    MOUSSE, 102
MEASUREMENTS AND METRICS, 207
MEATS
    See Beef, Ham, Lamb, Pork
MELONS, 134-136
    See individual names
METRIC MEASUREMENT, 207
MICHIGAN, 61, 66, 69, 73, 75, 132, 140,
    142-143
MICROWAVE OVEN, 2, 6
MIDSUMMER FRUIT BOWL, 14
MILE HIGH CRACKED PEPPER STEAK,
    182
MINIATURE REUBENS, 64
MINNESOTA, 147
MINT JULEP, 126
MIRLITON, 149
MISSISSIPPI, 115, 123, 170
MISSISSIPPI LEMON BARBECUE SAUCE,
    170
MISSISSIPPI MUD PIE, 123
MISSISSIPPI RED BEANS AND RICE, 115
MISSISSIPPI VALLEY FRIED CATFISH, 72
MOCHA COOLER, 77
MOCHA PUDDING, 202
MOLASSES GLAZED PÁN YAMS, 120
MONTANA, 39, 43
MONTANA CALICO BEAN SOUP, 43
MONTEREY BAY ARTICHOKES, 31
MONTICELLO SALAD, 112
MOULES MARINIERE (sailor's mussels),
    98
MOUNT HOOD CHERRIES JUBILEE, 33
MOUSSE
    chocolatetown cloud, 103
    fresh berry mousse, 32
    Massachusetts cranberry mousse,
      102
MUFFINS, SUNDAE, 42
MULBERRIES, 131
MULLED WINE, IVY LEAGUE, 106
MULLET, 154
MUNICH BEEF SPAETZLE, 205
MUSHROOMS, 146
    beef Stroganoff, 90

fresh mushrooms Boursin, 99
marinated mushrooms, 20
salad Loretta, 20
shallot-stuffed mushrooms, 100
sliced mushrooms, equivalents, 204
snowbird shrimp, 51
stuffed mushrooms Florentine, 100
stuffed Pennsylvania mushrooms, 99
MUSKELLUNGE, 154
MUSSELS, 161
    beachcomber's mussels, 98
    gathering and cleaning, 161
    moules mariniere, 98
    steamed mussels, 97
MUSTARD GREENS, 144
MUSTARD SAUCE, 119

N

NEBRASKA, 64
NEBRASKA GRILLED REUBENS, 64
NECTARBERRIES, 36
NECTARINES, 136
NEW AMSTERDAM PUFFED PANCAKE,
    82
NEW ENGLAND BEACH BAKE, 187
NEW ENGLAND CLAM CHOWDER, 85
NEW JERSEY, 79, 88, 104-105, 140-141, 144
NEW JERSEY STONE FENCE PUNCH, 105
NEW MEXICO, 40, 43, 53, 144
NEW MEXICO HUEVOS RANCHEROS, 40
NEW ORLEANS MILK PUNCH, 124
NEW ORLEANS OYSTER LOAF, 113
NEW ORLEANS PAIN PERDU (French
    toast), 110
NEWPORT SHRIMP SALAD, 19
NEW YORK, 18, 82, 85-86, 88, 93, 106,
    142-144, 146, 189
NOAH'S ARK SOUP, 62
NO-COOK POTATO SALAD, 63
NOPALES, 146
    nopales Mexicali, 146
NORTH CAROLINA, 120, 192
NORTH WOODS SAVORY BEEF PIE, 65

O

O'BRIEN STEW, 195
OCEAN PERCH, 154
    poached Pacific perch, 27